Religious and Political Ethics in Africa

Recent Titles in
Contributions in Afro-American and African Studies

Masters of the Drum: Black Lit/oratures Across the Continuum
Robert Elliot Fox

Africa's Agenda: The Legacy of Liberalism and Colonialism in the Crisis of African Values
Harvey J. Sindima

Negritude and Literary Criticism: The History and Theory of "Negro-African" Literature in French
Belinda Elizabeth Jack

Prospects for Recovery and Sustainable Development in Africa
Aguibou Y. Yansané, editor

The Black Press in the Middle West, 1865–1985
Henry Lewis Suggs, editor

Of Dreams Deferred, Dead or Alive: African Perspectives on African-American Writers
Femi Ojo-Ade

Digging the Africanist Presence in American Performance: Dance and Other Contexts
Brenda Dixon Gottschild

Development Strategies in Africa: Current Economic, Socio-Political, and Institutional Trends and Issues
Aguibou Y. Yansané, editor

Langston Hughes: Folk Dramatist in the Protest Tradition, 1921–1943
Joseph McLaren

The Rules of the Game: Struggles in Black Recreation and Social Welfare Policy in South Africa
Alan Gregor Cobley

The Problem of Embodiment in Early African American Narrative
Katherine Fishburn

African Horizons: The Landscapes of African Fiction
Christine Loflin

Religious and Political Ethics in Africa

A Moral Inquiry

HARVEY J. SINDIMA

Contributions in Afro-American and African Studies,
Number 188

GREENWOOD PRESS
Westport, Connecticut • London

Library of Congress Cataloging-in-Publication Data

Sindima, Harvey J.
Religious and political ethics in Africa : a moral inquiry / Harvey J. Sindima.
p. cm.—(Contributions in Afro-American and African studies, ISSN 0069-9624 ; no. 188)
Includes bibliographical references and index.
ISBN 0-313-30703-2 (alk. paper)
1. Church and state—Africa. 2. Political ethics—Africa. 3. Christian ethics—Africa. 4. Africa—Church history. I. Title. II. Series.
BR1360.S566 1998
291.5'62'096—dc21 97-43937

British Library Cataloguing in Publication Data is available.

Library of Congress Catalog Card Number: 97-43937
ISBN: 0-313-30703-2
ISSN: 0069-9624

First published in 1998

Greenwood Press, 88 Post Road West, Westport, CT 06881
An imprint of Greenwood Publishing Group, Inc.

Printed in the United States of America

The paper used in this book complies with the Permanent Paper Standard issued by the National Information Standards Organization (Z39.48-1984).

P

In order to keep this title in print and available to the academic community, this edition was produced using digital reprint technology in a relatively short print run. This would not have been attainable using traditional methods. Although the cover has been changed from its original appearance, the text remains the same and all materials and methods used still conform to the highest book-making standards.

For my wife

Contents

Acknowledgments

I am very much indebted to my fellow struggler in faith, a partner in work, and companion in life, my beloved wife, Gertrude. She encouraged me to write the book and always wanted to know how much progress I had made. She has done more for the writing of the book than I can say in a few words. I heartily thank her for the interest she has in my work, the encouragement she gives, and the love she continually pours on me. As a token of my appreciation for everything she does this book is dedicated to her.

Introduction

One of the most difficult issues confronting the modern nation-state is the role organized religion can play in politics, or rather to what extent, if any, can religion or religious authorities be involved in state affairs or influence government policies. This is an age old debate on the relation between religion and the state. The issue has been a topic of public debate mostly in the West as the question of the relationship between church and state, but the topic also arises in other parts of the world and with other religions such as Islam and Hinduism. The topic involves many issues: state support of religious observances and holidays; state funding of religious institutions such as schools, hospitals, orphanages, etcetera; the state paying salaries of clerics and other church officials; legislation affecting particular religious and moral teachings; and others. These issues must be seen in the light of the rights of individuals to free assembly and worship, but also free expression. The state's guarantee of religious liberty implies guarantee of religious pluralism. Above all, the independence of the modern nation-state, which is often secular, raises the question of what role religion has in politics.

Several issues emerge when considering the relation between organized religion and the state: secularization, individual rights, and pluralism. As society becomes more and more secular, the marginalization of religion from the public arena becomes the norm and the attempt by religion to assert its influence, moral or otherwise, on society is regarded as an intrusion into public life. With secularization, religion becomes a private matter with no impact whatsoever on public moral discourse. The question of religious influence becomes even more difficult in a secular state where religious pluralism must be maintained. Neither can the state nor the general public favor one religion over others. The solution, in theory, is to maintain a separation of religion and the state, as in the American model. In practice, however, the separation is difficult to maintain. In the American model, for example, the calendar used in the country is Christian, Gregorian to be specific, which allows for Christian observances and holidays. The observance of Sunday and Christmas as holy days have become days of rest for the whole nation. Christian symbols abound in public places, including the legislature, a chaplain in the houses of Congress, and display of the nativity scene or the cross in public places during high holidays. Laws passed by Congress often reflect the Jewish-Christian influence of the American heritage. The Christian right influences American politics. It is general knowledge that the Christian right was a strong factor in the 1980 presidential election and that it was they who led Ronald Reagan to the White House. The Republican platform at the 1996 Convention in San Diego, California, reflected the values of the Christian right. When judged by its practice, the American model is, on the contrary, very Christian although the state does not intervene in matters of faith or regulate religious practices. One thing the American model does, is to discourage religious pluralism. In short, the separation of religion and state is a very complex issue.

Although the idea of a secular state, along with the issues of secularization and the privatization of religion, are of Western origin, dating back to the Medieval period, these problems have found their way to other parts of the world. The idea of a secular state has marched to many corners of the globe including Islamic regions. In Africa, where traditionally the idea of religion as a matter of private concern is unknown, echoes are now being heard about the separation of religion from public life, and that religion should not influence or interfere with the running of the state. Indeed, it must be acknowledged that sometimes religion has created serious problems in politics or the running of the state. Religious intolerance has cost too many lives in history. On the other hand, religion has also inspired individuals and nations to greater things.

The issue of religion and politics, or church and state, is a topic of concern for many in Africa. A quick look at a few places will show how widespread the issue of religion and politics is in Africa: from Nigeria and Sudan, where conflicts between Christians and Muslims seem to have no end; to Egypt, where the Copts have for hundreds of years cried for constitutional guarantees from a state that is predominantly Muslim; to Ethiopia where Muslim voices have been suppressed for centuries; to South Africa, where Christianity was used to legitimize oppression of blacks by a handful whites; and to many countries in between where Christian leaders are pressing for human rights and political participation. The issue of the relation between church and state is rife in Africa. In most places the state feels that religious leaders should concern themselves with the spiritual welfare of the people and not meddle in politics or interfere with governing the country. In other words, there should be a separation between temporal and spiritual powers. However, human suffering, along with pressing political and economic issues, are making it clear that Christians cannot remain uninvolved with the concerns of their country. The question for Christians is no longer whether or not they should participate in politics, but what is Christian responsibility in society and towards civil authorities? Or, on what grounds can Christians, or any other group, call for accountability of those in power?

These issues are not new; they have been with Africans since the days of colonialism but the church-state relationship has really become "a problem," or sharpened, only since independence. What is at stake in this problem is human life and its dignity. The question is: How can a society structure itself in such a way that its moral fiber continues to safeguard the dignity of persons and thus ensure itself a better future? The question demands immediate attention because the church-state issue centers on a fundamental question, namely, what constitutes a community?

A community is built on some basic symbols or a framework of shared meanings. Basic symbols are not chosen arbitrarily, they are born; they arise out of a particular way of understanding the world. Therefore, to grasp how people decide to live together, involves interpreting the symbols which inform their vision of life since symbols are about a people's vision or destiny. Clergy see that the symbols constituting life together have been emptied of their meaning by the body politic or the state. Life has lost its value. It is expendable: people have died in hundreds in civil wars in Angola, Ethiopia, Liberia, Mozambique, Sudan, Somalia, Liberia, and Sierra Leone. People are dying from starvation, disease, poverty caused by mismanagement, corruption, and power struggle. In their pastoral ministry, clergy experience first hand the pain and suffering of the people; the clergy see that people lack basic necessities such as food—the granary is empty, and they cannot afford the staple, and children do not have enough blankets or clothing because of sky-rocketing prices resulting from devalued currency and high inflation rates. Traders use the sad economic conditions and foreign exchange difficulties to exploit the people. Other problems arise, including increasing unemployment, and shortages of medicines, beds, and other facilities for proper medical and nursing care in hospitals and clinics. In their pastoral visitations, clergy go to overcrowded hospitals where they see patients sharing a bed or the space under a hospital bed, in hospitals that do not have medicines and where the equipment does not work because the government cannot afford to replace it or buy spare parts. While the majority suffer in these poor conditions, the elite and the wealthy go to private hospitals where everything is available. Clergy hear parents worry about overcrowded classrooms and falling educational standards. Pastors and priests see and hear many things which the elite–the wealthy and powerful, politicians, and government authorities–do not know because they live lavishly away from scenes of human torment and misery, and because of the power the elite have, the people fear to tell them the true nature of things. Being closer to, and among the people, clergy see that all symbols of good life and human dignity have disappeared. Clergy feel obliged to let the authorities know about the true nature of things, and to ask them to rectify the mistakes which have had serious repercussions for the economy, justice, and general harmony of society. Certainly, these issues pertain to the manner of governance, but pastors do not question the authorities' ability to rule, they only appeal to the leader's responsibility to the people. It is behind this background that the church's involvement in politics, hence the church-state conflict in Africa must be understood.

This book has been inspired by the activities of the churches in the 1990s in a number of countries: Benin, Congo Brazzaville, Democratic Republic of Congo, Malawi, Kenya, Sudan, and Zimbabwe. Catholic bishops took the lead through their pastoral letters in which they openly expressed solidarity with the people in their struggle for economic and political justice. In Benin, Congo, and the Democratic Republic of Congo, bishops chaired reconciliation talks. The Catholic Church was also very instrumental in bringing to the negotiating table the two warring parties in Mozambique. The talks led to the signing of a peace accord in Mozambique on 4 October, 1992, thus ending a sixteen-year civil war, and thereby opening discussions which led to the first multiparty general elections held in November 1994. In all these countries, the bishops received wide support from students and clergy of other denominations, but those in authority questioned the motives of the bishops in leading the church to be involved in economic and political issues.

This book has been written as a resource for students and readers in African politics and ethics, especially those interested in the relation of church and state. An attempt has been made to show that there can be harmonious relationships and areas of cooperation between religious leaders and secular authorities. Hopefully, too, that this book has clarified to some "concerned" Christians or uncertain clergy, the nature and extent of the mission of the church and individual Christian responsibility towards society and the state. Through investigation and analysis of some key concepts in political theory I discuss the following terms: politics, nation, state, power, governance, ethnicity, and military rule. The question of church and state is Western and Christian in origin, but I have also included a discussion of the encounter between Christianity and Islam because the meeting of these two Semitic religions has had negative effects on national politics in some countries. I have examined the politics of Nigeria and Sudan as case studies in the Christian-Muslim conflict in politics. Having made a survey of the African political situation, I found it instructive to see how many patterns and practices with respect to church and state go back in time to the early years of the founding of Christianity itself. Focusing mostly on the early documents, I have examined the history of the Christian tradition from the New Testament through the fifth century into the early Medieval period, to ascertain the attitude of the early church to civil authorities. Since Protestants pay close attention to the works of the Reformers, the attitudes of Luther, Calvin, and Knox to princes have been briefly outlined. Discussions of church and state often do not include the Orthodox tradition, but that is not the case in this book although the consideration is limited. Since the question of church and state concerns politics, it is illuminating to explore the development of political theory and the beginnings of secularization of the state as seen through the works of Marsilius of Padua and William of Ocham in the early period, and of Niccolò Machiavelli and Thomas Hobbes later. This book being a Christian project, it was only proper to inquire into scriptures for guidance on Christian responsibility in politics, accountability of leaders, and the relation of the church to the state. Finally, I have outlined the basis for political ethics in Africa. In other words, I have developed political ethics grounded in the values of African culture.

This book is about the political responsibility of leaders towards their subjects, and the relations between organized religion and the state. It is a comprehensive study of church and state. I do not presume, however, that African leaders, politicians, or people of influence and power will read this book, but I hope readers will find this a modest resource towards understanding the nature of politics and individual political duty in the modern nation-state.

1

Church and Politics in Africa

THE CHURCH IN COLONIAL AFRICA

The church-state problem cannot be fully appreciated unless seen through the missionary and colonial experience of the African people. In colonial Africa, the missionary hegemony worked hand in hand with the colonial powers. Missions were one of the three agencies of the colonial machinery, the other two being commerce and government. African novelists have shown how well the three worked together. In his novel, *The Poor Christ of Bomba*, a book which first appeared in 1956, Mongo Beti shows the relation between mission work, government, and commerce. Father S. Drumont builds a mission station in Cameroon. After many years of preaching comes Monsieur Videl, a young colonial administrator, tours Fr. Drumont's missionary field, acquainting himself with his area of administration and surveying for a road to be constructed. Fr. Drumont is not excited by the young administrator's attitude towards Africans, and like many of his parishioners, Fr. Drumont is concerned, indeed worried because the construction of the road will mean forced labor, particularly in the villages along the road. A few of Fr. Drumont's parishioners, those who have disposed themselves to some European items, are happy that those commodities will become available locally. The book is about a failed missionary work since Fr. Drumont's imported Christianity does not take into account African values or religious life, thereby failing to capture or convert the hearts of the Africans to whom he has dedicated a good twenty years of his life. Discouraged that he has failed to truly convert the Africans, Fr. Drumont packs his bags and goes home to Europe for good.[1]

When the matter of imported Christianity is put aside, we notice that missionary work paved the way for establishing colonial influence and administration in the hinterland, which in turn prepared the area for trade and commerce. Missionaries were important to colonial authorities because they established and funded schools. This is one of the reasons colonial administrators had a keen sense of obligation towards missionaries. The other reason was that in most cases, missionaries came from the same country as colonial administrators. In some areas, the government did not permit missionaries of other nationalities to operate within the country for fear that such missionaries would not support the government's colonial policies. The Flemish Scheut Missionaries, for instance, were actively supported in their missionary work in Congo by the King of Belgium. In fact, *Directives for Government Agents in the Congo*, specifically stated that "government agents whatever their opinions, are under strict obligation to help Christian missionaries especially in the regular frequentation of the mission schools by their pupils."[2]

The mission school was a critical institution for both missionaries and the government. It was through schools that missionaries and colonial administrators launched an onslaught on African value systems and ritual practices.[3] A few illustrations will suffice: missionaries preached against polygamy, taught against it in schools, and the government prohibited it; missionaries prohibited clitoridectomy in Kenya, the government banned it, too. Bénézet Bujo says that in Congo Free State, church and state were very severe on ancestor veneration. In September 1923, the Superior of the Belgian Congo Mission issued a document to take action against certain African practices and rituals which were considered to not promote public order; those "included offering to spirits and ancestors; cooperation in ancestor rituals; dancing and hunting ceremonies; magical or religious rites on occasion of a birth, or the appearance of the child's first teeth, or circumcision, or a girl's puberty, or marriage, or illness. Likewise forbidden were traditional rites in honor of the ancestor performed before a hunting or fishing expedition, and carvings representing the spirits of the dead."[4] Customs proscribed by the church were outlawed by the government as harmful to public order. Africans had to carry out some customs or rituals secretly for fear of missionaries and government officials. The school was the right place to begin to instill that fear and hate for African values, customs and the past—attitudes that became characteristic of educated and alienated Africans.

Even more important was that mission schools educated persons who joined the government as civil servants in various junior positions such as clerks and interpreters. Missionaries boasted of producing qualified people who became employed in the government. In Malawi, for example, missionaries claimed: "it is perhaps in the sphere of the church that Africans have had the fullest opportunity of bearing responsibility."[5] In turn, the task of the government was to ensure security for missionaries and their stations. It was the question of security which ushered in colonial rule in some places in Africa; Malawi is a good example. At first, the British government was not interested in colonizing Malawi because of its poor natural endowment. Since the land had no copper, gold, or other minerals, it would cost the British treasury more to run it than it was worth. It was therefore not in national interests to bring the country under British rule. Up to 1889 "the only Britons interested in imperial expansion in this area were the missionaries and their supporters. From their earliest days in the country they sought government support."[6] Repeated calls for protection, and ten thousand signatures from Scottish clergy and elders led Scottish members of Parliament to urge Parliament to change its mind and declare Malawi a British Protectorate. Missionaries wrote that their interests, hence British interests, were at stake in the country. Arabs (who had been in this part of Africa for centuries) had increased their presence, and the Portuguese pushed in closer to the Scottish mission in the south. In short, the Arabs and the Portuguese were encroaching on British interests. If the British did not claim the land, it would fall under Arab or Portuguese control, so argued the missionaries. Fearing that their influence in the region would be diminished by the nearby Portuguese, the British declared Malawi a Protectorate.

During the colonial era, the church and state had much in common, since their mission was the same: to "civilize the backward people of Africa" through true religion and principles of civilization. For missionaries to carry on this "noble" task they needed protection from both the "warring tribes" among whom they lived and from other Europeans competing against them in the area. This was the role that colonial government played. Colonialists and missionaries shared the belief that they were destined to fulfill divine purpose in Africa. Cecil Rhodes, a colonialist in South Africa expressed this messianic view as follows: "only one race was destined to help in God's work and to fulfil his purpose in the world . . . and to bring nearer the reign of justice, liberty, and peace."[7] David Livingstone likewise said: "We come among them as members of a superior race and servants of a government that desires to elevate more degraded portions of the human family. We are the adherents of the benign, holy religion and by mere consistent conduct and wise patient efforts become the enjoinders of peace to a hitherto destructed and downtrodden race." Many in Europe shared these feelings and they saw "in colonial enterprise, the triumphant alliance of the three Cs—Commerce and Christianity bring civilization to black Africa which was at the mercy of the pagan monarchs and slave trading Arabs."[8]

The preparation for a harmonious relation between the two institutions was long in the making for wherever missionaries established their station, they not only preached the gospel, they also exercised judiciary powers. Mission stations were mini-colonies with complete executive and judiciary systems. The head of the mission station was also the chief executive and judge, disregarding and undermining the power of all traditional authorities.[9]

Missionaries continued to "rule" till they handed their power to the colonial government when it was established. The church-state relationship went further: when the colonial government decided to have African representation in the legislative councils, they turned to missionaries to represent African interests.

Alexander Hetherwick, one of the early missionaries to Malawi, admits in *The Romance of Blantyre* that Africans saw no difference between colonialists and missionaries for both treated them with contempt and had no respect, just plain insensitivity and prejudice for the dignity of the African. When Africans began the fight against colonialism, they were told by missionaries that, as Christians, they were obliged by the Bible to obey their rulers. Africans were bombarded with distorted interpretations of scriptural texts urging them to obey civil authorities. These exhortations were made before and during the struggle for independence. In Mozambique, even three years before the beginning of the armed struggle, the archbishop of Lourenço Marques (now Maputo) told his faithful: "Do not allow yourselves to be seduced by fantasies or led astray by evil counselors who feed your dreams of independence to utopias of economic and cultural prosperity. As citizens of the Portuguese nation for the last four centuries, it is within the framework of that nation that you should aspire to material, cultural and moral progress by cooperating honestly with the Portuguese authorities and obeying their orders."[10]

There were few exceptions where missionaries spoke against the ill-treatment of the people.[11] Noteworthy is the statement issued by Blantyre Synod of the Church of Central African Presbyterian concerning unrest in Nyasaland (Malawi):

> Federation has produced a deep and widespread feeling of unrest. Fears for future security and political stability have increased and in many cases are proving to be well founded . . . all their fears expressed in former years against Federation being instituted are being realized . . . the old boast that Nyasaland is a land without a color bar is no longer true. . . . The increase in special police activities and widespread employment of police informers directed against essentially law-abiding people . . . school children are questioning their teachers, prominent visitors with known liberal views have been followed round the country. . . . Europeans have been asked to report on the activities of their colleagues, sermons are subject of special police reports, reputations are viciously maligned with no possibility of answer in regard to truth, public meetings cannot be held without informers or detectors being present.[12]

Calls to obey civil authorities ceased to be heard once it became obvious that nothing was going to stop Africans from achieving independence. Missionaries started projecting a new image: the saving of souls, the issue

Christians were to be concerned with, was no longer the only thing that really mattered! Missionaries suddenly became concerned with the African condition and urged their parishioners to participate in the political process. Missionaries even started supporting political parties financially and otherwise: Catholics in Malawi were behind the Christian Democratic Party; while the Presbyterians supported the Malawi Congress Party, the party which led the country to independence. These examples could be multiplied elsewhere in Africa. Why this sudden turn around? The main reason was the church's own self-interest; its popularity was at stake, therefore its future. If it did not switch sides, it would have no place in the hearts of many in the future. Furthermore, it would not be a moral authority in the new society, a role which the church had belatedly recognized.

The church in Africa has been characteristically slow in identifying itself with the people's struggle for freedom and dignity. This practise raises a number of questions: could it be that the church's leadership has been too comfortable and thus out of touch with the suffering of the people? Could it be because of fear of the powers that be—the concern for self-preservation? Does it mean the African church has no message for present historical circumstances? These questions were basically true of the post independence era, but from the 1980s the church took a new attitude. In a number of countries the church started playing an active role, speaking on behalf of the people as did the bishops in Kenya, Malawi, and Sudan; and taking a leading role in national reconciliation talks, such as those in the Republic of Congo (Brazzaville), Mozambique, Togo, and Democratic Republic of Congo. Ugandan Bishops set an example in the 1970s under the rule of terror of Idi Amin, and the churches of South Africa presented a formidible challenge to the white minority government in the late 1970s and through the 1980s.

In most of Africa, there is widespread recognition that the church has much more to offer even in the present serious social, economic, and political crisis. The church cannot afford to stand aloof in some countries, the church is perhaps the only hope the people have.[13] It needs to develop theological and political ethics to deal with these problems. With clear political ethics and serious biblical hermeneutics, the church could contribute greatly to the well-being of the people by offering constructive ideas in many areas of society. The significance of the church in society must be made manifest in the everyday experience of the people. It is unfortunate that "the church has been slow in giving the guidance which African nations have needed in working out their national aspirations as independent states. Instead many a church leader has found himself largely jumping on the band wagon and in accepting opinions mooted by politicians."[14] Nonetheless, the church is now rising to its responsibility. Now the church is taking seriously the Confession of Alexandria that as a community of forgiven sinners it has "no choice but to continue the struggle for full liberation of all men and women, and the societies."

CLERGY AND POLITICS IN INDEPENDENT AFRICA

With few exceptions in colonial Africa, the African clergy participated very little, or not at all, in politics. There were a few exceptions such as the Malawian martyr, John Chilembwe, Ndabaning Sithole, and Bishop Abel Muzorewa in Zimbabwe. Most clerics did not get involved in politics because they believed politics concerned itself with earthly things; moreover, politics was considered a "dirty game" in which decent people should not get involved. This lack of involvement in the political struggle identified clerics with the oppressors. In independent Africa, the African clergy have slowly assumed a different position, taking active roles in politics although not to the degree of the rest of the population. The clergy have spoken on issues of concern for the people. Some clergy have joined politics and have sought or accepted positions of leadership, examples include the Rev. C. Banana, who became the ceremonial president of Zimbabwe, and Reverend Father Vincent Damuah who was invited by Flight. Lt. J. J. Rawlings to become a member of the Provisional National Defence Council after the December 31, 1981, *coup d'etat* in Ghana. In an interview with the *Christian Messenger*, a Ghanaian paper, Fr. Damuah responded to the criticism that he had involved himself in politics instead of seeking the spiritual welfare of his flock:

> Who are my flock? Are they not the suffering, impoverished Ghanaians who have been left uncared for by the church? Those priests who are criticizing me for doing politics are the very people who are rather doing politics than the professional politicians. Let me ask you one question: Is the Pope not a head of state with envoys all around the world? Is this not politics? Politics is no sin. It is a selfless opportunity to serve and to be served. It is an opportunity to fight and die gallantly for one's country when time comes. I am therefore ready to die for Ghana to let the revolution succeed.[15]

Individual clerics, church councils and assemblies have addressed social, political, and economic issues facing their countries: Ugandan bishops addressed the malpractice of the regime of General Idi Amin; Nigerian Christians denounced the malpractice of their government in the 1980s—particularly during the Biafran Civil War. Ecumenical councils have not been quiet either: National Christian Councils have spoken against abuse of power and suffering of the people. The All Africa Conference of Churches (AACC) has continually made statements against violations of human dignity, denounced oppression, and called for justice towards the weakest members of society. The AACC has not only issued statements but also sent its envoys to different countries to support local church leaders in their struggle against abuse of power by dictatorial and totalitarian leadership. Justice and liberation were the main subject of the Third Assembly of the AACC held in Lusaka in 1974. Meeting under the title, "Living no longer for ourselves but for Christ," the assembly called on the member churches not to condone evil by giving a blind eye to structures of injustice.[16] On the Catholic side, the Symposium of Episcopal Conferences of Africa and Madagascar (SECAM) held a meeting in Dakar, Senegal, (10–11 May 1979) to discuss justice.[17] Almost a decade later, SECAM organized the Pan-African Seminar on Justice and Peace that took place in Lesotho, 29 May to 3 June, 1988.

This concern for the well-being of the people, or the call for justice, is all likely to cause suspicion among political leaders. Politicians wonder why the church *now* seeks to champion issues concerning the human condition? Where were these "moral authorities" when the people needed them during colonial rule? The general conclusion made by politicians is that clerics have contempt for African political leadership, for they were quiet during colonial rule. In some countries the church has been accused of working in alliance with overseas governments, and/or "dissidents" to break law and order with the intention of disturbing the prevailing peace, harmony, and unity. In 1979, José Chipendo, the current General Secretary of the AACC, commented that "there are sufficient grounds for rulers in the newly independent countries to suspect the church. The church, through the centuries, has supported the status quo and stood against change. . . . The church's resistance to change is still fresh in the memory of our leaders. Unless the church shows signs of repentance, it cannot be counted on in building new nations."[18]

Prior to the 1990s, the state in post colonial Africa was not only critical of the new moral superiority of the church, but was swift in silencing the clergy and firmly enforcing the doctrine of non interference. One broke the silence or disregarded the doctrine at a great personal peril and price. Through the doctrine of non interference and harsh enforcement of silence, the state managed to instil fear upon the leadership of the church. Consequently, for a very long time the message from pulpits was: "render to Caesar what belongs to Caesar and to God what is God's!" Popular, too, became Romans 13:1 "Everyone must obey the state authorities, because no authority exists without God's permission, and the existing authorities have been put there by God. Whoever opposes the existing authorities opposes what God has ordained." Relations between church and state went well as long as the church stayed out of politics and concerned itself with spiritual matters. Things were even better when the church became involved in community development projects such as building schools and medical clinics, running youth hostels, introducing cottage industries, or social service work such as helping the poor, relief projects for victims of natural disasters, floods, hunger, or war. The church was encouraged by the state to seek help from overseas "donors," agencies, and "partners," including the founding churches to support social service projects. In brief, in the post-independence era, the state accommodated the church as long as the church remained within the limits prescribed by the state.

What did the idea of non interference and the "law" of silence mean for the church? These practices paralysed the church, and in some countries the church was put in the back pockets of politicians. The function of the church became sanctioning the activities of the powers that be, and the church did all it could to avoid conflict—not to disturb the "prevailing national peace, harmony, and unity." In the quest for a harmonious relation with the state, the clergy avoided addressing controversial issues. With glaring corruption in both the public and private sectors, abuse of power, and lack of human dignity, the church pretended not to see that there was anything wrong in the country! Instead, the church was grateful to the state for the freedom of worship enjoyed! The church pledged its loyalty to the state and the (ruling) party, even as public funds were channelled to serve personal interest of the powerful, while the majority of the people could not meet basic needs such as food and health services, and unemployment was extensive and growing. Loyalty was vouched even while some languished in detention for years. How could the state be assured loyalty when some of its top leaders and executives displayed ethnic prejudice, thus fueling divisions among the people? For far too long, moral decadence seemed not to concern the church. The primary concern of the leadership of the church was to ensure that the word of God was proclaimed; but what does the word of God say about the cry of the people? The words of the prophet Jeremiah (8:11) come true again: "They have healed the wound of my people lightly, saying 'Peace, Peace' when there is no peace."

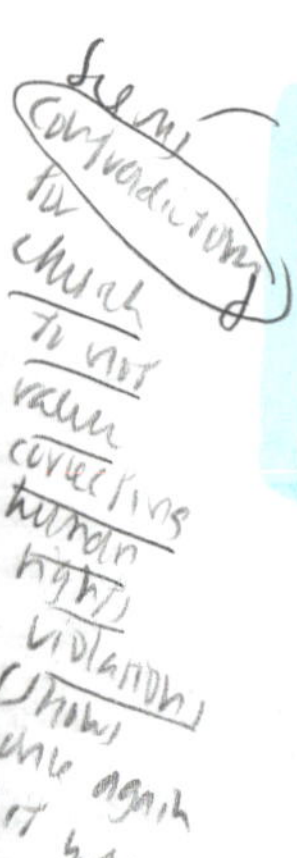

In the 1970s and early 1980s some churches took the idea of maintaining law and order so seriously that on their own, or in full collaboration with the state, they reprimanded any clergy who raised the question of accountability of the leaders of government or the party. The church was, and still is in some countries, afraid to do something which might lead the state to curtail the privilege of preaching the gospel. Does the Bible not say that God hates all worship which ignores evil and acquiesces in oppression? God, through the prophet Isaiah said: "When you lift your hands in prayer, I will not look at you. No matter how much you pray, I will not listen, for your hands are covered with blood. Wash yourselves clean. Stop all this evil that I see you doing. Yes, stop doing evil and learn to do right. See that justice is done—help those who are oppressed, give orphans their rights, and defend widows" (Isaiah 1:15–17; see also Jeremiah 7). The prophet Amos says when people worship but pay no attention to injustice and oppression, their worship only multiplies sin:

> The Sovereign Lord says, people of Israel, go to the holy place in Bethel and sin if you must. Go to Gilgal and sin with all your might. Go ahead and bring animals to be sacrificed morning after morning, and bring animals your tithes every third day. Go ahead, and offer your bread in thanksgiving to God, and boast about extra offerings you bring. This is the kind of thing you love to do.
>
> You people hate anyone who challenges injustice and speaks the whole truth in court. . . . I know how terrible your sins are and how many crimes you have committed. You persecute good people, take bribes, and prevent the poor from getting justice in courts. *And so, keeping quiet in such evil times is the clear thing to do.*
>
> The Lord says, I hate your religious festivals: I cannot stand them. When you bring burnt-offerings and grain-offerings, I will not accept the animals you have fattened to bring to me as offerings: I do not want to listen to your harps. Instead, let justice flow like a stream, and righteousness like a river that never goes dry.[19]

As if the church leadership never read this, they took active steps to enforce the law of silence. Clergy persons could be transferred away from the capital or center of activities, as the Presbyterian Church of East Africa did to Timothy Njoya for his outspoken criticism of corruption in the government and the private sector in Kenya. A cleric who dared speak the truth could even be sent into exile for what fellow ministers perceived as a seditious sermon which would make the church look like it was conspiring against the state. This is what happened to Peter Kaleso, a Malawian Presbyterian minister who did not mince his words; he was advised and "helped" by church authorities and friends to go into exile. The Presbyterian Church missed an opportunity for faithful witness when it failed to stand by and support Kaleso. He was not the first Malawian Presbyterian minister to suffer banishment. In 1974, the church cooperated with political authorities to remove Stephen Kauta Msiska, then principal of the Presbyterian Theological College, from office and the ministry. Rev. Kauta Msiska was banished to his village on the allegation that he had told students in a homiletics class not to wear President Banda's badge (a pin with a picture of Dr. Banda's face) sold by the ruling Malawi Congress Party. The party officials and other authorities considered Rev. Kauta's alleged remark seditious and he was prohibited from engaging in any form of institutional ministry. These stories sound like the story of Amos and Amaziah: "Amos has conspired against you in the midst of the house of Israel; the land is not able to bear all his words. . . . O sear, go, flee away to the land of Judah, and eat bread there; but never again prophesy at Bethel for it is the king's sanctuary and it is the temple of the kingdom" (Amos 7:10, 12–13).

For far too long church leaders treated the church as if it were an extension of the state. Through their words and actions, church leaders promoted the ideology of the state, although the church claimed political neutrality. Homilies on church and state relation refuted any claim to neutrality; the church was fully assimilated into the state. This lack of distance from the state turned Christianity into a state or civil religion. The task of political (civil) religion is to justify and glorify the state by interpreting national ideology using religious language. The church integrated the symbols of the nation so as to help unify the population. Zephania Kameeta, a Namibian pastor, says that those who seek to preserve "law and order" are the "messengers of this world." "There are many voices in the church of Jesus Christ. The voices of false prophets call the church to adapt itself to the evil conditions in this world. Many Christians do this, and regard it normal Christian living. They go even further, and preach that obedience to God demands such accommodation to the structures of the world."[20]

At great risk and personal cost, a few clerics distanced themselves from the practice of political religion. These called on Christians and political leaders to lead a responsible life and stop the dehumanization of the people. In South Africa this challenge was taken by many clergy, although belatedly. They preached against making Christianity an ideology of the state, or developing what they called "state theology," which was "the theological justification of the status quo with its racism, capitalism and totalitarianism. It [state theology] blesses injustice, canonizes the will of the powerful and reduces the poor to passivity, obedience and apathy. . . . It does this by misusing theological concepts and biblical texts for its own political purposes."[21] Not only did South African church clerics criticize "state theology," but also "church theology," the theology of churches which liked to point out the evil but in such a timid, guarded, and cautious way that their words ended up being support for the state. "Its criticism, however, is superficial and counter productive because instead of engaging in an in-depth analysis of the signs of our times, it relies upon a few stock ideas derived from Christian tradition and then uncritically and repeatedly applies them to our situation."[22]

The commitment of the South African clergy to the political liberation of their people was impressive, for numerous clerics were involved and they used all their resources including intellectual. The fact that there were many of them in the struggle did not make it any easier, for they put their lives on the line and their jobs in jeopardy. The good thing about having so many of them committed to the struggle was that they supported each other, which was not the case in most other countries where it was, and still is, a lonely and risky business to denounce the evils of the state. The list of those who have suffered humiliation from their own churches for denouncing evil is too long to be catalogued here. Those courageous people have been ridiculed as having received a "due reward for being pretentious enough to challenge the state," as it was said to Archbishop Tchidimbo of Conakry, Guinea, who spent years in prison. For others the "due reward" was loss of life! Here we remember, among others: Michael Kayoya, a Burundi priest, who died in a firing squad (a total of 17 Burundi priests were executed following the 1972 Hutu rebellion); Cardinal Bayenda of Congo Brazzaville, and Archbishop Luwum of Kampala, Uganda, both of whom were murdered; and the leaders of the Ethiopian Orthodox Church who died in prison and elsewhere when Mengistu Haile Mariuam seized power in 1974.

What is to be done? In the face of repression and human suffering, should the church acquiesce in exchange for the liberty to proclaim the Gospel? Is not acquiescing itself a sin which stands in the way of proclaiming the gospel? Does not the suffering of many, present a moral challenge to the church?

NOTES

1. Mongo Beti, *The Poor Christ of Bomba* (London: Heinemann, 1971).
2. *Receuil à l'usage des fonctionaries et des agents du service territorial au Congo belge* (Bruxells, 1930), 57f.
3. I have discussed the impact of mission education on African culture in "Liberalism and African Culture," *Journal of Black Studies* 21, 2 (December 1990). Also in *Africa's Agenda: The Legacy of Liberalism and Colonialism in the Crisis of Africa's Values* (Westport: Greenwood Press, 1995), chap. 2.
4. Bénézet Bujo, *African Theology in Its Social Context*, trans. John O'Donohue (Maryknoll, New York: Orbis Books, 1992), 44.
5. Memorandum submitted to the Bledisloe Commission in April 1938 by the International Missionary Council of Nyasaland, 6.
6. John McCracken, "The Nineteenth Century in Malawi," in *Aspects of Central African History,* T. O. Ranger, ed. (Evanston, IL.: Northwestern University Press, 1968). See also his book, *Politics and Christianity in Malawi 1875–1940*: *The Impact of the Livingstonia Mission in Northern Province* (London: Cambridge University Press, 1977), 158. Also see Hetherwick, *The Romance of Blantyre* (Dunfermline, Scotland: Lasodine Press, n.d.), chap. 5.
7. Quoted by Saimon Maimela in, "The Concept of Israel," *Africa Theological Journal* 15, 2 (1986):83.
8. Jacques Maquet, *Power and Society in Africa* (London: World University Library, 1971), 242.
9. Hetherwick, *The Romance of Blantyre*, 31–32. Although the General Assembly of the Church of Scotland condemned assumption of civil jurisdiction by missionaries at Blantyre mission, the practice did not die out. Every mission station continued to practice civil jurisdiction over all Africans at the station.

10. Francis Hourtart and Andre Rousseau, *The Church and Revolution* (Maryknoll, New York: Orbis Books, 1971), 251.

11. Scottish missionaries at Blantyre mission joined Malawians in their rejection of the Federation of Rhodesia and Nyasaland. They also wrote to protest the government's treatment of the people. See my book, *The Legacy of Scottish Missionaries in Malawi* (Lewiston, New York: The Edwin Mellen Press, 1992), chap. 6.

12. *Why Not Be Fair*? London. n.d. Federal High Commissioner, 43–44, 46.

13. Jean-Marc Ela has discussed at length the idea of the church being the people's hope. See his *African Cry* (Maryknoll, New York: Orbis Books, 1986), chap. 5.

14. Bishop J. Henry Okullu, *Church and Politics in East Africa* (Nairobi: Uzima Press, 1982. Reprint), 12.

15. *Christian Messenger* 4, 3 (March 1982):1.

16. See the resolutions and recommendations of the assembly in the AACC Bulletin, 1974.

17. Resolutions and recommendations of the meeting appeared as "Seeking Gospel Justice in Africa," *Spearhead* 69 (December 1981).

18. José B. Chipendo, "Theological Options in Africa Today." In *African Theology en Route*, Kofi Appiah-kubi and Sergio Torres, eds. (Maryknoll, New York: Orbis Books, 1979), 69.

19. Amos 4:4–5; 5:10–13, 21–24. Paraphrased by Zephania Kameeta, *Why O Lord: Psalms and Sermons from Namibia* (Philadelphia, PA: Fortress Press, 1986), 52. My emphasis.

20. Ibid.

21. *The Kairos Document. Challenge to the Church: A Theological Comment on the Political Crisis in South Africa* (Braamfontein, South Africa: Kairos Theologians, 1985; Grand Rapids, MI: Eerdmans, 1986), 17.

22. Ibid., 25.

2

Politics and the Idea of a Nation

The African condition is very complex; the problems are many and seem to feed into each other in an endless and vicious circle: political problems produce economic crisis which cause civil unrest, ethnic prejudice, and linguistic tensions as people scramble for what seems to be an ever diminishing national economic pie. With very few exceptions, African economies are in bad shape and most of them have had to be propped up by foreign aid as national gross products slide backwards to preindependence times. Even the once bright spots of Africa—Ghana, Kenya, and the oil rich Nigeria—have had their economies regress. Africa is not doing well in trade; its share of world markets has fallen by half since the 1970s. These economic problems have led to political instability, and they have been the pretexts for coups and plots. The countries which have so far been spared from these problems have mounting political turmoil and economic problems, and it is hard to tell what is going to happen in those places. It seems that both the ancestors and God have turned their backs on Africa. The cry, "How long O, Lord?" seems to get no reply.

When one looks at all the problems Africa is facing, the inevitable questions are: What happened? Or, what is not happening in Africa? The explanation often given about Africa's problems is that there is a leadership crisis. It may well be, but how did it all begin? Africa is not the only continent with ethnic and linguistic, or even religious problems: India, Malaysia, Thailand, all of Asia, has these problems but Asian countries are economically well off. Africa is not the only place to have experienced military takeovers; Latin America and Asia have. Africans are not the only people to have experienced totalitarian governments, or paternalistic rulers. How about Singapore? Is it not doing better than countries with a similar leadership in Africa? These problems are not peculiar to Africa but the puzzling question is: why are African countries not doing better when countries in other parts of the world are? It is true that one of the reasons Asian and Latin American countries are doing well is because of large support from the West. Nothing surprising there: due to historical connections and Western interests, but is the way Africa has taken the only possible path?

In this chapter and the next, I have investigated what might have happened to Africa. This is done by examining some key concepts in political theory, which although of Western origin, have become common stock of African political language and systems. The investigation focuses only on those terms that have influenced political institutions and government apparatus, the practice of law, etcetera. This is because contemporary African nation-states were created by Europeans, and African governments to this day are, by and large, European institutions. Take, for instance, the idea of a parliament with a sergeant of arms, a mace, and a speaker; a judicial system whose judges wear black robes and white wig; and an infamous "special branch" internal security force—are not all these near duplicates of Westminster and Whitehall? In order to fully appreciate some of the issues the continent is facing, and to make an informed critical assessment of the nature of things, it is well to start by clarifying some basic concepts such as politics, nation, nationalism, and state. The idea behind discussing these terms is not to suggest that a clear understanding of these terms from their Western origin will solve Africa's political problems; rather, that a study of these terms might provide an insight into what happened or might have happened. No doubt, these terms have acquired particular meanings and nuances in their African context, and that is what makes it even more important to explore their meaning as Africans use them.

POLITICS

To speak of politics is to refer to life together; that is, how people live or interact in a given context. Behavioral and structural patterns are developed to enhance, monitor, and guide a manner of living together and these patterns are seen in politics. What is meant by politics? The term *politics* is one of the most unpopular and abused words in Africa today—it has a very negative connotation. This negative meaning is not new, but is something of the postindependence era. The present social strife and economic crisis have only confirmed how most people viewed politics even in preindependence days: that politics is a "dirty" game which no good and honest person gets into. The politician was perceived as a greedy, mendacious, and corrupt person, one with low moral standards. The

Malawian word for politics, *ndale*, expresses these negative connotations: cunning, dishonest, conceit, and underhanded. To be referred to as *wandale* (adjective), is to be thought of as not an honest and reliable person, but a person with whom one has to be careful, one must be on the lookout for he or she is a deceitful and crafty person, or an exploiter. *Wandale* is also used to denote a "party" leader, and in most cases the negative connotation seems to fit, especially for those in the higher echelons of the system who seem to be corrupt morally and otherwise. During the years of a single party system in Malawi, (the party) *wandale* implied absolute power—one dared not say "no" when asked for anything, or else. Whatever *wandale* said, one did, no questions asked. Although the local party branch *wandale* may have been an honest person, people still felt they had to be careful, watchful to the point of self-censuring speech and deed before the party authority. Is politics really negative as it has been depicted?

It is interesting to note that *ndale* or *wandale* is never used in reference to traditional chiefs, village heads, or members of the council of elders. It appears that *ndale* only refers to practices and ways of relating within what are perceived as foreign, Western, social, political, and economic systems. *Ndale* and *wandale* are terms which emerged with the coming of colonialism and may have initially referred to the way whites related to Malawians. Etymologically, *ndale* derives from wrestling: it describes the calculated moves and blocks a wrestler makes to knock the opponent off balance and onto the ground. Thus in ordinary speech, *ndale* means slick, crafty, shrewd, sly, tricky, deceptive, and underhanded, or simply, to block someone. However, depending on the intonation, *ndale* can also mean a crack in a wall or ground. In both cases, the idea is that there is no unity, wholeness, or harmonious relations in which trust can exist. Given people's experience with "Western" systems of common life, perhaps *ndale* is a correct description and translation of politics. Before making such a characterization of Western politics, however it is proper to examine the meaning of politics in Western thought.

The Western understanding of politics derives from the Greek word, *politike*. Implied in this term is the notion of the *polis* which means city-state or town with the *polites*, citizen, who was a free member of the *polis*. (In ancient Greece women, though free, were not considered members of the *polis*.) It is also worth mentioning that the word *state* only appeared in the course of modern Western history; however, the notion of state itself was implicit in *polis*. Therefore, *politike,* referred to both the theory (science) and practice of the city-state and its members. Also implicit in *politike* is the modern idea of society. The Greeks had no word for society, accordingly, *politike* meant both theory and science of society as well as state.[1] This understanding of politics as a science (*techné*) of the *polis* is what Aristotle and Plato considered the only civilized form of human dwelling.

Building on Aristotle's understanding of society and state, the liberal tradition defines politics as the science of how people organize their societies and how society should be organized. Since politics is about organizing society, it concerns itself with issues relating to law, economics, and government.[2] This understanding of politics is limiting and narrow since it abstracts politics from everyday reality, that is from the people, and concentrates power in the hands of those in the areas of law, economics, and government. Politics is an everyday reality in which everyone is involved; politics is about how people live together, in a family, village, town, or wherever people are. Politics is about how people work together. Politics is about building networks of relations between people; a way people communicate among themselves as they live together. How people communicate or fail to do so, is reflected in their social relations and the kinds of social and political structures and institutions they create for themselves. For instance, when people do not relate very well among themselves, be it in a family, village, or the workplace, fear characterizes their relations and this fear is reflected in the kinds of channels of communication they develop, or fail to develop, among themselves. Fear creates poor channels of communication resulting in distrust and this is always destructive and paralysing.

NATION, NATIONALISM, AND ETHNICITY

The term, nation, is no longer popular as it was during the struggle for independence when the idea of peoplehood created a consciousness and an identity which inspired nationalism. The concept of nation and the spirit of nationalism as they are known today, was created by colonialism. This is to say that a European policy of divide and rule created nations in Africa. Families, ethnic communities, and kingdoms were divided arbitrarily to bring together different ethnic groups in order to create a territorial administrative unit. These different groups brought together against their will, soon began sharing a common experience, which created for them a common identity and history. From their common experience, in the shared immediate past—the experience of disrupted social structures and cultural values—emerged a consciousness of their life together, thus a sense of oneness as a people, but without dignity and history because of colonial subjugation. In the years following the Second World War, this feeling of common identity led to a sense of peoplehood and therefore nationalism.

This bringing together of different peoples under one administration was very much in line with the Western view of nation. In Western thought, *nation* is not something biological, although there may be some familial relation and cultural heritage, but the emphasis is on social formation emerging from common historical recollections. Nation is not a territorial area of power with institutions for administration as a state; it is a community of communities, a network of feelings of people in a particular physical, historical, and social formation. It is a community that is created, or rather, reasoned out, and not given by birth. Interestingly, the word nation itself means birth (*nasci*, in its Latin origin), but this birth is a social awakening to a particular human grouping. Nation and nationalism evolved in Europe, especially in Britain and France from the late eighteenth and early nineteenth centuries, as a result of economic and political revolutions in those countries. What emerged from those revolutions was a social, economic, and political stratification, a model of living together dependent on the "middle wealthy." This system replaced feudalism which had previously been the dominant way of life. To the European, "nation" therefore, meant liberty and freedom. The new social order had metaphysical roots: the equality of all people, the belief in universal order, and the sense of history as the unfolding of a progressive purpose. But unlike the old social organizations, the tribe and the feudal system, the new order was secular. The monarch and the Pope, or the court and the church, had lost power to a new consciousness. The new social formations, however, shared strong historical and social identities: a common language, culture and history, homogenous ethnicity, and boundaries that followed after the first three identities.

Tribalism and Ethnicity

Up until the 1990s, when some Eastern Europeans started asserting their will and started to demand self-determination, ethnic conflicts were characterized as an African phenomenon; something the "uncivilized tribes" of Africa did, and they were called *tribal* conflicts. Note that in Europe the same phenomenon is called *ethnic* conflict. Simply put: *tribes* are in Africa while ethnic groups are found in Europe. Applying the word *ethnic* to Europeans is a new thing altogether, for as far as Europeans were concerned, they had passed the stage of identification by origin and descendance; the old traditions had passed away after the coming of modernity. The socialization, hence the identity of a modern European was determined by economic circumstances, urbanization, education, and political participation. Africans being rural, still under traditional political organization, and uneducated (in the Western sense), were tribal. From a scholar's point of view, the distinction between tribe and ethnicity hinges on Weber's distinction between traditional and modern societies. It is known, though, that the colonial Europeans did not use this distinction; their understanding of a tribe was based on the view that as Europeans they were "civilized," having passed through the Enlightenment and industrial revolution.[3] Africans on the other hand, were "primitive," therefore still tribal. Today many African scholars and some Westerners too, object to the use of the term *tribe* because they consider it rooted in European prejudice.[4] In this chapter the term tribe will be used in its generic or basic understanding and its European usage in Africa.

Nation may be contrasted with tribe, which is an ethnic community defined by blood ties (no matter how remote), language, culture, and patterns of feelings rooted in the physical soil of origin of the group. The contrast made here does not imply that the idea of an original group—tribe and language—disappear in a nation-state. Britain and France are both composed of original tribal groups which were formed and reformed by waves of conquests, the last wave being that of the Scandinavians from the north, carrying the last fling of conquests from Normandy to Britain in 1066. In the wake of these upheavals, two communities framed particular languages and shaped each other's consciousness as a people by their continuous wars. It was language, above all, which served as the bond of unity between the people of each particular group. Language identified the old blood kinship of the tribe.

Tribe is the most ancient social organization, and most stable form of human society. It is usually composed of clans, kinship groups, and (extended) families. There is a strong sense of kinship and family solidarity since all members trace their biological lines to common ancestors. Members also share common traditions and the sense of the sacred, beliefs, and practices. It is within the security of a tribe that one develops a sense of identity, purpose, and meaning in life. Economically, it is a self-contained community. The size may vary but tribes do have defined territorial boundaries with or without a highly stratified political organization and military power. There are some exceptions, of course. In precolonial Africa, some tribes covered vast areas, they were nations in themselves, having one language, culture, political authority, and sacred history.

When colonialists started taking control of Africa, they found centralized kingdoms, stateless societies, and a variety of other cultural forms and political organizations, all of which involved a high degree of loyalty. Europeans believed that it would be difficult to govern people with strong loyalty to their ethnic group, but most importantly they believed that African political and economic structure would be an impediment to Europeanization (modernization) of Africa. For ideological and administrative purposes, colonialists created tribes as well as nations in Africa. While the rise of nation in Europe signaled liberty and freedom to Europeans, in Africa nation meant a forced gathering of people for subjugation by Europeans. To argue that Europeans created tribes, is not to deny that Africans did not see themselves as units sharing land, language, and culture. These three categories, land, language, and culture, fostered kinship systems that provided physiological and spiritual support to the individuals constituting the group.

Beginning with the partition of Africa along European territorial interests, Europeans divided ethnic groups, bringing together people with different ethnic background into administrative units called *tribes*. This is to say, *tribes*, as invented by Europeans, were territorial entities with cultural and linguistic differences. Even when the members of the tribe seemed to speak one language and share a common culture, it was only at a superficial level because the *language* and *culture* they shared were categories imposed on them by Europeans for political control. To illustrate, the people characterized as the Alomwe tribe in Malawi belonged to various language groups and had no common ancestry, but Chilomwe became the language of the Akokhola, Amarenje, Thakwani, and others who had been grouped together as members of the Alomwe. Similarly, all people in northern Malawi were categorized as Tumbuka although they did not even speak the same language. The real Tumbuka were members of the Ngoni groups that settled in the country in the later part of the nineteenth century, while the rest of the northerners were of the Maravi kingdom dating back to the fifteenth century. Tribe in its basic sense implies a kinship system but that was not always so with the tribes Europeans invented in Africa. It appears that the location of a group at the time of the colonization process defined the classification of the tribe. The people in northern Malawi became Tumbuka by tribe because of their location and not a common ancestry and heritage.

Tribe, as defined by Europeans, became the framework for institutional hegemony. Through constant usage of the term in school and government business, Europeans managed to make tribe the most powerful identity of people with a shared colonial experience. Curricula created a common language for the tribes that had been invented. In northern Malawi, Chitumbuka became the language of instruction, preaching, and government business. Thus Chitumbuka, the language colonialists imposed on all the people in northern Malawi, facilitated categories of understanding and governance according to the European way of seeing things. At the same time, Chitumbuka expedited the internalization of European values and worldview to such an extent that at the beginning of the struggle for political independence, the idea of tribe was stronger and more appealing than that of nation. One's social and political organization was defined by tribe. In fact, the African elite had to put aside the idea and primacy of tribe to achieve unity and mobilize the people in the struggle for independence.

When the struggle for independence started, nationalists pushed forward the idea of nation which they understood as a community of communities in which people had become aware of themselves as colonial history had made them. Political rhetoric emphasized the idea that the people of a given country were one because they belonged to one nation. Kenneth Kaunda's "One Zambia, One nation," political slogan is an example. The elite came to understand nation as a historical calling to fulfill the feelings and aspirations of those who constitute it and to do so by drawing on a people's potential. The elite did not question whether a political and economic organization of Europe would fit African ways of life; they took it for granted that just as it had worked in Europe to bring freedom and prosperity, it would work the same miracles in Africa. Thus "Building the Nation" became a dominant theme of many political parties for many years beyond the struggle for independence. In Malawi, "Building the Nation" was the theme of every annual convention of the Malawi Congress Party, the only party during the thirty years of the first republic. *Malawi News*, the official paper of the party, had "Building the Nation" as its motto. In adopting the concept of nation, the African elite did not pay attention to the historical and cultural factors which had given rise to the concept in Europe. Although there were some who knew that the concept of nation had risen on the ashes of feudalism, they ignored that this way of being together favored a few and that it was guided by the principle of capital formation.[5]

The idea of nation is in trouble in Africa today. The problem started right at the establishment of nations when different ethnic groups were forced to live together under a single administration. Inside this single administrative unit, the different tribal and ethnic groups were further divided for the colonial authorities knew that it would be much easier to control a group of tribes than a united people. As if tribal divisions were not enough, the authorities encouraged tribal hostilities by favoring one group over the rest, describing one as more intelligent or hardworking than others, a practice which Henry Okullu termed "chosenness" of the supertribe.[6] Similar ethnic divisions and hostilities were encouraged and followed in hiring for the civil service: administrators came from one ethnic group or region; the army was full of people from one region; good domestic servants in homes of Europeans came from a particular tribe. In creating a nation, colonialists also created "tribalism," that strong ethnic affiliation and allegiance which overrides the feelings for nation and directs obligation to the ethnic group or region of origin. Tribalism carries the idea of competition between tribes, hence the idea of doing things according to tribal sentiments. There is nothing bad in identifying oneself as a member of a particular tribe or ethnic group, for these are simply social, cultural, political, and linguistic groupings of people with a shared value system and concept of the world. What is wrong with "tribalism," is that it forms ethnocentrism, that curse which emerged with the European rule of divide and rule. This is to argue that in inventing tribes, Europeans also created tribalism, the tribal factionalism that seeks to relocate goods and services in a situation of competition for scarce resources. They invented tribes by grouping together related ethnic peoples and emphasized ethnic identities so as to create "tribes" to function within the colonial framework, for Europeans wrongly believed that Africans would work well as tribes since they had no notion of peoplehood or nation.

The white minority government in South Africa and Zimbabwe copied very well the colonial system of divide and rule to form a nation. Whites in these countries divided the indigenous people into tribal groups, played one against the other, and sharpened ethnic differences. The idea of homelands in South Africa fed on ethnic differences. Whites in South Africa believed they would create a stable nation, not by dividing the people arbitrarily but along ethnic lines. In this plan, South Africa would be a federation of nations, with whites controlling the federation. They not only divided people into ethnic groups but fanned the flames of ethnic suspicion and militarily supported the conflicts. The white minority government was responsible for the ethnic bloodbath the world witnessed between the Inkatha, a Zulu ethnic group, and the African National Congress, a party comprised of all ethnic and linguistic groupings, including whites, in South Africa. The government was responsible in every respect: they created it, and continued to support Inkatha, financially and otherwise, and they had biblical and theological justification for their evil practice.

Colonialism, with its system of divide and rule, favoring and playing off one group against the other, and using a strong arm, managed to keep the lid on the monster of tribalism which it had created. Postindependence Africa has not been so lucky; the beast came out not long after independence and in many countries it is influencing, if not determining national destiny. A number of variables unleashed the beast. Some clans and ethnic groups feel they are not receiving a fair representation in national government or getting a fair share of the "national cake," and such groups sometimes decide to opt out of the national boundaries. National government is evaluated in terms of which ethnic group dominates it—from which tribal group or region are the people in key positions in government. Government programs are evaluated the same way because dominant groups control the distribution of goods and services. The allocation of goods is a way of building or strengthening political support at ethnic grassroots levels. People at the grassroots level expect one of "their own" in the upper echelons of government or the party to deliver goods and services to his or her people or region. There is pressure for the elite to elevate the ethnic group or find rationale for unproportional distribution of services and goods to one region. Political parties are not free from ethnic interest and conflict, and that is why they, too, are assessed on how they distribute power. Thus tribalism may exist within a party, and sometimes perceived or real unequal distribution of power between various ethnic groups may lead to a split within the party itself. Civil wars in Africa must be understood from the angle of dissatisfaction and preferential treatment on the basis of ethnicity. The Biafran, Sudanese, Somali, Burundi, and Rwandan civil wars were expressions of deep dissatisfaction with the colonial arrangement of nation and with the distribution of material benefits in the postcolonial state. In Rwanda, the Hutu are about 85 percent of the population while the Tusi are 15 percent but during the presidency of the Tusi, the Hutu have not had equal access to employment and education.

It is ironic that in building *nations*, colonialists also introduced tribalism, a practice that would undermine the idea of nation. Colonialists were not alone in doing this: missionaries played a significant role in deepening ethnic differences, although it was not all their fault. Colonial policy was to allow Christian missionaries into certain ethnic group(s) and areas not under Islam. Obviously, those under Christian missionaries received Western education and some skills. This made those who were exposed to Western values feel "superior" to the other ethnic groups. This is what happened in Nigeria between the Muslim north, the Hausaland, and the Christian southeast, the Igbo. But it also happened in areas where missionaries were dominant in one ethnic group, and the "chosen" felt they were "civilized" because of their exposure to European values. It was not only tribalism that missionaries encouraged but also "detribalization" which happened through conversion and education. The converted often looked down on traditional culture and values as "heathen," and instead, glorified European values.

The struggle for independence developed an understanding of the ideology of nationalism because people faced a common enemy—colonialism. Experience had taught the people that it was easy for their colonial masters to deal with them as long as they brought their grievances as individual groups. The people realized that they were making it easy for colonialists to continue to control their destiny. There was a need, therefore, for unity transcending local loyalties of clan, ethnicity, and region, hence the birth of a nationalism. Speeches and resolutions of the first Nyasaland African Congress in 1944, reflect this realization: "In the past grievances and other vital matters affecting the country and the people have been presented to the government and/or other authorities by local organizations who were interested only in their local worries. It is considered that the time is ripe now for the Africans in this country to strive for unity so as to obtain the greater development of the peoples and country of Nyasaland."[7]

This awareness was universal in Africa and it intensified after the Second World War. As in the First World War, Africans were drafted to fight on the side of their colonial masters, and this time around, there was hope that things would be better after the war. Their hope was based on the promises of colonizing governments that its victory against an evil empire would bring peace and justice for all. But after the war, Africans were forgotten and their economic and political condition did not really improve. Just as it was after the First World War, the Europeans with whom they fought side by side in the war, were recognized by the metropolitan country for their valor on the battlefield. Some were given positions in government, others assigned to the colonial service as administrators, while others retired with handsome pensions, including land sold to them at a cheap price in the colonial country. The end of the Second World War made it very clear that colonial administrators did not have much interest in the economic, social, and political well-being of Africans. To make things worse, employment became difficult after the Second World War because of a number of factors: (1) there was little or no subsidy from the metropolitan country as it was itself trying to rebuild its own economic infrastructure in the wake of the destruction of the war; (2) there had been an increase in the amount of large estate farming and this altered land tenure systems in the rural areas, resulting in a massive exodus of people from villages into estates and urban areas as wage-laborers; (3) there was inflation after the war; and (4) there was growing urbanization, with an emerging middle class, because of Western education and local entrepreneurship. However, local business enterprises were too small and weak to absorb the people from rural areas and school leavers.

The end of the Second World War brought widespread dissatisfaction with colonialism. European exploitation and the harsh colonial practices and regulations removed any respect people may have had for the metropolitan country. In British colonies the people felt betrayed by Britain; it had not kept its prewar word of tutelage, according to which at an appropriate time the colonies would become self-governing. Colonialism had lost its justification and authority even for modernist Africa who had believed transformation was possible through the system. The elite, who had up to now fought for their own acceptance within the colonial structure and/or pleaded the grievances of tribal or regional associations that had sprung up between the two world wars, began agitating for more than transformation in education and welfare, and for progress. With the exception of Liberia's True Whig Party founded in 1860, political parties appeared in most of Africa only after the Second World War. Initially, nationalists did not seek independence; it was after the people had seen that the colonial system did little towards transformation that self-government and independence became a concern. Even then, only radicals sought self-rule. In French Africa, some nationalists, including prominent leaders such as Houphouët-Boigny, opposed independence at the Bamako Conference of the Rassemblement Democratique Africain (RDA) in 1946. Like many modernists and African deputies in French Parliament, he preferred membership of the French Communauté with a federal executive in Paris not in Dakar.[8] In fact, French Africa sought independence only after President Charles de Gaulle had changed his mind in 1959 following the realization that French economic interest could best be preserved by granting independence.

Nationalism on a large scale emerged after the Second World War, and it grew out of a general dissatisfaction with colonialism, starting from the rural areas, then into urban centers and trade unions (which had appeared to address the poor working conditions of the urban people) and to the political and bureaucratic elites. African nationalism was anticolonial nationalism since it was against the practices of colonialism which brought together people of different loyalties and background: chiefs, professionals (teachers, the few doctors, and lawyers), clerks, trade unions, various corporate and tribal associations, entrepreneurs (shopkeepers and traders), the urban workforce, and the rural smallholder farmers. African nationalism was also a moral nationalism for it was a movement for justice, dignity, and the right to self rule.

The idea of self-determination embodied in moral nationalism had been advanced by the religious faithful in both Christianity and Islam long before nationalism itself became popular. From the earliest times of Christian evangelization, there were African converts who did not want to be under the authority of missionaries for a number of reasons which can be summed up as treating the African without respect and dignity or simply as inferior. Such Africans founded their own churches mostly by breaking from the missionary churches, although some established their own churches without having first been members of mainline churches. These churches came to be known as Independent Churches, because of their origin and aspiration to be independent from whites.[9] The prophetic movements of the Liberian William Wade Harris, Garrick Braide in the Niger Delta, Simon Kimbangu in Congo, and many other African prophets, were powerful examples of the spirit of protest and independence which was to be the spirit of African nationalism. These leaders suffered imprisonment under colonial authorities: the French (Harris), the British (Braide), and Belgian (Kimbangu).[10] From 1913 to 1915, Harris crusaded on foot carrying a cross, Bible, and a bowl for baptism from Liberia, Côte d'Ivoire, Ghana, and back to Côte d'Ivoire. Arrested in September 1921, for preaching and performing healing miracles, Kimbangu "was tried of subversion and sentenced to one hundred and twenty lashes to be followed by execution. The death sentence was commuted by the King of Belgium. He was flogged and sent to Lubamba prison where he died in October 1951."[11]

"Independent Churches" is a broad spectrum title that includes churches of various sizes and orientation such as "Ethiopian," messianism, or millenialism such as that of the Watch Tower movement to which Elliot Kamwana belonged when he prophesied the First World War. Kamwana, a Malawian who had been attracted to millennial teachings in South Africa, came home to proclaim the message of his new faith which emphasized believers' baptism, the corrupt nature of governments and historic churches, and the end of the age, that is, the coming of the millennium in October

1914. This prophecy concerning World War I angered the colonial authorities; they called it a message of sedition. Kamwana had also managed to upset missionaries in the historic churches with his message of believers' baptism. The missionaries conspired against him and fabricated malicious reports against him to the colonial authorities who were already unhappy with him. The result was that Kamwana was deported to South African in 1909, but he secretly managed to reenter Malawi and this time around the colonial administration exiled him to the Seychelles Islands together with his followers where they remained until their release in 1937.[12]

Other Independent Churches are like mainline churches in doctrine and practice. Whatever their orientation, Independent Churches gave hope in a situation of political denial and economic insecurity. In a time when open political expression was dangerous or prohibited, the leaders of these churches spoke on behalf of the people when they raised issues of justice and equality. In some countries the leaders of Independent Churches, such as John Chilembwe of Malawi, were the first nationalists.[13] Some of the leaders were influenced by outside ideas such as Garveynism. The influence of Marcus Garvey in east, west, and southern Africa was enormous. Many intellectuals in Anglophone Africa read Garvey's journal, *The African World*, which appealed to the people of African descent to rebuild Africa to its glorious past—independent and free, politically and economically. In as much as these churches sought to be self-governing, they were forerunners of moral nationalism. The Mahdist movement in Islam was similar, for it too, sought to break with tradition and embrace new doctrine. With their message of African dignity, control, and independence, religious movements became seedbeds for nationalism, that is, nationalism as a protest movement towards independence.

Nationalism as a movement towards self-rule emerged from anticolonial coalitions. These united forces radicalized political parties where they had been allowed such as in Francophone Africa. Before the Second World War, parties meant practically nothing to the rural people since parties favored the political elite. In Francophone Africa parties were a means of choosing representatives who sat in the French National Assembly—during the Fourth (1946–1958) and Fifth Republics (1958 to the present), respectively—as deputies for their countries: Houphouét-Boingy (Côte d'Ivoire) was a deputy for thirteen years and Léopald Sénghor (Senegal) for two, four-year terms. Note that in the French electoral system the people voted for a party in a multi-member list system, while in the British single-member constituency system, voters elected an individual candidate. Up to the 1950s political parties were transformist; only a few of them agitated for independence. It must be pointed out, however, that in French-speaking Africa independence was constitutional but incompatible with belonging to the French community. France had a problem, namely, how to reconcile liberty and empire by stressing equality. Under the French idea of equality, fraternity, and liberty, equal treatment was to be accorded all citizens of the empire regardless of their place of origin and color. To hold the empire together or encourage fraternity, citizens outside France had representation in Paris for *départments*. That arrangement failed and the 1956 *loi cadre* reforms legally acknowledged that failure. On 28 September 1958, Francophone Africa went to a constitutional referendum over whether to remain within the French community or seek independence. President Charles de Gaulle warned that any country voting against Title XII of the Constitution of the Fifth Republic should be willing to "take the consequences." Only Guinea voted not to accept the Constitution and chose independence while the rest elected to become autonomous republics within the French community with France controlling foreign policy, defense, and currency. President de Gaulle remained faithful to his word: he gave harsh treatment to Sékou Touré and his Parti Démocratique du Guinée (PDG). Title XII did not remain in force for long; it was amended in 1959 and each country negotiated its independence with France and remained within Communauté renoée.[14]

In the 1950s nationalist leaders started appealing to various disenchanted groups and the larger population for a moral struggle against colonialism, which they deemed to have no right to be determining their destiny. Nationalists appealed to political interests of various associations and ethnic groups. From the 1920s Africa saw the birth of many organizations and associations: youth, students, women's, farmers, ethnic, crafts, professional groups, and credit and trade unions. Most of these associations and organizations were small and sometimes short-lived, but they provided a feeling of self-determination and preserving tradition since they were local. It was from these associations that political parties, nationalism, and sometimes trade unions grew. Nationalists appealed to all these associations, especially trade unions, thus attracting the urban working class. Trade unions had been agitating in many parts of Africa in pre-World War II but closer working relations with dominant parties came only on the eve of independence. Trade unions were strong but often did not get involved in political activities, they however, contributed a great deal to the rise of nationalism and the quest for dignity and self-determination that independence sought to bring.

In the last decade towards independence, nationalist leaders became dogmatic about their understanding of loyalty to the nation. Nation was the community of communities within colonial territory, and it was to this entity that loyalty was to be given and not the old attachments to tradition, ethnic, and clan groupings. Most nationalists wanted to wipe out the old loyalties, because they believed multiple loyalties were incompatible with development and modernization, and above all, the idea of modern statehood. These nationalists feared old loyalties would prevent positive identification with the territorial nation as defined by colonialism, which had now become their new identity. Ajayi says, "As the European administrators became more and more effective, the colonial boundaries, arbitrary as many of them were, began to acquire some significance for the African. Each territorial unit was becoming the focus of some national loyalty."[15] While most nationalists wanted to get rid of old loyalties, others did not see it that way: Joseph Kasavubu and his Abako leaders in the Democratic Republic of Congo, for example, "conceived of the Congolese nation as an aggregate of distinctive loyalties based on 'ethnic, linguistic, and historical' affinities . . . . [and they] favored the maintenance and preservation of all intermediate groups."[16] The goal of most nationalists, however, was "the creation of larger, economically and technologically developed nations able to take their places in a basis of equality with other nations in the world."[17] To achieve this goal, national solidarity was necessary and that could not happen with old loyalties and their parochial ethnic groupings which often produced "negative tribalism" that went back to the beginnings of colonial power.

While most nationalists denounced old associations and loyalties, they exploited them for political support, thus strengthening rather than weakening the hostilities planted by colonialists. As political campaigns intensified in the years leading to independence, so did the rivalries and hostilities. Once again, it was at the instigation of the about to go colonialists, who believed the country would be well served if a particular ethnic group took control. Colonialists started planting fear, telling one group the future would be secure for one group and not the other. This was the case in Uganda where the British favored one ethnic group over the rest. In postcolonial Africa these divisions have played themselves out to the point of destroying the nation. It has not all been the indigenous people playing on the idea of "chosenness," the "better than thou," attitude of the superior ethnic group. Henry Okullu says that since independence in East Africa, the encouragement of tribalism by foreigners has taken a new and interesting dimension; some foreigners have sided with certain ethnic groups. "The explanation is that certain tribes are accused of being 'unfriendly,' therefore if they took a leading role in the government they would not be able to look after the economic interest of Western investors—or to look after Eastern economic interests." But Okullu also says that certain situations have forced foreigners to go along with ethnic divisions. "Say, for example, a business concern wishes to Africanize a management post, the firm would be very reluctant to appoint to such a post a person who comes from a tribe which will not carry influence with those in government."[18]

What we see is that from the beginning of the "new nations" there was never serious concern obligation to the nation. There is nothing wrong in emphasizing one's ethnicity and being loyal to it, but it is of utmost importance to recognize, and particularly for those in authority, that nation is a community beyond the ethnic community. Indeed, the contemporary nations are not of Africans own making, they emerge from historical circumstances which have forged people into nation-states. The nation is not a marketplace from which one gets items for one's people and them alone, which is the idea of clientelism inherit in tribalism. Politicians and public officials should not use nation as a slogan, but should show loyalty and obligation to it. There should not be any conflict between nation and ethnicity because if the nation is served well, and justice is practiced, no ethnic group should suffer want. When people begin to think of nation as a "pie," for which ethnic or regional groups scramble, that announces the beginning of the end of the nation for no one will feel responsible for or obligation to the nation.

Prejudice of any sort—tribalism, regionalism, or racism—has a negative impact on national economy. When a nation is torn by tribalism, it becomes economically weak. Tribalism always over and under-allocates resources causing a weakening of the domestic economy. This over-and under-allocation is best seen in hiring practices. To illustrate, tribe *A*, wanting to improve the status of its members, hires most of the senior technical and managerial staff from its own tribe regardless of qualification. Tribe *A* has over-allocated by over-recruiting from one tribe, its own. At the same time, tribe *A* has under-allocated causing a swell in unemployment and an uneven distribution of available goods and services in the rest of the country.

In tribalism there is an overwhelming tendency to overlook qualification and experience when hiring in order to advance the tribe. When widely practiced, the favoritism of tribalism can affect productivity because of the deficiencies that the employees may have and the lack of motivation due to the absence of competition from rival ethnic groups. Productivity (P) is measured by average output (AV) per unit time (T) or the average of what each employee produces in a given time, say per hour or day. Thus P=AV over T. Since tribe *A* did not minimize human resources by hiring according to merit and competency, production cost goes up because of inefficiency in the production process. Efficiency (E) means the price of goods and services (PG) considered as approximately equal to average total costs (TC), and the minimum resources (R) needed to produce a wanted product. Therefore E=PG=TC over R. Since qualification and skill were not considered when hiring, efficiency becomes impossible as employees are paid for doing little for a given time: too many employees with little or no qualification. "Too many cooks spoil the soup," as the saying goes, only worse in this case since the cooks do not even know how to cook! This leads to losses resulting from average total costs. The employer absorbs these losses by increasing the prices of goods and services. This makes the products out of reach for most consumers and the firm becomes uncompetitive at the home market, and in the case of the government revenue is lost.

The major problem with African governments is that they are inefficient at the technical and bureaucratic levels, and part of this inefficiency can be attributed to tribalism, regionalism, and clientelism (the preferential treatment of friends and relations). These cost a nation a great deal in terms of economic and human resources. Here are the costs of tribalism and they could be applied to regionalism and clientelism: (1) tribalism prevents economic efficiency of a society *as a whole* because the combination of output with total value does not equal average total costs, given the limited resources; (2) tribalism wastes human capital by giving preferential treatment in not hiring the most qualified and skilled. This becomes the source of economic inefficiency, dissatisfaction, and conflict between various ethnic groups as goods and services are not allocated equally. To become efficient, in the technical and bureaucratic sense, Africa needs qualified people to take positions of leadership besides cutting overspending and taking other measures. Rival tribalism must be given up for pride and loyalty to one's culture and ethnicity without preventing national development.

NOTES

1. Aristotle, *Nicomachean Ethics.* Martin Ostwald, trans. and intro. Indianapolis: Bobbs-Merrill Publishing, 1962; Scott Buchanan, edited with Introduction, *The Portable Plato* (New York: Penguin Books, 1981), Ernest Barker, *The Political Thought of Plato and Aristotle* (London: Oxford University Press, 1906); Ernest Baker, *Greek Political Theory*, 4th. ed. (London: Methuen, 1951), chap. 1 and 2.

2. Roberto Mangabeira Unger, *Knowledge and Politics* (New York: Free Press, 1975), 4.

3. I have discussed the problem of the European self-understanding under the concept of "civilization." See my book *Drums of Redemption: An Introduction to African Christianity* (Westport, CT: Greenwood Press, 1994), 104–5.

4. Bates makes the distinction between tribe and ethnicity based on the idea of modernity. See Robert H. Bates, "Ethnic Competition and Modernization in Contemporary Africa," *Comparative Political Studies*, 6 (January 1974): 457–484.

5. Basil Davidson, *The Search for Africa: History, Culture, Politics* (New York: Times Books, 1994), 259.

6. Okullu, *Church and Politics in East Africa* (Nairobi: Uzima Press, 1982. Reprint), 48.

7. Robert I. Rotberg, *The Rise of Nationalism in Central Africa: The Making of Malawi and Zambia 1873–1964* (Cambridge, MA: Harvard University Press, 1965), 183.

8. Elenga M'uyinga, *Panafricanism or Neocolonialism* (London: Zed Press, 1982), 34–37.

9. I have discussed the subject of Independent Churches in *Drums of Redemption*, 127–134

10. Ibid., 85–88.

11. Ibid., 88.

12. Harvey J. Sindima, *The Legacy of Scottish Missionaries in Malawi* (Lewiston, NY: Edwin Mellen, 1992), 76–77.

13. For a full discussion of John Chilembwe, see George Sherperson and Tom Price, *Independent African: John Chilembwe and the Origins, Setting, and Significance of the Nyasaland Native Rising of 1915* (Edinburgh: Edinburgh University Press, 1958).

14. R. S. Morgenthau, *Political Parties in French-Speaking West Africa* (London: Oxford University Press, 1964), 73–74.

15. J. F. A. Ajayi, "The Place of African History and Culture in the Process of Nation-Building in Africa South of the Sahara," *Journal of Negro Education* 30, 3 (1961): 209.

16. Rene Lemarchand, "The Basis of Nationalism among the Bakongo," *Africa* 31, 4 (October 1961): 347.

17. Ajayi, "The Place of African History," 211.

18. Ibid., 50.

3

State and Civil Society

In this chapter we will seek to understand the nature of governance or the capacity of the state to establish and maintain the common good. In this respect, we will address the issue of efficiency, exploring how a state becomes an efficient machinery for delivering the common good. Attention will be given to the state in postcolonial Africa but the colonial state will also be discussed. The state is an ensemble of institutions of government—administrative, technical, political, and economic institutions—for the welfare of the people. The chapter will, therefore, be concerned with the nature of the state in Africa and its capacity to respond to demands and pressures of various societal groups, its ability to mediate social demands and maintain institutions, and be effective in conflict resolution and administration. The success—or failure—of a state depends on its ability to establish and maintain effectively the institutions of government, administrative and technical, and to discharge political and economic functions towards national development. The state is distinct from society and economy, but it asserts its control over economic and social interactions, and actually structures economic and social relations. The state does this out of concern for the common good, and this obliges it to maintain internal and external security, to generate revenue, and to achieve dominance over alternative forms of social organization. The ability of the state to achieve these objectives depends on its legitimacy and internal cohesion, economic conditions, and the degrees of social mobilization. The examination of the nature of the state in Africa will be made in light of these introductory remarks. There have been various forms of state in Africa: colonial, postcolonial based on the Westminster and Elysée Palace, one-party, and military states. We will discuss each of these types of states and the evolution from colonial, independent state to single-party and military governments.

A regime defines the state, or at least the way it wants society to perceive the nature and function of the state. However, there are certain fundamental concepts concerning the nature of the state. In general, the state is that part of the people concerned with the maintenance of law, the promotion of the common welfare, and administration of public affairs. It is that part of society which specializes in the interests of the whole. Through the constitution, people put the state in power to carry out its duties and responsibilities in accordance with the will of the people as expressed in the constitution. This means that, except under military rule or government take over by force, the people are governed by individuals they themselves have chosen, and entrusted with a power to command. Leaders are chosen for functions of determined nature and duration, and are monitored by the people through representatives in the national assembly. The people who are invested with executive power, the administrative officials, are the governing organ *in the state*, because people have made them the deputies for the whole. The responsibility of the national assembly, then, is to express the will of the people and to provide checks and balances on the functions of the state. The people are the very substance, the essence if you will, of the state. They are above the state; they are not for the state, the state is for them.

The state is not an individual or a group of people with power to administer the nation; the state is a set of institutions combined into a machinery working for the common good.[1] As a "machine," the state has no brain, spirit, or feeling; its character, personality, and attitude are those of its administrative officials. This machinery is not above the people but conducts its duties with authority from the people and only by virtue and to the extent that it meets the requirements of the common good. When the state no longer regulates itself in accordance to these requirements, it loses its authority for it is no longer for the people. It becomes concerned with self-preservation—or better, the preservation of those who run it—distinct both from public order and welfare which are its immediate end, and from the common good, its final end. In self-preservation power is abused and consequently social justice, or the common good, are not enforced. Public welfare and the general order of law are essential, but the common good includes: promotion of good human life by providing public commodities and services as well as those nonmaterial things that help foster full human existence, or personhood, namely, cultural values, wisdom and knowledge, virtue, moral rectitude, and spiritual pursuit. In brief, those things which bring happiness, peace, and freedom.

At the center of the church-state tension is the question of power. The church and state both have power and appeal to symbolizations of power. The state does not have power of its own, but is entrusted with power. The state uses power to safeguard private interests of the "general public." The term *state* itself is a symbolization of trusteeship of the power of the persons constituting the state. In liberal political theory, the state is the symbolization of private wills. This is to say that the state is a will above contending private wills, therefore the main task of the state is to avoid a dictatorship of private interests (wills). The state carries out its duty through means of public rules, and by enforcing laws and rules, the state promotes the "common good" and controls hostility between people of different interests.

Perhaps Hobbes expressed most succinctly the need to form a state, or commonwealth as he put it, to regulate the claims of contending wills so that there may be peace in society.

> The only way to erect such a Common Power . . . is to confer all their power and strength upon one Man, or upon one assembly of men, that may reduce all their Wills, by plurality of voices, into one Will; which is as much to say, to appoint one Man, or Assembly of men, to bear their Person; and everyone to own, and acknowledge himself to be the author of whatsoever he that so bears their Person, shall Act, or cause to be Acted, in those things which concern Common Peace and Safety; and therein to submit their will, everyone to his Will and their judgement. This is more than Consent or Concord; it is a real Unity of them all, in one and the same person, made by covenant of every man with every man, in such a manner, as if every man should say to every man, "I authorize and give up my right of governing myself, to this Man, or to this Assembly of men, on this condition, that you give up your right to him, and authorize all his actions in like manner."[2]

Hobbes identifies this idea of the state and its duty as sovereign monarch (*Leviathan* chapter 18), and Hegel refers to it as universal (bureaucratic) class and the crown. The monarchy was to Hobbes the most stable and orderly kind of government. Like Machiavelli before him, Hobbes believed in absolute power of the monarch. Since he maintained people were radically egoistic by nature, Hobbes argued that the monarch and force behind the law was the only power able to hold society together. For Hobbes, as for Machiavelli, there is nothing in human behavior to inform people about living together well. Moral obligations can only derive from law and government by a powerful monarch or Prince. The ideas of Hobbes and Machiavelli on the running of the state relate closely, especially on issues of power and government. Hobbes in many ways systematized Machiavelli's social philosophy.

It is to be noted that Hobbes's commonwealth or state implies a surrender of private wills to form a General Will, which transcends all wills and has absolute power over all. This is the basis of Rousseau's Social Contract and the sovereignty of the monarch: "the social pact gives the body politic an absolute power over all its members; and it is this same power, which directed by general will bears . . . sovereignty."[3] Rousseau's state was but the Hobbesian Leviathan, crowned with General Will.

Sovereignty is a two-sided concept with bad and good sides, depending on how the sovereign perceives the nature of the office to which he or she has been called. The problem with the concept lies in the idea of absolute power. When this power is used to protect and enhance the common good, monarchy is good, for it embodies the will and wishes of the people. On the other hand, the monarch can use absolute power to oppress the people who should be the final judges of the stewardship of government officials since they entrusted the monarch with power to administer justice. This happens when the monarch no longer feels accountable to the people. Simply put: a repressive monarchy ceases to be accountable to the people since it robs the people of their responsibility to supervise the state. Repressive monarchs, despots, use absolute power to impose their will on the people; accordingly, they have no checks and balances on their administration, hence the corrupt nature typical of authoritarian rule.

THE COLONIAL STATE

What does the discussion of political theory have to do with the African reality? It is always claimed that Europeans left a democratic form of state in Africa. From what has been said above concerning the nature of politics and the meaning of the state, it is hard to see how the legacy of colonialism could have been democratic by any means. To begin with, the people had nothing to do with the coming into existence of the colonial government that had power over them. Colonial rule survived by command, maintenance of rigid hierarchies, and the attitude that colonial, governments knew best. Everyone who lived through any part of the colonial period knows that the system was highly centralized to the point of being quasi-military and the tendency everywhere was towards paternalistic bureaucratic authoritarianism. Further, the colonial government had no system of multi-party politics; the British, the French, and later the Belgians, were pressured into multi-party politics by African political activities. Strikes and other forms of instability decreased the value of colonial bases, disrupting full exploitation of trade and investment opportunities. When multi-party politics finally happened, in very few cases did the people elect the members of the Legislative Council (each British colony had its own Legislative Council) or deputies in French Parliament. Moreover, even fewer Africans received ministerial responsibility in colonial governments; the few who did were in French colonies. The Legislative Council itself was not a body which provided checks and balances for the colonial administration.

The colonial state was an absolute monarchy answerable to no one except the home government it served and along whose requirements it was organized. Colonial governments did not hide this fact about administering "natives"; colonial administrators acted in the interests and only at the dictates of Westminster and Elysée Palace. Indeed, they later introduced "opposition parties" in the Legislative Council but it was not there by the will of the people and did not represent the people. In Malawi, Zambia, and Zimbabwe, the "opposition party" was part of the colonial machinery representing the interests of white farmers. In short, the colonial administration was not a representative form of government, and in most places African political activity was banned; where it was permitted, people could not electorally compete in a political system that was monopolized by European administrators and others. Abuses of freedoms and instances of lack of human respect by the colonial government are too many to enumerate, but suffice it to say these were the factors that galvanized the people in the struggle for independence.

Gus Liebenow says it can be correctly argued that the British and the French at least had some resemblance of a "democratic" government by the twilight of colonialism.[4] That cannot be said of the Belgians, the Portuguese, the Spanish, and the pre-World War II Italians. The Portuguese under Salzar, the Spanish under Franco, and the Italians under Mussolini did not permit competitive political groups to challenge the monopoly of the fascist parties in their respective countries. It should not have been expected therefore that the situation in Angola, Fernado Po, or Eritrea could have been more liberal than in the situation in the metropole. Elections, where they did occur, were confirming plebiscites conducted to give the regime the appearance of legitimacy. African participation was token where it was permitted. In contrast, the Belgians had a long history of multi-party democracy at home, but until about two years prior to independence they denied this form of government to people in their colony, Belgian Congo. The country was governed by a troika: the colonial administration, the Roman Catholic Church, and the Union Minière du Haut Katanga, an industrial corporation.

THE STATE IN INDEPENDENT AFRICA

The politics of independence have been those of despair. Independence only changed the faces of the leaders in government, but not the nature and practice of the state, and this was true even in places where only a few white civil servants remained. The colonial state machinery remained intact after independence because African civil servants had been trained, even though at a junior level, to maintain the colonial state apparatus. Most of them had a good education compared to the rest of the population. Their education along with their positions in government gave them contempt for African values and instead they aspired Western ones. The fact that civil servants were trained only at junior levels meant that there was a serious shortage of trained and experienced African personnel. By comparison, Francophone Africa was a bit better; trained there were more and experienced Africans than in English-speaking colonies. The French established more universities and institutions of higher learning. (The number of educated people during the colonial period remained very low. In 1958 there were only about 20,000 Africans enrolled in universities, with a limited number in secondary schools and by 1960 only 3 percent of school-age children were in school).[5] Likewise, Anglophone West Africa could and did fill most senior administrative and technical positions with trained and qualified indigenous personnel. In the rest of Africa the new leaders were faced with the choice of either retaining white administrative and technical staff until local people had been trained for the position; or recruiting expatriates on contract under technical assistance agreements with the former metropolitan.

This approach was not well-received by politicians, trade-unionists, and the general population, who demanded immediate filling of public service with Africans. The demand for immediate Africanization led to localization of most administrative positions, especially highly visible positions. Accelerated promotions led senior clerks into taking chief administrative positions and top policy-making positions, including permanent secretaries, and the foreign service. The Africanization of the public service was very rapid in most of Africa excluding Côte d'Ivoire and Malawi where the process was deliberately almost as slow as it was in the colonial times; people had to prove themselves for senior administrative and technical jobs. The Africanization of the civil service has been criticized in and outside Africa for mismanagement and inefficiency. While that is true in some cases, what must be realized is that Africans inherited huge European state bureaucracies with few trained and qualified administrative and technical personnel, and without sufficient material resources to run them. With a shortage of qualified personnel, so much energy was spent in keeping the huge state machinery going that necessary administrative reforms were not undertaken. The new leaders had no time to formulate economic policies that would help with operating the state bureaucracies which they had inherited. They also needed to satisfy political demands of the electorate, among which was seeing African faces in government offices since it was Africans who were now in control of government.

The leaders of the postcolonial state in Africa had other problems with the state machinery they had inherited. It appears that the brevity of exposure to a parliamentary system prior to independence did not allow nationalist leaders to become aware of the problems inherent in a state machinery modeled on the institutions of the metropolitan countries in the post-1945 period. This meant that the machinery would be costly to run and difficult to staff given that during colonialism Africans gained no experience operating a governmental system on a national scale in addition to lacking a high level of technical and administrative skills. If nationalists were aware of these problems, they may not have been cognizant of how difficult it would prove to change the state bureaucracy and parliamentary system towards the task of nation-building, effectively dealing with poverty, and raising the Gross National Product (GNP). At any rate, they decided to follow the Westminster and Elysée Palace forms of government, and with these they also inherited a crisis that had started with the creation of the nation-state, namely, the disintegration of society that would result in serious social structural breakdown manifesting itself in poor government and poverty. By opting for Western forms of government and state bureaucracy, nationalist leaders accepted a system which was antithetical to the dreams of independence and African ways of life. The principles governing the colonial state directed all activity towards the metropolitan center and fostered the center's interests and values. The colonial state was there to channel resources home to Europe and not to deal with African poverty and national infrastructure. Commenting on how much British colonial states channeled resources to the home government, David Fieldhouse says a "rough calculation suggests that between 1945 and 1951, Britain extracted some 140 millions (pounds) from its colonies, putting in only about 40 millions under Colonial Development and Welfare Acts."[6] Fieldhouse also says that in the 1950s when Belgium Congo had only about 1 percent foreigners, "95 percent of total assets, 82 percent of the largest units of production and 88 percent of the private savings belonged to foreigners. . . . Here then was a society in which about 110,000 whites and a very few large overseas firms controlled almost the entire modern economy."[7]

These are the kinds of problems African nationalists inherited at independence. National independence was a transfer of poverty which would continue and become evident in the 1970s and 1980s, as the international terms of trade continued to favor Europeans resulting in a deep decline of Africa's export earnings. Illustrating this point in his book *The Black Man's Burden*, Basil Davidson says, "In 1975, for example, a ton of African copper could buy 115 barrels of oil, but in 1980 only 58 barrels; a ton of African cocoa could buy 148 barrels of oil in 1975, but in 1980 only 63 barrels; a ton of African coffee could buy 148 barrels of oil in 1975, but in 1980 only 82 barrels."[8]

Not long after independence nationalist leaders realized that they could not implement the dreams of independence by following the rules of the state machinery. Frustrated by the system or by their inability to change the system, they started blaming it on the opposition, thereby blaming the parliamentary system which they had inherited. Nationalist leaders started patching up the system to "fit African traditional political systems," but this in fact was an attempt to curb opposition and domesticate the body politic. This "traditional" form of politics and government was not quite "traditional," neither was it Western. The problem was that when the leaders decided to appropriate traditional models, it was to establish a paternalistic form of government in order to exercise absolute rule and eliminate opposition. This was contrary to traditional forms of government which were not paternalistic.

It is not popular in the West and in some African circles to say that current African problems cannot be understood without taking into account the colonial period. It is argued that it is a cop-out, an attempt to blame colonialism for the mismanagement and corruption of the current leaders. This may be true to a degree, but are Africans the most corrupt people on earth? Colonialism has a lot to answer for why nationalist leaders did not choose a different form of government at independence. Basil Davidson is correct in his assessment of the impact of colonialism in Africa. Davidson says that colonialism in Africa set out to deny and eventually eliminate the continent's precolonial history. Africa was a continent without history, therefore the European project in Africa "taught that nothing useful could develop without denying Africa's past, without ruthless severing from Africa's roots."[9] To this end, Europeans found willing accomplices among Africa's European oriented elite, the "modernizers," who were in constant conflict with traditionalists, including chiefs. The modernizers had bought into the idea that anything traditional was by definition primitive. It was this group of elites that was at the forefront of the independence struggle, and this group imposed European models on new Africa. To them, there was nothing "out there" to help the new Africa move towards modernization, so they proceeded to purge what was deepest and most authentic in African culture: "Africa would prosper upon condition of rejecting itself. The future was not to grow out of the past, organically and developmentally, but from an entirely alien dispensation," observes Davidson.[10] One still hears the comment to the effect that traditional Africa has nothing to offer modernity, so Africa keeps looking elsewhere rather than into its culture and tradition for solutions for present ills. Traditional ways have become quaint in these days of the cry for multi-party democracy. Multi-party systems *may* solve the question of repression but I am not sure that Africa's political and economic crisis will be solved. Senegal has a number of registered parties; Gambia had them too before the military takeover in October 1994; Mauritius has a multi-party system; and Zambia joined them with the 1991 election of Frederick Chiluba as president (ending the three-decade rule of Kenneth Kaunda); but in 1990 the economies of these countries were not much better than those of Ivory Coast, Malawi, and Kenya, countries with single party systems since independence. (The latter two went multi-party in 1994 and 1992 respectively.) The only exception is Botswana, and there we may have to look at factors other than a multi-party system for the country's great economic success. Multi-party politics succeeds in removing the problem of repression but not the problem of moral crisis, and this may be the area in which traditional values and wisdom may help Africa.

The idea of the nation-state as a means to create forms of administration and governance that will enable the continent to get out of its current crisis is in trouble. The idea of the nation-state has not worked for the simple reason that it does not belong there, and does not correspond to traditional forms of governance which had allowed the continent to survive for thousands of years. While accepting blame for some of the failures of the African leadership, it is important to remember that nation-states in Africa have not worked in part because such political and economic organizations presupposes a "middle strata capable of dominating society and its economic sources of wealth; and these indispensable 'middle strata'—whether 'bourgeois' or 'middle bourgeois' or even 'petty bourgeois'—were precisely what the histories of Britain and France had produced over the past 150 years."[11] These classes later produced a "working class." Thus we see that inherent in the concept of nation-state is organizing the people on a bourgeois-capitalist system. At independence African countries did not have a sizeable "middle strata" to effect a smooth running of the nation-state which they had inherited.

ONE-PARTY STATE

Now let us follow the evolution from Westminster or Elysée Palace style of government to the so-called African type. Several things happened which led to this move, and the precipitating factors were not the same and universal; even for those which were similar, there were some nuances particular to each country.[12] To take Francophone Africa, for instance, there the new states inherited the centralizing tradition of the French. Africans there participated in elections and parties as far back as the time of the French Third Republic (1870–1940) when the évolués of the four communes around Dakar, Senegal, participated in the elections. The parties and the parliamentary institutions they participated in, however, were French parties which organized branches in the territories. The point is that Africans participated in parties as long as those parties were affiliated with parties in France. The reason France did this was to centralize political activity in France and to divert the territories from engaging in their individual political parties. At independence, the new Francophone states adopted the centralizing practice of France. Although Africans in French territories had the experience of voting in party politics, they did not have the background of a competitive party system as in countries under British rule. In a way,

Francophone Africans really did not inherit competitive party-politics for they had never voted for individuals but parties. On the other hand they had higher levels of electoral participation than in Anglophone Africa.

The history of parties in Africa is a post-World War experience. It was stated in the previous chapter that with the exception of the Whig Party of Liberia founded in 1860, parties emerged in most of Africa in the post-World War II period. There were a few parties established during the first quarter of the twentieth century: the African National Congress in South Africa formed in 1912 was a coalition of Africans, European, and Indian settlers; the National Congress of British West Africa was established in 1917; and the National Democratic Party of Nigeria was founded in Lagos in 1923. As indicated in chapter two, most political parties evolved from differing interest groups, economic and cultural associations, voluntary organizations, and other movements concerned with everyday things. These African parties never really functioned as political parties in colonial politics for two reasons: (1) initially, the parties were not concerned with issues of representation in the colonial parliament but with issues of justice; but (2) when the parties started talking about no taxation without representation, the colonial government did not permit the parties to have candidates for parliamentary or local elections. Instead, in British Africa, the other groups that functioned as parties and had candidates besides the colonial party candidates, were settler parties found especially in southern, central, and east Africa. These parties defended their interests, which included internal political affairs, and they were responsible for the colonial government's passing of racist laws covering education and social services.

In the years leading to independence, African parties emerged as uniting and mobilizing forces. While in some places parties were country-wide, in others they were regional or even ethnic, functioning as a galvanizing power. The revolutionary parties—those parties that won independence by the barrel of gun—of Angola, Guinea-Bissau, Mozambique, and Zimbabwe were not only the galvanizing powers, but the very force towards independence. How countries became one party states after independence differed: for some such as Mauritania and Chad, it was by default in the sense that they were the party that won all or almost all the seats in parliament; while elsewhere there was no party organization to compete with the ruling party—this was the case in Côte d'Ivoire, Guinea, Mali, Niger, and Liberia. In other situations, such as Malagasy Republic, Kenya, and Uganda, the dominant party won a majority of the seats in the legislature, but the opposition existed. There were other instances where the party composed of settlers and colonialists was abolished soon after independence—since it was a party of foreigners—thereby making the dominant party all the more powerful. This was the case in Malawi. It must be pointed out, though, that the one-party system in Malawi was by act of Parliament which passed the Enabling Act on 17 May

1966. Act no. 23, the Republic of Malawi (Constitution) Act, was passed two years after the country had earned its independence from Britain.[13] There was a stipulation in the Republic Constitution to cater to European interests because of their electoral role, which was to be abolished by the independence constitution.[14] In some countries the one-party state was *de jure* while in others it was *de facto*. The *de jure* parties include the Front de Libération Nationale (FLN) in Algeria, the Mouvement National de la Révolution in Congo-Brazzaville, the Convention People's Party (CPP) in Ghana, and the Tanganyika African National Union (TANU) in Tanzania.[15]

The mandate for a one-party state was clear in some countries such as Tanzania. In others countries, such as Ghana, the mandate was uncertain. The degree to which one-party systems operated differed from country to country. In Tanzania, TANU (after the April 1964 union between Tanganyika and Zanzibar, TANU was known as Chama Cha Mapinduzi (CCM)—Revolutionary Party) permitted considerable intra-party competition, while in Kenya, opposition was allowed in the legislature, and in other countries (Ghana, Guinea, etcetera) these situations did not prevail. The ideological basis for single-party systems varied too, and was strong in some countries (the Parti Démocratique de Guinée in Guinea for example) and weak in others (the Parti Démocratique de Côte d'Ivoire in Ivory Coast). Legalizing of a one-party state did not happen immediately after independence. Countries evolved into single party states, and two of the reasons were: (1) the strength of the ideological underpinnings after independence, and (2) the move away from political pluralism. After independence a number of African countries sought to find ways to address the emerging economic disparity in society resulting from the problems of colonialism and its market economy. As I say in *Africa's Agenda*, "The challenge," before nationalists,

> was now to engage liberal economics and political theory in order to find a mode of production and political theory that would enhance African values. Liberal political theory and economics had proven antithetical and destructive to African values and way of life. . . . Given the basic presuppositions of liberal economics—power, competition, private ownership, and control of the means of production—African nationalists saw that this system could not foster African values, especially community and the dignity of persons. . . . For them, such a system had to be communal. Such a mode of production already existed in traditional society; nationalists called it African socialism.[16]

Various brands of African socialism emerged after independence, some leaning towards Leninism (Sékou Touré in Guinea), or influenced by the dialectical materialism of Karl Marx (Nkrumah's scientific socialism in Ghana) or Marx and Pierre de Teilhard de Chardin (Senghor in Senegal), or de Chardin alone (Kaunda's humanism in Zambia).[17] Nyerere's *Ujamaa* was rooted in traditional society. It was not until the 1970s that a number of ruling parties identified themselves as strongly Marxist-Leninist in doctrine. The degree to which party ideology influenced national economic decisions depended on the strength of the party and particularly on the charisma and dominance of the party's leader who was the party ideology's architect, ideologue and state president. Technocrats, civil servants in general, tended to be cautious in implementing economic decisions of the ruling party. Most of the time they carried out the decisions for fear of losing their jobs.

As varied as the issues were that led to one-party systems in Africa, they can be summed up as failure to accommodate opposition arising from a dislike of the government or from ethnic and regional issues. Even more serious was the mistaken view of the nature of power and functions of the state. The state having been initially democratically elected, drew no distinction between itself and the body politic, the people. That is to say, "the (ruling) Party" became the state. The party-turned-state misinterpreted its success as a mandate to control all dimensions of society and consequently took upon itself the tasks which should pertain to (civil) society and its various organs.

This practice produced a "paternalistic state," which by its very nature is authoritarian because it assumes absolute power—the monarchy of Rousseau. I use the term "paternalistic state" to include various forms of government. The paternalistic state goes beyond the normal function of the state, which is to supervise from the political point of view the common good and security. It directly organizes, controls, and manages, to the extent it judges the public welfare to demand, all forms—economic, commercial, cultural, academic research—of the life of civil society. The paternalistic state determines which activities are good for civil society. While the state may have competence and skill in certain areas—administration, legal, and political—it cannot control all endeavors such as the arts and sciences, for instance. Therefore its paternalism stifles creativity, but above all abrogates the freedom of organization and expression of its citizens.

The paternalistic state can exist only by effectively eliminating all opposition and politically domesticating the people by presenting them with symbols, values, and projects around which they rally and find some identity. This is the same political strategy that was used in the campaign for independence, but used this time to depoliticize the people. This process prevents the people from participating in meaningful politics. The state uses its absolute power to silence those who do not become domesticated by designating them rebels, dissidents, and other labels which make them look like troublemakers, people who do not appreciate what their government is doing. This is why the paternalistic state is prone to abuse of power and authority to accomplish its goals.

Here we see the evolution to a one party-system state, a system common in most of Africa since the mid-sixties, and which by 1984 was present in twenty-five countries—more than half of all countries in Africa. What was the rationale supporting the single-party system? At independence, the new African state faced many challenges, the main one being nation-building. This task demanded that pre-independence parties which were based on ethnicity, language, religion, region, or other divisive factors, should be banned for the sake of national unity. Any political opposition organized along those divisions threatened the stability of the new state. The problem of poverty required unified action to achieve greater productivity and create effective systems for distribution of goods and services. The limited pool of educated people had to be fully maximized in the development process for the common good and not be drawn by ethnic, regional, or any other factional politics. Regional or ethnic politics often led to secessionist demands, as was the case with the Buganda in Uganda and the Igbo in Nigeria. These were some of the arguments for the shift towards single party-systems.

Critics of the new state at home and abroad cried foul, claiming dictatorship because opposition was not permitted. Nationalist leaders argued that it was for the survival of the state. They could also cite examples from the West: Britain had one party ruling in both the Depression years and during World War II; and from 1935–1945 the British never went to the polls. The United States virtually ignored the constitution during the first hundred days of the New Deal.[18]

The party thought it had a mandate for change and development, but felt that opposition stood in the way to fulfilling this mission. To eliminate or restrict opposition became an obsession with nationalist leaders. Much energy, intellectual and otherwise, went into justifying and legitimizing having a one-party system. The argument was heard everywhere that departure from multi-party parliamentary systems did not imply rejection of democracy. Julius Nyerere argued against those who objected to a one-party system, saying, "to minds modeled by Western parliamentary traditions and Western concepts of democratic institutions, the idea of an organized opposition group has become so familiar that its absence immediately raises the cry of 'dictatorship'."[19] Nyerere and other nationalist leaders justified single-party systems on the grounds of traditional societies where broad popular political participation was practiced, and politics was directed towards achieving consensus rather than continued polarization and proliferation of opinions and groupings within society.

One party systems are not undemocratic by nature, but obsession with power leads to undemocratic practices. As during the colonial period, no real opposition exists under a one-party system: elections become routine plebiscites in which the people are asked to give legitimacy to the party;

parliamentary sessions become occasions to sing self-praises, and for the party to pat itself at the back. Indeed, accomplishments ought to be celebrated and heros acknowledged, but mistakes, too, ought to be pointed out. The problem with a one-party system is that this corrective voice is not allowed, the one who voices it is either expelled from the party and/or detained. The fears that make everyone toe the party line give the party a false self-understanding and sense of security. The absence of organized opposition makes the party believe it is popular. This is why multi-party campaigns in the late 1980s and in the 1990s have often taken one-party systems by surprise. Fear depoliticizes the people; it makes politics uninteresting and that results in low voter turnouts, which has been characteristic in single-party elections throughout Africa.

In the 1980s most parties began experiencing a decline in membership, influence, and function because of a growing state machinery. Inefficiency increased as the result of corruption and incompetence, or because of decentralization. Military intervention also reduced party power. Some military regimes either suspended or dissolved political parties. Another reason for the decline of the party is the emergence of the pro-democracy movement throughout the continent in the 1990s. Whether or not the ruling party is returned to power as happened in Kenya, the pro-democracy movement is limiting the power of the dominant party and the presidency, and strengthening competitive-party politics. Where the ruling party lost in multi-party general elections (Malawi and Zambia) considered free and fair, the rules of the game of politics have been redefined, and so far, in the best interest of the people.

MILITARY STATECRAFT

The idea of soldiers in government is a postcolonial phenomenon. During colonialism a number of countries did not even have a standing army of their own; they had to create armies at independence. The French military policy was to create regiments which were not identified with a particular territory but could be moved from country to country or be sent wherever they were needed. The British, too, had some colonial regiments which were similar to French regiments in Francophone Africa. In east and central Africa the British had the Kings African Rifles (KAR) and in west Africa there was the Royal West African Frontier Force. In both the French and British regiments the officer corps were Europeans and it was difficult for Africans to be commissioned as officers. In the British regiments, Africans were passed for promotion by Goan Indians who entered with lower level officer rank in the KAR. When armies were created at independence, many did not have commissioned officers, a fact which hastened the Africanization of the army in order to have African officer corps. African armies, then, are very young armies without a long military tradition.

The military did not engage in politics during colonialism, but the regiments were used to put down protests or rebellions. When these regiments needed support to accomplish a mission, the colonial administrators asked their home countries for help since the security needs of the territories were in the hands of the metropolitan country. This happened more with the French whose policy was to centralize and manage the defense needs of all territories. Accordingly, they did not send just the regiments to carry out missions, but if need be, units of the French army became involved. The French continue to maintain military assistance agreements with all Francophone Africa except Guinea, and to this day France maintains military bases (called "facilities") in a number of Francophone countries. On a number of occasions, French troops have intervened in several Francophone countries: Central African Republic, Chad, Gabon, Mauritania, and Zaire (now Democratic Republic of Congo). Although British troops have not been involved in events in Africa, the British air force was called into Kenya 1952–56 to crush African opposition. Although soldiers were not politicized during the colonial era, they defended the colonial government not because they understood their role as serving the government to maintain stability, but simply because they were a colonial army.

Since independence soldiers have changed their image and role as they have become politicized and involved in governance as rulers without militarization of the state. Since 1960, soldiers have led coups. The picture of coups in Africa looks messy and bloody. In 1966 Milton Obote, then Prime Minister of Uganda, seized power from President Sir Edward Mutesa; Prime Minister Chief Leabua Jonathan took control of Lesotho in 1970 by defying the will of the electorate and deposing King Moshweshwe II; in 1973 King Sobhuza of Swaziland abolished the constitution. In the violence that accompanied most of these coups, heads of states were killed. This happened in Togo (1963), Chad (1975), Ghana (1975), Liberia (1980 and 1988), and Burkina Faso (1988). In other cases the head of state was detained as in the case of David Dacko (Central African Republic in 1965), Maurice Yam'ongo (Upper Volta now Burkina Faso in 1966), Alphonse Massamba-Débat (Congo-Brazzaville in 1968), Modibo Keita (Mali 19 in 1968), Mohammed Haji Ibrahim Egal (Somalia), Grégoire Kayibanda (Rwanda in 1973), emperor Haile Selassie (Ethiopia in 1974—he is believed to have been killed a year later by lethal injection or by poison upon the order of Lieutenant Colonel Mengistu Haile Mariaum who seized power), and Daddah (Mauritania in 1978). Some leaders were forced into exile: Nkrumah of Ghana in 1966; Obote in 1971 and 1982; General Yakubu Gowon of Nigeria in 1975; Idi Amin of Uganda in 1980; Jaffar al-Nimeiri of Sudan 1985; Mengistu Haile Mariaum in 1991.

There have been other successful coups elsewhere in Africa: Niger, Rwanda, Somalia, and others. If military coups have not occurred, then civil wars often have as in Nigeria, Burundi, Somalia, and the long standing war in Mozambique. In Ethiopia, as in Somalia and Mozambique, the devastation has been made worse by hunger and warring factions who prevent relief from getting to the people. The factions supply food to their own soldiers, thus increasing suffering and mass loss of innocent lives. In some countries coups have been repeated: Benin (1963, 1965 in both November and December, 1967, 1969, 1972), Burundi (1966, 1976, 1987), Central African Republic (1965, 1979, 1981), Congo-Brazzaville (1963, 1968, 1977), Ghana (1966, 1972, 1978, 1979, 1981), Nigeria (1966 in January and July, 1975, 1983, 1985), Sierra Leone (1967 on March 21 and March 23, 1968, 1969, 1992, 1996), Sudan (1958, 1969, 1971 on July 19 and July 22, 1985, 1989), Burkina Faso (1966, 1974, 1980, 1987), and the Democratic Republic of Congo (1960, 1965).[20] In Nigeria military governments have fought each other for long periods, from 1966–1979 and from 1985 to the present. The longest military regime was Mobutu Sese Seko's government in Zaire, which was in power from 1965–1997.

The reasons that are often given for staging a coup are the deterioration of the economic and political situation of a given country. The real motives, however, are not always clear, but before getting into details about the motives, one thing that can be said is that the military has control of the means of institutionalized violence in society—arms, and weapons can, and do, succeed in destroying the people's will, their sense of self and destiny. The history of military coups has shown that the one who has command of organized violence controls the destiny of a nation. In Africa, coups have been carried out by battalion commanders, who afterwards bring in senior officers "to minimize the disruption to the army's internal command structure and to give respectability to the regime; this happened in Ghana in February 1966 and in Nigeria in both January and July 1966, though not in Mali in late 1968 or Liberia in 1980."[21] The Liberian and Sierra Leone coups showed that the coup leaders in Africa are not exclusively commissioned officers. With the exception of Ghana's counter-coups of 1979 and 1981 by Flight-Lieutenant Jerry Rawlings, coups in Africa have been military coups. There is a psychological factor involved in military coups: once a coup occurs, another coup is always a possibility. Benin had six coups in a nine-year period (1963–1972); Burkina Faso experienced four coups in seven years, even though the country had been democratic from 1960 to 1980. Henry Bienen identified three phases of military intervention:

> an initial stage during which the military may for the first time make overtly threatening demands on the government of a new nation; it may settle

> conflicts between civilian contenders or it may itself take over the government. . . . The next phase can be considered one in which there is a struggle for stability after seizure of power. . . . The third phase is institutionalized intervention. . . . Military coup may become the accepted way of getting political change for groups with the armed forces, for certain civilian leaders and for citizens who remain by-standers to coups. Dahomey, now Benin, Congo-Brazzaville, Sierra Leone, and Nigeria had all at least three successful coups since independence.[22]

The motives for military intervention are many and more complex than the simple economic and political mismanagement often cited by coup leaders. This is not to downplay these factors; they are important because the army shares these interests with society, which is one of the reasons a coup is sometimes welcome by general society. However, Ruth First has observed that "whatever the political background to a coup d'état, when the army acts it generally acts for many reasons, in addition to any it may espouse."[23] Studies also show that personal motives (ambition and the fear of professional advancement may not come) corporate reasons, ethnicity, regionalism, or other factional issues are factors in a coup, and in some cases the ideological motive plays a role. External interest and support, such as the involvement of a foreign government or neighboring African country is a factor. Guinean forces went into Liberia (1979); a Guinean rescue unit went into Sierra Leone (1981); Libya went into Chad supporting President Goukouni Oueddei; Senegalese troops went to Gambia in 1981 to protect President David Jawara following a police coup; Tanzanian soldiers toppled Idi Amin to bring back Milton Obote (1979); in 1981 Tanzania thwarted South African mercenaries backed military operations in Syechelles to overthrow Albert René and replace him with James Mancham, the former Prime Minister; Tanzania stationed 600 troops in Mozambique, and in 1985 Zimbabwe had 10,000 soldiers in Mozambique supporting Samora Machel in his struggle against RENAMO (Mozambique National Resistance or MNR).

Military intervention is not entirely the fault of soldiers' some political situations, or rather the actions of civilian leaders invite a coup. For instance, when a civilian government is weak and feels threatened by the opposition or dissidents and then calls in soldiers instead of seeking a political solution, it makes soldiers feel that they have the power to unify the state. So why not take over political leadership and unify the country? The army learns, too, that intervention is acceptable. Any civilian government that does not negotiate but uses force or generally relies on the army is likely to be toppled by those who control the instruments of violence. Conversely, when a civilian government seeks to weaken the power of the army by making some sudden unexplainable cuts in its budget, or angers the army by not increasing salaries and by limiting benefits, or by either dismissing or not promoting its high ranking officers, the army may stage a coup. Civilian leaders have to walk a tightrope with the army, balancing between over reliance on soldiers to settle political issues and not provoking them either out of fear or jealousy of high ranking officers.

How a military government rules, that is, establishes authority and legitimacy, depends on its own self-understanding, and the goal of its intervention, whether it is a transitional (caretaker) regime, revolutionary, or a corrective regime. According to Martin Dent, the difference between the three types of regimes is as follows: a caretaker regime pledges to restore constitutional integrity, or be constitution-makers (as happened in Nigeria, Benin, and Congo); a corrective regime aims at putting in order profound deficiencies created by the civilian leadership (Ghana under Flight Lieutenant Jerry Rawlings, Burkina Faso with General Thomas Sankara); and a revolutionary regime seeks to restructure society in order to end the prevailing order of the elite rule.[24] While the revolutionary regime is a distinct idea, the performance of its military leaders does not differ from any kind of military rule. Examples of revolutionary regimes are Jamal Abd-al Nasser in Egypt and Jaffar al-Nimeiri in Sudan.

Are military rulers more successful than their civilian counterparts? Evidence shows that military regimes fare no better than civilian governments, and the success of a military regime or the length of its government depends on the soldier-rulers' knowledge of the rules of the craft of statesmanship. They must be politicians to rule for after the dust has settled, they have to find power and legitimacy beyond weapons of violence. Legitimacy is earned or given; it cannot be coaxed from the people, it has to be freely given. To govern, soldier-rulers have to learn to secure networks of political relations; they must find support in civic society by courting people of influence, professionals, students, trade unions, various organizations and groups, but also civil servants and different state bureaucracies. They may, too, form an alliance with the police. More often than not, soldier-rulers have a false self-understanding of their relation to civil society. As civilian rulers, they confuse the absence of opposition for popular support and take that absence as a mandate for their programs. In reality people are afraid of detention, trial by a military tribunal, or execution by firing squad, abuses of power often associated with military regimes. When soldiers take over, they promise to rid the country of corruption and improve the economy. Soon, however, soldier-rulers learn the lessons civilian leaders find: the state machinery has rules and life of its own and those rules cannot be changed by imposing military discipline.

After the honeymoon period of an overthrow of an unpopular regime, the army also finds that it has to secure power and authority beyond that which arms can provide. Like the civilian government, it must gain the popular support necessary to rule. Once in government, "the military organization immediately becomes vulnerable to social and political pressure from which it was hitherto . . . protected, and is required to operate under conditions and for purposes for which it was not designed."[25] The military style of command through hierarchies is not readily adaptable to civilian politics and life; its specialized training and relatively insular experience poorly prepares the army for tasks of governing, that is, the act of constant negotiations among vested interests, and tradeoffs. Bienen has observed that "when armies come to power in Africa, their leaders, be they ex-noncommissioned officers from the colonial forces or new graduates from Sandhurst [England], St. Cyr [France] and Fort Gordon [USA], do not show any particular skill in manipulating political groups via persuasion, flexible policies, and bargaining abilities."[26]

When the military takes over, it does not realize that the acceptance of the coup was not because of the popularity of the military group per se, but rather the lack of popularity of the preceding civilian or military government.

> To the extent, moreover, the destruction of the preceding regime was broadly accepted, it has been perceived by the participants as a mandate which the military was obliged to share with other significant dissident groups in society. Thus the very group that had applauded the military intervention and provided it with popular acceptance is among the first to criticize any effort on part of the military to give itself unlimited mandates in terms of both time and scope of responsibilities.[27]

To illustrate, Gus Liebenow says the Ghanaian market women cheered most enthusiastically the second coming of Rawlings during the 1981 New Year's Eve coup because he pledged to eliminate corruption. Months later, the same women found themselves engaged in violent confrontation with Rawlings' troops who were attempting to deal with market corruption, which had become a way of life among the market vendors. A similar kind of reaction to a coup happened in Liberia. Master Sergeant Doe came into power in April 1980, after a violent military coup which had been preceded by a year of mass opposition demonstrations against the rule of President William Tolbert led by students, clergy, and journalists. Within a short period of Doe's presidency, the People's Redemption Council banned all political activities for five years. Doe's military had turned against the activities of various groups of people who paved the way for the coup.[28] In order to contain popular discontent, the military government turns to coercion, threats, and military justice, which only succeed in creating more disenchantment and dissent in the general public and in some quarters of the military itself—another coup follows.

The reasons which account for the failure of military regimes are many, but a few illustrations will throw some light on their problems. Military regimes enter promising to return governance to civilians within a certain specific period, but usually they do not. Ghanaians and Nigerians had that promise from the leaders of each military coup. Major General Ibrahim Babangida spent seven years preparing the country for a return to civilian rule, but at the end of the period he annalled the results of the June 1993 general elections in which Moshood was the apparent winner. In August Babangida stepped down leaving the government in the hands of fellow military officers as a transitional government. In November, General Sani Abachi, the defence minister, overthrew the transitional government and banned all political activity, lifting the ban in June 1995. Abachi, too, is not in a hurry to hand the government to civilians, despite the international pressure in the aftermath of executing nine environmentalists in November 1995. Rawlings took eleven years to have multi-party elections on November 3, 1992. Many never fulfill their promise for they are toppled by fellow military officers in another coup. The unfulfilled promises raise suspicion and distrust in the general public because the very people who claim to be the defenders of the constitution usually suspend it when they seize power. Rawlings did what many military regimes do not in their attempt to find broad-based legitimacy, that is, he held presidential elections. Usually, the soldier-rulers build a national party that is associated with and controlled by them. This happened in Egypt, Mali, Somalia, Togo, and Zaire.

The weaknesses which lead to the downfall of civilian governments also affect the military leadership. The usual reasons for a coup are corruption and mismanagement, but the army also falls victim to this. When in government, the top military officers get easier access to privileges associated with state power (including legal means of acquiring property); this creates a gulf between the senior and junior officers. The general population may be unhappy with the leadership because of decisions that the leadership may make for the common good of the nation, but which necessarily satisfy the narrow interests of the military. Ethnic, linguistic, and religious problems also trouble military leaders. All segments of society may not be proportionally represented in the top military cadre. Linkages between the top military officers and influential members of their own ethnic or religious group within the civilian population creates tension within the army itself and the whole society. In an attempt to take control of one or all of these problems, so as to avoid the kinds of problems which led to the downfall of the preceding rule, governance goes to one person, a form of personal rule, or a narrowly based junta concerned with tightly controlling both the military and the society. This form of leadership further alienates the top leadership from its own primary constituency. Any of these factors, or a combination thereof, may be cause for a cycle of coups.

To conclude, despite the claim to moral authority, military governments fail to produce a cleaner, honest, and efficient government. Stories of increased salaries for the army, arbitrary repression, arrests of dissidents, and manipulation of the media have been characteristic of military regimes. In addition, corruption and kickbacks have been observed in many military states. Military governments have not been more economically successful than civilian regimes. In seeking legitimacy, military governments have been drawn into politics, a game for which they are not prepared nor have the skills. There are a few cases where political stability has emerged under military government. The continuing saga of Nigerian politics is an example. There have been so many coups, so many soldier-rulers who have ruled that if military governments had moral integrity, as they claim, Nigeria would have the cleanest government in Africa. On the contrary, corruption and political instability continue to plague the country in astronomical proportions. There is corruption within the military itself; there are no effective political structures; administrative controls and judicial powers have been undermined by military governments to the extent that everything is unpredictable, both at the national and local levels. Soldiers in Nigeria have been so politicized that they define and control politics, even including who may take political office. In October 1990, President Babangida told the National Electoral Commission that electoral competition would be limited to two parties, one of which would be "a little to the left, the other a little to right of center."[29] Things have become so bad that Nigerians wonder whether there will ever be political "normalcy."

From the example of Nigeria we see that in the end, military governments are no more disciplined and have no more moral integrity than the civilian governments they oust.

THE STATE AS AN ECONOMIC MACHINE

The state in Africa is a very powerful economic institution. With a very small and weak private sector at the time of independence, the state emerged as the single largest employer. It had access to and controlled all domestic resources and investments funds from abroad. The state expanded its economic power by getting into industry and agriculture, and through nationalization of companies, which in fact was the "statization" of the private sector. With all this expansion, the government became the engine of economic development. To be fully involved in the development process, some countries, Malawi for instance, started what is known as an "development account." This is an account on investments expenditure incurred in expanding the government capacity system. This account is to be understood differently from a "revenue account," from which current government costs, salaries, and other expenditures are drawn. This account is financed by government revenues and tax indexing. A development account on the other hand, is funded by external donors.

In order to lessen the burden on their capital (investment) expenditure or development account, while at the same time expanding state economic power, former British colonies worked through parastatals, which are state invested organizations which operate on a profit and loss account. The parastatal sector grew rapidly for two reasons: (1) the relative weakness of domestic capitalism, and (2) the new governments' attempt to end foreign control of the economy, which in some cases meant nationalization of foreign-owned companies and establishment of new public enterprises. "The new enterprises offered government leaders a more flexible instrument of development than the government department, which was subject to full panoply of parliamentary and treasury control."[30] Parastatals were those new enterprises, and they expanded the state apparatus enormously in the area of economic development. The government became involved in many enterprises, too many in some cases: transportation (air, road, and railways), electricity, housing, mining, retail, banking, and many others. Governments overextended themselves, and as in the state bureaucracy, governments had neither personnel nor the experience necessary to move from a mostly private economy to a completely public-controlled one. The result was that many parastatals or other state-owned businesses operated at a loss and they contributed to growing external debt, accounting for almost half of the debt.

Parastatal organizations have to show the profit and return on capital in a fiscal year. The state is a shareholder, although there may be other partners; as such, it is entitled to appoint directors, to sit on the board of directors, which meets from time to time to approve the policy of the parastatal. Most of the appointments to the board were, and still are, political. In most cases, people are appointed to the board because of political connections rather than knowledge or competence in the enterprise of a particular parastatal. Parastatals, particularly those which report profits, are open to abuse because they have considerable freedom in how they spend money, whom they employ, and what prices they set. It is this freedom which has led parastatals be characterized by cumbersome administrative procedures, misappropriation of funds, the hiring of people on ethnic lines, and all forms of abuse and corruption. Besides problems of qualified personnel and poor financial management, parastatals have another problem, namely, the relationship between parastatal staff and civil servants is uncertain and weak.

Parastatals played a very significant role in the development of most African states. Again, let us draw examples from Malawi, a country which extensively utilized parastatals. Examples are: Capital City Development Corporation (the responsibility of CCDC was to establish the infrastructure of the new capital city area on behalf of the government through the building of houses, roads, offices, and service sites), Malawi Railways, Air Malawi, and the Agriculture Development and Marketing Corporation (ADMARC) (a parastatal charged with the development of traditional agriculture through pricing and buying of crops and selling them on the international market). Through parastatals, the Malawi government managed to keep its own investments at about a third of the total for the economy in 1978 (and this rose to 40 percent in 1980), which was the same as it had been in 1973. Besides parastatals, other investments came from the commercial sector.[31]

This expansion of government responsibilities in economic development, and the simple fact that the state was the major employer, soon created problems for the state. Salaries, pensions plans, and other benefits were better in parastatals, facts that had a serious demoralizing effect on civil servants. In conditions of scarcity, low wages, and greed—moral bankruptcy—anything is done for money or as a means to make money. Civil servants and bureaucrats began asking and receiving bribes in exchange for favors, services, or even jobs which the power, authority and influence of their position could deliver. Nepotism, ethnicity, and regionalism made things worse. People from one ethnic group or region took all the top positions in certain parastatals. Incompetence among the bureaucratic elite, particularly among political appointees, was destructive to the national economy since the state and parastatals were the major employers. Soon, these abuses were also happening in private companies or corporations. The extent of abuse of power or conflict of interest differed from country to country and it depended on how each state enforced discipline; but even in those countries where strict discipline was enforced corruption prevailed.

Parastatals showed government innovation but because of losses and the reasons mentioned above, in addition to national economic problems and mounting debt, governments closed some parastatals. In the 1980s many governments were pressured by the International Monetary Fund (IMF) or the World Bank into the closing or divestiture of those nonprofit parastatals that had not been closed earlier. This was part of restructuring programs prescribed by multilateral financial institutions as cure for ailing economies. By the 1990s forty-five countries were committed to privatization of parastatals. Privatization was slow in countries such as Malawi, Rwanda, Somalia, and Swaziland, while in other places, especially Francophone states, there was serious interest in privatization. Some countries were slow in implementing the privatization programs because of the lack of will power by politicians and bureaucrats who feared the loss of employment and benefits. The lack of sufficiently developed capital markets and the difficulty of establishing an effective administrative machinery also hindered privatization programs.[32] Divestiture programs would weaken the power of state control over the economy; this also explains why some countries were slow in implementing the programs although they were aware of the need to overhaul parastatals. While some countries feared divestiture programs, President Houphouët-Boigny (of Cote d'Ivoire) implemented them in order "to regain firm control over the whole of the patrimonial system [by] the bringing to heel of the country's political class and the drying up of the sources of clientelist enrichment."[33]

The people who were hit hardest by the mismanagement of public funds were the local people, smallholders, the very people who worked hardest for national development. The powerful, the bureaucratic elite, grew affluent on the backs of poor traditional farmers. People saw the corruption, the greed, of those in the civil service or parastatals, but they had neither the power nor the influence to do anything about it. The church went on with business as usual, blessing the flag on Flag Day, or attending state banquets and functions as if there were no corruption in the country. The church capitulated in its responsibilities to both the people and the state.

THE STATE AND CRISIS

African states have been in perpetual crisis irrespective of their ideology. Revolutionary as well as conservative states had to deal with crisis in all dimensions of governance: administrative, technical, political, and in regulating social relations.[34] The 1950s and 1960s were years of independence in Africa, while in the 1980s and 1990s African states experienced economic and political crises of historic proportions. The problems of Africa seemed to be ongoing in a vicious cycle: there was a huge external debt, high interest rates, inflation, and low commodity prices on top of severe droughts. According to a 1993 World Bank report, Africa has been experiencing constant slower average annual Gross Domestic Product (GDP) growth rates since the 1970s. The sudden and rapid rise in oil prices in 1973–1974 and again in 1979–1980 had very serious effects on already weak economies, especially those without a strong industrial base. Industrial and agricultural productivity decreased due to the rise in oil prices. To keep the economy afloat, most countries borrowed heavily from international financial institutions, and some countries even took loans from commercial banks such as Chase Manhattan, Barclays, and others. This heavy borrowing was increased by the low commodity export prices of the 1980s. The high level of indebtedness did not reduce the expanding government deficit, which was the reason some countries had sought external funding in the first place. The situation became worse as prices rose while buying power went below to the pre-1970s levels. In fact, people were better off in the late 1960s and early 1970s than they were in the 1980s. Domestic policy adjustments failed to correct the situation; many countries appealed to the IMF for assistance with international obligations and to avoid national bankruptcy. The IMF introduced austerity measures, recommending devaluations in order to stabilize economies but not all structural adjustment programs were successful. Almost all economic reforms led to the loss of legitimacy of states, and weak governments faced protests, riots, and increased opposition groups since the people felt the state was incapable of governing. Presidential appeals for peace and stability went unheeded and presidential decrees for economic recovery failed. Weak states were unable to withstand the political instability rising from the effects of the structural adjustment reforms of the IMF.

What was happening to the economy had serious impact on politics. Since the 1970s Africa had been torn by civil wars, protests for human rights, and demands for the accountability of public officials. The late 1980s were years of agitation for political participation to form parties and to contest elections. These events affected institutions of government since states were grappling with economic problems such as inflation, generating economic growth, and ensuring stable trade relations. People interpreted what was happening as the government's failure to carry out its function of regulating social and economic interaction and political behavior because it lacked the capacity to enforce contracts, control corruption in the public sector, and define the rules for resolving economic and political conflict. With its legitimacy undermined, the state was unable to plan and implement national policies, maintain law and order, and enforce norms of social behavior. The economic and political crisis affected the judicial system, too; there was no enforcement of contracts or due process because of bribery and corruption—the state had failed in its capacity to maintain institutions of government. Administratively, the state had not carried out its responsibility to take care of its own. Public goods were not delivered; food, health care, and education suffered cuts under the austerity budgets of the IMF. Civil servants' morale and motivation dropped because of low salaries and lack of incentive.

The 1980s brought so much hardship that public dissatisfaction with government and the people's protest were only natural. Economic difficulties decreased the ability of leaders to govern since they could not use state resources to maintain their core constituencies of support. In these ways, the economic crisis made political leaders more vulnerable to demands for change by weakening their ability to control dissatisfaction or to shore up political support through the use of patronage, rents, and access to spoils.[35] As leaders increasingly became unable to claim broad-based legitimacy or the loyalty of traditional support groups, political regimes demonstrated their inability to dominate and lead civic society as they had done in the past. As more and more people increasingly questioned the ability of the leaders to govern, civic organizations appeared everywhere and demanded accountability and participation in politics and government. With their authority and legitimacy undermined, regimes resorted to repression and brutality in responding to protests and demands. Repression and coercion further revealed the inability of the state to define and establish "the rules of the game," and resolve conflicts, thereby demonstrating inability to interact effectively with civil society.

While the economic crises of the 1970s to the 1980s were worldwide, striking hardest at the weak economies of non-Western states, the problems preceded the new states of Africa, revealing the economic weaknesses of colonial rule. The colonial government operated on the idea of maximization of profit through exploitation and state management strategies of development. At independence, the new leaders adopted the policy of state management of development strategies, encouraging industrialization and state control of economic institutions, and using, among other mechanisms, state industries (through parastatals), joint ventures with state capital, nationalization of foreign investments, protection, regulation, marketing boards, and widespread subsidies. The new states sought to stimulate industrial and commercial development through extensive investing and an interconnected economic activity. This interlocking of economic institutions encouraged the development of weak and inefficient industrial and agricultural sectors, and this eventually destroyed the capacity of states to acquire resources from the economy.[36] When one sector of these interlocked economic institutions failed to perform to expected levels, the whole economic infrastructure was effected. Leaders found that the economic crisis that ensued could not be dealt with through deficit spending or external borrowing, and things became more difficult when the worldwide economic situation took a downward turn. The policy of state control of the economy became seriously questioned.

The economic crisis was a crisis of the state to impose its authority over government and civil institutions. "Institutions," says Douglas North, "are the rules of the game in a society; more formally, they are the humanly devised constraints that shape human interaction. In consequence, they structure incentives in exchange, whether political, social, or economic."[37] These rules evolve over time through the interaction of the state, economy, and society, but it is the state which ultimately authorizes and enforces the rules to establish stability. This is one of the purposes of the state: "to reduce uncertainty by establishing a stable (but not necessarily efficient) structure to human interaction."[38] With the economic crisis of the 1980s and 1990s states found themselves without resources to enforce the "constraints that shape human interaction," and often states suddenly changed those "constraints" in order to contain dissatisfaction within various institutions of government and civil society. Institutional instability was widespread: civil servants disenchantment because of low salaries, ethnic and regional conflicts, informal markets, lack of the rule of law, and the presence of armed struggles caused already weak states—Ethiopia, Liberia and Somalia—to collapse.

In weak states the leaders had lost legitimacy to make and enforce rules of the game. Strong states, on the other hand, used their power to entrench themselves and centralize authority in the person of the presidency. Such states accomplished that by abruptly changing the rules of the game through manipulation of the constitution. Entrenchment did not work because disenchanted groups in urban areas mobilized to contest governance, to demand the state's greater responsiveness to civil society, thus ending government mismanagement of the economy, centralization, and abuse of power. Coalitions of different civil groups—business, lawyers, trade unions, Non-Governmental Organization (NGOs), university students, religious and pressure groups—demanded democratization of the government. States responded to those demands by passing laws that restricted individual's and group's rights to engage in organized political activity. The print media was carefully watched, for it was prohibited by these laws to print "seditious" material. Radio and television were no problem for the states for they were state-owned; they broadcast government versions of stories and events. As during colonial days, the governments passed repressive laws under security acts and the police (and sometimes the army) was given unlimited powers. Demands to end authoritarianism were supported by international financial and humanitarian organizations concerned with violations of human dignity. International money lending and aid-giving institutions withheld all forms of assistance except humanitarian to pressurize the states into the democratization process. It was through the pressure of the international financial institutions that government authorities in Malawi and Kenya reluctantly started talking of the possibility of multi-party systems.

THE PRESIDENCY

In the above paragraphs the discussion concerned the crisis of the state, referring to states as strong and weak. The discussion should actually be about strong or weak presidencies, and not states, since to speak about the state in Africa is not only to refer to an ensemble of institutions with rules and regulations, rights, duties and power under the authority of the constitution, but also to allude to the head of state, the president.[39] To varying degrees, the state apparatus is directed and controlled by the president: the cabinet, parliament, the judiciary, and the ruling party make their decisions according to the wishes of the president. Unless under external pressure, policy makers and technocrats do what the president wants and likes, for the country is identified personally with the president. For example, at one time it was almost impossible to imagine Malawi without

Kamuzu Banda, Kenya without Jomo Kenyatta, or Côte d'Ivoire without Félix Houphouët-Boigny. These men had extensive powers and authority, most of it invested by the constitution they indirectly framed for their people in constitution drafting committees which carried out their wishes. Malawi's Republic Constitution in 1966, gave Dr. Banda unlimited flexibility in governance; the constitution said the president would act "on his own discretion and shall not be obliged to follow advice tendered by any other person." There were other powers given to the president: he would appoint all senior civil servants, including judges, control all contracts undertaken by public corporations, and appoint three cabinet ministers who were not Members of Parliament.[40] The president had such enormous powers that the country was the president and sometimes Dr. Banda, as other presidents with similar powers, ran his country as a personal estate.

The African state has been a personal rule or monarchy of Hobbes, the princedom of Machiavelli, about which I spoke at the beginning of the chapter.[41] Machiavelli's ideas about an effective ruler are worth recalling at this point. According to him, a successful state is the one founded by a single person, who creates laws and government that determine the national character of the subjects. "But we must assume, as a general rule, that it never or rarely happens that a republic or monarchy is well constituted, or its old institutions entirely reformed, unless it is done by only one individual; it is even necessary that the one whose mind has conceived such a constitution should be alone in carrying it into effect."[42] There is practically no limit to what a powerful ruler can do, as long as the rules of the game are understood. There is no standard to judge the acts of such a ruler, except the success of political obedience for enlarging and perpetuating the power of the state. Machiavelli's ruler can use "cruelty, perfidy, murder, or any other means provided only they are used with sufficient intelligence and secrecy to reach their ends."[43] "It is well that, when the act accuses him, the result should excuse him, and when the result is good, as in the case of Romulus [his murder of his brother] it will always absolve him from blame. For he is to be reprehended who commits violence for the purpose of destroying; and not he who employs it for a beneficent purpose."[44] Here we see how fitting the image and character of the Prince is to some African leaders. That some African presidents have been cruel, disrespectful of human dignity, and even murdered to advance their ends, induce fear, and eliminate opponents is testified by the reports of human rights organizations such as Amnesty International.

As Machiavelli stated, the monarch or prince (the president) defines the rules of the game in line with his personal ideology and political convenience. The constitution is indeed binding for everybody, but the president can amend or suspend parts of it to allow for his own political ends or action. There is no authority to which the personal ruler is answerable save his own; there are no checks and balances since they follow impersonal rules. Hence personal rule is the authoritarian. By authoritarian is meant "an arbitrary and usually a personal government that uses law and coercive instruments of the state to expedite its own purposes of monopolizing power and denies the political rights and opportunities of all other groups to compete for that power."[45] In personal rule the focus is on centralization and concentration of power in the office of the president while institutional checks and balances are eliminated or weakened and political participation is limited to a single party, the ruling party. Whereas authoritarian governments curtail political rights, they tolerate "non-political rights—such as the right to worship freely, the right to possess private property, and the right to choose one's occupation at will."[46] The strength of the state in person rule does not lie in the public system of rules or institutions of government, but in the power or the political will, skill, ability to mediate between different interest groups, effective regulation of political institutions, better judgement, and fortune of the president. Personal rulers survive by rewarding their lieutenants, patrons, associates, clients and supporters who may limit or undermine their authority and power through non-cooperation. These groups form the "system" of personal rule—the patron-client system.[47]

Personal rule is not unique to independent Africa. The colonial governor practiced some form of personal rule in spite of being answerable to higher authority at home. According to Jackson and Rosberg, personal rule is a transitional stage between the breakdown of the old regime and the establishment of the new.[48] The European modern state was preceded by strong personal rule of the late medieval period, the Renaissance and the civil and religious wars that followed. After this period absolutism became a common rule in Europe. The idea of personal rule as transitional seems to be correct especially when we look at post-Kaunda Zambia or post-Banda Malawi, countries where the ruling party was defeated in multi-party general elections. However, in countries where the ruling party was returned to power, personal rule does not seem to be transitional; Kenya is a case in point. Kenyatta dominated the politics of Kenya until his death in 1978. His vice-president, Daniel Arap Moi, took over the presidency, despite the fact that Kenyatta had attempted unsuccessful constitutional changes to prevent Moi who is from the minority Kalejin ethnic group, from becoming president. Moi had learned very well the rules of personal rule from Kenyatta: he had learned how to build a clientele system by pursuing a political strategy through distribution of state patronage and moving quickly against the opposition. "He moved some members of his own and other minority groups into positions of power and moved against some close associates of Kenyatta. [He knew] state patronage, ethnic arithmetic, and regional political autonomy similar to that of Kenyatta before him."[49] When multi-party politics and elections came in 1992 and 1997, Moi simply appealed to these constituencies to retain him in power, and thereby continue personal rule, albeit with some limited checks and balances because of the opposition representation in parliament. On the whole, even after multi-party elections Kenya, is still under personal rule of Moi.

Most politicians say they entered politics because they wanted to serve their people, and that is true in some cases. What is evident, though, is that many who become politicians seek or accept political appointments in government with the intention of being a beneficiary of patronage resources through clientelism. As mentioned earlier, clientelism is a system in which there is a patron-client relationship of mutual assistance and support between a leader and his or her associates and supporters. The patron-client relationship is not of equals, but recognized and as accepted leader-subordinate. The leader builds alliances and collaborates with different groups within state and civil society. Those who specifically benefit patronage are individuals with power or who hold positions of influence: cabinet members, party and army officials, high ranking civil servants, and parastatal executives and senior administrators. These officials in turn also build their own subordinate clients. Through this network of patronage, the leader is linked to the whole of civil society in a hierarchical manner. In this extensive relationship, the leader expects steadfast political loyalty in exchange for patronage resources. Clientele loyalty is not simply given, it is earned and will last as long as the leader remains trustworthy and in control of the state apparatus from which the resources derive.

This is what is meant by saying that clientelism is a system. It is not a system because it is an institution with rules or laws governing it, clientelism is a system because it is a structure, although nebulous. It is a system based on the availability of resources which enable the leader to respond to the interests of various constituencies. The system has a capacity to alter or enhance state and loyal policies and maintain political stability while at the same time increasing corruption. Jackson and Rosberg are correct in identifying this amorphous structure as lying between "civic society" and the "state of nature."[50] Clientelism is not endemic to personal rule, as a matter of fact, clientelism is found in many other systems and in situations other than politics. Given the strength of the presidency and personal rule in Africa, however, clientelism plays a significant role in shaping the nature of the state.

African personal rules emerged from the collapse of the colonial regimes. However, I see the path to personal rule being charted by nationalism, the struggle for independence, to be specific. Personal rule in Africa evolved from the personality cult of the Weberian charismatic leader that developed during the struggle for independence, when some nationalist leaders embodied and championed the cause of their people. At independence, most of these nationalist leaders became the obvious choice by their party to become heads of state, and just as they had personalized the cause of independence, these leaders started to do the same with their new offices. There was no separation between the office and the individual. Although some may have foreseen the problems of such personalization of the office, most of the people accepted it because of the political socialization during the struggle to independence. The nationalist leaders had been presented to the people, or had risen through their party, as symbols of national unity, or as the ones with the interest of all at heart. Now as presidents, there was a sense of being the guardians of the people. Banda used to call himself "Nkhoswe (guardian) number one" of all the women. Some nationalists, like Kenyatta, had demonstrated the love of their land and people by sacrificing personal comfort during the struggle for freedom.

The path to personal rule described above applies to nationalist leaders who became presidents. Those who became presidents through coups or plots were not obvious leaders of their people but by demonstrating a strong will, decisiveness, employing patronage to build a clientele, and by using all those things mentioned above when I discussed Moi's ascent to personal rule. Some presidents such as Idi Amin (Uganda) and Francisco Macias Nguema (Equatorial Guinea) used coercion and force to induce terror to build personal rule. There are different types of personal rule; Jackson and Rosberg have identified these forms in Africa: prince, autocrat, prophet, and tyrant. However they came to the presidency and however they established personal rule, one thing is clear about the character of personal rulers: they are individuals with a great desire and love for personal power, and they go to a great distance to acquire power. This is why they become the axis of state power and have a commanding presence on the political stage. They are all-imposing and demand attention. They are the spirit behind the party and government; they do not have to be physically present for their wishes to be known or implemented. They are the watchful eye that sees every movement, the ear that is down to the ground, hearing everything. Personal rulers have incredible power. These persons love power so much that they hold on to it even after their political authority has dissipated and their charisma has been routinized, as Weber noted.[51] This attitude to power stands in the way of an orderly transition government and transfer of the reins of the presidency.

POWER AND MORAL BANKRUPTCY

One would not like to agree with the popular negative saying that "power corrupts; and absolute power corrupts absolutely," yet this seems to be the case: power and corruption appear to be two sides of the same coin—politics. Good and decent politicians seem rare and far between; they all become corrupted by the power they acquire, and in some cases the very means by which they get that power is corrupt. Is power really negative? One gets the impression that those who exercise authority understand power as instrumental, that is, as a means to one's end or capacity, and I believe this is what Hobbes meant in his definition of power: "The power of a man, to take it universally, is his present means, to obtain some future apparent good; and is either original or instrumental." Hobbes identifies two forms of power: natural and instrumental. "*Natural power*, is the eminence of the faculties of body, or mind: as extraordinary, form, prudence, arts, eloquence, liberality, nobility. *Instrumental* are those powers which acquired by these, or by fortune, are means and instruments to acquire more: as riches, reputation, friends, and the secret working of God, which men call good luck. For the nature of power, is in this point, like to fame, increasing as it proceeds; or like the motion of heavy bodies, which further they go, make still more haste."[52]

Hobbes further says that power is about domination, human value, success, and dignity. Power is everything for Hobbes. People use power to achieve their desires but since human desires are infinite, the quest for power itself increases. "I put a general inclination of all humankind, a perpetual and restless desire of power after power, that ceaseth only in death. And the cause of this, is always that a man hopes for a more extensive delight, than he has already attained to; or that he cannot be content with a more moderate power: but because he cannot assure the power and the means to live well, which he hath present, without the acquisition of more power."[53] With everyone seeking power, and more power, there emerges a free-for-all fight for power. Hobbes calls it "a fight of one against all." In short, Hobbes maintains that power is about self-interest; it is personal and at the same time a source of conflict in society.

The views of Hobbes are reiterated by Max Weber, the founder of the discipline of sociology. Weber's interest was in social structures and organization but in studying political structures, he observed that all political structures seek power for prestige: "The striving for prestige pertains to all specific power structures and hence to all political structures. The striving is not identical simply with 'national pride' . . . and it is not identical with the mere pride in the excellent qualities, actual or presumed, of its own political community or in the mere possession of such a polity."[54]

Weber also observed that the conduct of political structures may sometimes be influenced by internal dynamics of power within the political structures themselves: "The power of political structures has a specific internal dynamic. On the basis of this power, the members may pretend to a special 'prestige,' and their pretensions may influence the external conduct of power structures."[55] Weber further noted that political structures and bureaucracy have the same notion of power; they both understand power as a means for expansion. For a bureaucrat, expansion of power "means more offices, more sinecures and better opportunities for promotion." In politics and bureaucracy, expansion means control, domination, and/or imperialism as in the case of powerful nations.

The idea that power is capacity to dominate is deeply entrenched in liberal politics. Roberto Unger, a contemporary Brazilian critic of liberal political theory, notes, "Power is capacity to command, to subordinate the wills of others to one's own will. Glory is the winning of admiration, applause with which one is favored." Agreeing with Hobbes, Unger shows that the orientation towards glory or material success which comes with power is a source of perpetual hostility in society.

> The first source of hostility, given the scarcity of material resources, is the desire for comfort. There are not enough of the goods people want in order to be comfortable. They must therefore scramble. Scrambling is all the more inevitable because men want not just to have, but to have more than their fellows. Only by fighting to get more can they be assured of keeping what they already possess. The reason for this is that the control of things is a tool of power.
>
> Power is the second cause of antagonism in society. The power of some is the powerlessness of others. The more one man's desire for power is satisfied, the more will his fellows' wish for it remain frustrated. The fight for power must be unceasing as the struggle for things.[56]

Here we hear Hobbes echoing Machiavelli whose political policy in *The Prince* assumed that people are by nature essentially selfish, aggressive, and acquisitive and that the effective motives on which a politician must rely are egoistic, such as the desire for security in the people and the desire for power in the rulers. According to Machiavelli, government is founded on the weakness and insufficiency of individuals to protect themselves against aggression of others unless supported by the power of the state. Machiavelli maintained that people are perpetually in a condition of strife and competition, which threatens open anarchy, and he argued that security is possible only when government is strong. Since people are by nature radically egoistic, the state and the force behind the law must be the only power that holds society together. The successful state, therefore, aims at security of property and of life before everything else, since these are the most universal desires in human nature.

In order to safeguard personal gains or to regulate the free-for-all fight of Hobbes and Machiavelli, the liberal state demands obedience: "By definition power requires obedience," says Unger.[57] In invoking law and order the state exercises its power of control. Law and order fall under a larger frame of control, that is, control of language. By language it is meant a mode of speech and a way of life. Unger reminds people that the one "who has power to decide what a thing will be called has power to decide what it is. This is true of persons as of things. . . . Properly understood, the system of public rules is itself a language. Every rule is addressed to a category of persons and acts, and marks its addressee off from others. To mark off is to name. To apply the rules to particular cases is to subsume individual persons and acts under the general names of which the rule consist. Hence, the theory of law is a special branch of the general theory of naming."[58]

What Unger is talking about can be illustrated by looking at some examples from the African context. The "pass law" in South Africa was aimed at identifying or marking off Africans so as to control and subdue them in the cities. We saw the same intention present in the idea of "homeland." Africans in South Africa never called their villages "homeland." This concept was an ideology, coined by the white minority power to create false consciousness and sense of security among Africans, and in so doing, subdue and control them. It was another way of "naming" or marking off Africans to subdue and control them through means of the law and psychological conditioning. We find another example in the terms "rebel" and "dissident," common in most African countries and used to label, mark off, and subdue political opposition. During the struggle for independence "terrorist" was used against Africans in the liberation movement. The term was popularized by the white minority government in Rhodesia (Zimbabwe) led by Ian Smith. In South Africa it was used almost exclusively on members of the African National Congress (ANC) as they engaged in the struggle for liberation and dignity. In all these examples, it was the state or "the Party," which named the people. The party has power to decide what "name" to give a person or group of persons and/or their acts. The Party can call any event subversive or any act seditious, and no one can oppose it. This means that the state has power to subdue a person or persons by applying rules under general names—laws. The state subdues or controls people under the pretext of maintaining law and order.

The main idea in politics is that power is instrumental, that is, power is about personal gain and glory or capacity, control, and domination. As a means of control, power gives its holders capacity to name, thereby to define both the legal and political vocabulary and language. Power gives people worth or value; it earns them dignity and respect. The self is the center, where things begin and end. We also see that power has a materialistic connotation. Orientation to materialism makes power a source of hostility between people because there cannot be enough material resources to go around when people are greedy. This is why the scramble for material things becomes a fight for power. The one with more power gets more material possessions. In a situation of a lopsided economic system, whereby a periphery country gets only a small profit from its trade commodities such as African countries do, the scramble for material possessions can only lead to a big fight for power!

The concept of power discussed here has no concern for ethical or moral behavior. The moral bankruptcy threatening African politics is rooted in this negative concept of power. As Machiavelli's Prince, presidents and politicians are indifferent to morality; they use immoral means to gain an end, proving Machiavelli correct when he says that the ruler, as the creator of the state, is not only outside the law, but if law enacts morals, the ruler is outside morality as well. Gibson Winter in his book, *Liberating Creation*, has discussed the problem of the concept of power in what he calls techno-society. His observations are very illuminating for what is happening on the continent. He says:

> In the techno-society, power is domination. It is power exercised by the stronger over the weaker, the technical expert over the ignorant, the corporate interests over local communities and economies. Power is imposition of the stronger will on the weaker. Power is hierarchical organization of life and activity by those who control capital, technology, and resources. The organicist heritage also celebrates hierarchy, but the hierarchy preserves the well-being of the parts. Organicist power is the quality of relations that pertain within the whole, maintaining bonds with the earth and sky, mortals and immortals. By contrast, the symbolization of power in the mechanistic world sanctions autonomy, independence, invulnerability, and superiority.[59]

Winter maintains that the idea of power as domination accounts for the serious spiritual problem in Western society, and we might add, it is having the same impact on African society, too. He also maintains that the struggle of non-Western societies is in fact a fight against Western spiritual bankruptcy.

> The spirituality of the techno-society is at war with the spirituality of peoples in the organicist heritage who aspire to self-determination and sovereignty. This is the shape of the struggle for colonization in the third world. Whether the colonization is political or economic, it expresses the ambition of the techno-society to subject all things to itself. This raises questions about the meaning of spirituality. *Lust for domination seems anything but spiritual.* However, the disfigurement of the human in the symbols of progress and domination illumines the ambiguity of spirituality and its vulnerability to distortion. Symbols conceal as well as reveal.[60]

A closer look at the concept of power as explored in this section reveals that it cannot be an organizing symbol for life together as a community or nation, for even when people come together as in Hobbes's commonwealth or in the modern corporate state (Unger), it is a coming together for self-interested reasons summed up in wielding more power for expansion. This is what we see with the bureaucratic elite in Africa who use their power to plunder public institutions and corporations. Expansion of the commonwealth or the state means more power to control and dominate a wider area for more resources and human power. This is what was behind colonialism.

Community is the heartbeat of African ways of life. A notion of power which does not pertain to building and maintaining community undercuts the African concept of life and community. If the current struggle for more and more power does not stop, or at least slow down, community will certainly be a thing of the past and the suffering of the powerless will abound as the powerful walk on the backs of the poor and rob them—there will be no justice.

NOTES

1. The idea of the state as a machinery working for the common good is from Jacques Maritan's *Man and the State* (Chicago University Press, 1951).

2. Thomas Hobbes, *Leviathan*, R. A. Waller, ed. (London: Cambridge University Press, 1904), Part 11, chap. xvii.

3. Jean-Jacques Rousseau, *The Social Contract*, Henry J. Tozer, trans. (London: Allen and Unwin, 1920), Book 11, chap. iv, 125.

4. J. Gus Liebenow, *African Politics: Crises and Challenges* (Bloomington, Indiana: Indiana University Press, 1986), 218–219.

5. Given by Peter Duignan and Robert H. Jackson, *Politics and Government African States: 1960–1985* (London: Croom Helm, 1986), 10.

6. David Fieldhouse, *Black Africa, 1945–1980: Economic Decolonization and Arrested Development* (London: Allen and Unwin, 1986), 44.

7. Ibid.

8. Basil Davidson, *The Black Man's Burden: The Curse of the Nation State* (New York: Time Books, 1992), 220.

9. Ibid., 42.

10. Ibid., 199.

11. Ibid., 205.

12. A number of scholars have given the reasons for the emergence of single party systems in Africa. Some of these scholars have also given typologies for distinguishing one-party systems. Their classification is based on the function of the dominant party in the post-independence era. Here I am informed by Henry Bienen, *Armies and Parties in Africa* (New York: Africana Publishing Co., 1978), chaps. 2 and 4.

13. See the *Malawi Gazette Supplement*, no. 4C, May 1966.

14. I discuss the problem of Malawi's Republic Constitution in my forthcoming book, *Malawi's First Republic: A Political and Economic Analysis*.

15. Information gleaned from Bienen, *Armies and Parties in Africa*, 46–47.

16. Harvey J. Sindima, *Africa's Agenda: The Legacy of Liberalism and Colonialism in the Crisis of African Values* (Westport: Greenwood Press, 1995), 89, 90.

17. Senghor was impressed by Marx's humanism but disagreed with him on the idea of class-struggle, Marx's poor image of peasants. Senghor was repulsed by his atheism. I have discussed these issues and Senghor's other views about Marx's economic theory in *Africa's Agenda*, 96–98. Also see pages 104–107 in the same book for an assessment of Kaunda's humanism.

18. Liebenow, *African Politics*, 226.

19. Quoted by Kofi Buenor Hadjor, *On Transforming Africa: Discourse with Africa's Leaders* (Trenton, New Jersey: Africa World Press; London: Third World Communications, 1987), 21.

20. Information about successive coups drawn from Henry Bienen, *Armies and Parties in Africa*, 10.

21. William Tordoff, *Government and Politics in Africa* (Bloomington, IN: Indiana University Press, 1993), 148.

22. Bienen, *Armies and Parties in Africa*, 5.

23. Ruth First, *The Barrel of Gun: Political Power in Africa and the Coup d'Etat* (London: Allen Lane, Penguin, 1970), 20.

24. M. J. Dent, "Corrective Government: Military Rule in Perspective," in S. K. Panter-Brink, ed., *Soldiers and Oil: The Political Transformation of Nigeria* (London: Frank Cass, 1978), chap. 4. Cited by Tordoff, *Government and Politics in Africa*, 162.

25. Geoff Lamb, "The Military and Development in Eastern Africa," *Bulletin of the Institute of Development Studies* 4, 4 (September 1972): 21–22.

26. Bienen, *Armies and Parties in Africa*, 113.

27. Liebenow, *African Politics*, 253.

28. Ibid.

29. R. Theobald, "Nigeria," *The National Register* (1989): 256.

30. Tordoff, *Government and Politics in Africa*, 135.

31. I have discussed Malawi's economy in full, and the subject of parastatals in *Malawi's First Republic* (forthcoming).

32. R. A. Young, "States and Markets in Africa." *Market and the State. Studies in Interdependence* (London: Macmillan, 1991), 169–70.

33. Y. A. Fauré, "Côte d'Ivoire: Analysing the Crisis," in D. B. Cruise O'Brien, J. Dunn, and R. Rathbone, eds., *Contemporary West African States* (Cambridge University Press, 1989), 72.

34. I am here following Merilee Grindle's assessment of African economy and politics in *Challenging the State: Crisis and Innovation in Latin America and Africa* (Cambridge: Cambridge University Press, 1996), chap. 2.

35. Ibid., 45.

36. Ibid.

37. Douglas C. North, and R. Thomas, *Institutions, Institutional Change and Economic Performance* (Cambridge: Cambridge University Press, 1990), 3.

38. Ibid., 6.

39. This is a paraphrase of John Rawls definition of institution. See John Rawls, *A Theory of Justice* (Cambridge, MA: Harvard University Press, 1971), 55.

40. See the Republic of Malawi Constitution Act, *Malawi Gazette Supplement*, no. 4C, 17 May 1966.

41. The idea of personal rule is from Robert H. Jackson and Carl G. Rosberg, *Personal Rule in Black Africa: Prince, Autocrat, Prophet, Tyrant* (Berkeley, CA: University of California Press, 1982). The concept is drawn from the works of Machiavelli, Hobbes, and Weber's analysis of charisma and authoritarianism.

42. Niccolò Machiavelli, *Discourses,* I, 9.

43. I am here following George H. Sabine and Thomas L. Thorson in their interpretation of Machiavelli's *Discourse,* in *A History of Political Theory,* 4th ed. (Hinsdale, IL: Dryden Press, 1973), 317–328.

44. Machiavelli, *Discourse,* I, 9.

45. Jackson and Rosberg, *Personal Rule in Africa,* 23.

46. Ibid., 24.

47. Ibid., 19.

48. Ibid., 5.

49. Grindle, *Challenging the State,* 66.

50. Jackson and Rosberg, *Personal Rule in Africa,* 40.

51. H. H. Gerth and C. Wright Mills, *From Max Weber: Essays in Sociology* (New York: Oxford University Press, 1980), 53, 54.

52. Hobbes, *Leviathan,* 72. Emphasis in the original.

53. Ibid., chap. 11.

54. Gerth and Mills, *From Max Weber: Essays in Sociology,* 160.

55. Ibid., 159.

56. Unger, *Knowledge and Politics* (New York: Free Press), 64, 65.

57. Ibid., 65.

58. Ibid., 80.

59. Gibson Winter, *Liberating Creation: Foundations of Social Religious Ethics* (New York: Crossroad, 1981), 102–103.

60. Ibid., 103. My emphasis.

4

The Early Church and the State

The problems of Africa are overwhelming and they seem to defy any political theory. For a person of faith, hope comes from religion but unfortunately, the most popular foreign religions in Africa, Christianity and Islam, have not been aggressive in attacking corruption and mismanagement. These religions have been domesticated by the state or the ruling party. As lamented elsewhere in this book, for a very long time Christianity has continually endorsed national ideology in the name of national unity. In its humble beginnings Christianity was the religion of the poor for it gave them hope. As one looks at what is happening in Africa several question arise: What happened to the revolutionary message, the idea of being on the side of the poor, those made hopeless by the powerful? Why has Christianity become a pacifier to the crying voices of Africa? How did Christianity lose its moral power? These are the issues addressed in this chapter and the next, and the discussion focuses on the attitude of the early church towards civil authorities, the development of civil religion and political theory during the Medieval period. This chapter examines church-state relation in the early church to demonstrate that the church-state problem is rooted in the history of the church itself. This inquiry is not undertaken to exonerate the church, but to put the problems into perspective, with the hope that the lessons from history will help the African church in its struggle against the powers that be, as it seeks to be the voice of the voiceless and the power of the powerless.

THE TWO KINGDOMS THEORY

From its beginning, the church has emphasized obligation of Christians to respect constituted civil authority. This was what was implied by Jesus when he said, "Render therefore to Caesar what belongs to Caesar and to God what belongs to God." As will be shown later, Paul, arguing in his letter to the Romans that there is no authority but from God, urged every Christian to be subject to the authorities; the authorities are ordained by God (Matthew 22:21; compare Mark 12:17; Luke 20:25). For Paul, as for the early church, respect for lawful authority was a duty no Christian denied, but this inevitably bound Christians to a twofold duty: to God and the constituted authorities. In case of conflict, however, the Christian was obliged to obey God rather than earthly authorities (Acts 4); and the authorities, too, were to obey God. It must be mentioned that the obligation to obey civil authorities was in part because of the protection the early Christians had since Christianity enjoyed the legal protection of Judaism from which civil authorities had not yet been able to distinguish it. For most Roman authorities, Christianity was a sect within Judaism and that is why Rome treated Jewish complaints against Christians as an internal problem (see especially Acts 18:12–17). Acts shows that Rome's legal attitude towards Christians was nonantagonistic (Acts 13:4–12; 19:23–41; 25:13–19, 25; 26:30–31). This attitude did later change as Jews drew a distinction between themselves and Christians (Acts 13:50; 14:2, 19; 17:5–6, 13; 18:12; 24:1–2; 25:1–3). Rome's later position grew from the recognition that the Christian way of life threatened traditional society (Acts 16:20–21).[1] Commenting on Rome's change of attitude, Everett Ferguson observes: "But Christianity started with several legal liabilities. It took its name from and was founded on a man who had been executed by Roman authority on a charge that amounted to treason. This was sure to provoke suspicion if not hostility in official circles. And then everywhere the teaching went, it seemed to provoke disturbances and riots, something neither Rome nor the local authorities could view kindly."[2]

Ferguson further comments that the accusation of Nero that Christians were responsible for the great fire of Rome in 64 C.E. (all subsequent dates are C. E., Common Era, unless otherwise indicated), was evidence that "the name" itself placed one in jeopardy. That this was true is affirmed by I Peter 4:16 which says, "However, if you suffer because you are a Christian, don't be ashamed of it, but thank God that you bear Christ's name." This indicates that "the name" was sufficient evidence for punishment.[3] The persecution—limited to Rome—that followed the fire was the first imperial policy to Christianity and it set precedence for succeeding emperors. early documents of Christianity single-out Domitian as the persecutor of Christianity. He persecuted selected individuals, including his cousin, the consul Flavius Clemens and his two sons, on the charge of atheism. Domitian also had the relatives of Jesus brought in for questioning. Concerning this account Eusebius says:

> There still survived of the family of the Lord the grandson of Jude, his brother after the flesh, as he was called. These they informed against, as being of the family of David; and the other officer brought them before Domitian Caesar. For he feared the coming of Christ as did Herod. And he asked if they were of David's line and they acknowledged it. . . . They were asked concerning the Christ and the kingdom, its nature, origin, and time of appearance, and they explained that it was neither of the world or earthly, but heavenly and angelic, and it would be at the end of the world, when he would come in glory to judge the living and the dead and to reward every person according to his or her deeds. At this Domitian did not condemn them at all, but despised them as simple folk, released them, and decreed an end to the persecution against the church.[4]

Emperors Trajan and Hadrian did not carry out large scale persecutions, but certainly punished Christians when brought before their courts. The letter of Pliny, governor of Bithynia in Asia, to Trajan and the reply of the latter make that point clear. Pliny had sought the emperor's counsel as to what to do with Christians brought to him. The policy he had adopted thus far towards Christians was to "ask them if they are Christians. If they admit, I repeat the question a second time and a third time, threatening capital punishment; if they persist, I sentence them to death. For I do not doubt that, whatever kind of crime it may be to which they have confessed, their pertinacity and inflexible obstinacy should certainly be punished. There are others who displayed a like madness and whom I reserved to be sent to Rome, since they were Roman citizens."[5]

The emperor's policy towards Christianity was to condemn those Christians brought before him but not to seek them out.

> You have taken the right line, my dear Pliny, in examining the cases of those denounced to you as Christians, for no hard and fast rule can be laid down, of universal application. They are not to be sought out; if they are informed against, and the charge is proved, they are to be punished, with this reservation—that if anyone denies that he is a Christian, and actually proves it, that is by worshipping our gods, he shall be pardoned as a result of his recantation, however suspect he may have been with respect to the past. Pamphlets published anonymously should carry no weight in any charge whatsoever. They constitute very bad precedent, and are also out of keeping with this age.[6]

In his rescript to Caius Minucius Fundanus, proconsul of Asia, Hadrian affirmed Trajan's policy towards Christianity.

> Now, if our subjects of the provinces are able to sustain by evidence this their petition against the Christians, so as to accuse them before a tribunal, I have no objection to their prosecuting this matter. But I do not allow them to use

> mere clamorous demands and outcries for this purpose. For it is much more equitable, if anyone wishes to accuse them, for you to take cognizance of the matters laid to their charge. If therefore anyone accuses and approves that the aforesaid people do anything contrary to the laws, you will also determine their punishments in accordance with their offenses. You will on the other hand, by Hercules, take particular care that if anyone demands a writ of accusation against any of these Christians, merely for the sake of labelling them, you proceed against that person with heavier penalties, in accordance with his heinous guilt.[7]

The impression we get from the New Testament is that Christians believed that the truth they held was revealed by God to guide them into salvation rather than any destiny the world afforded. Therefore they could not believe that religion imposed duties from which any emperor could absolve them and in the light of which admitted duty of civic obedience must be weighed and judged. This belief constituted a treasonable offense in the time of the Romans for they believed that the emperor was a civil authority and a divinity. From the vantage of the Roman authorities and citizens Christians were bad citizens, who showed no respect for the one who took care of their material needs, and also mediated for them before the gods. From the early church's perspective, the understanding was that there were two obligations and duties—spiritual, owed directly to God, and secular, owed to the emperor. These could be on occasion in opposition but not ultimately irreconcilable.

What we learn from the Gospels, Acts, and beyond about Christian attitude towards civil authorities is not a negative understanding but that the authority and power civic leaders had was from God. Furthermore, early Christians trusted that justice could be delivered by civil authorities. The apostle Paul appealed to civil authorities more than once. The persecutions of emperors Nero and Domitian did not change the attitude of the early Christians towards secular leaders because bad leaders were viewed as the representations of the evil power of this world. That is why the apologists (defenders of the Christian faith against wrong teachings and charges and attacks from the state) appealed to local civil authorities and emperors for fairness. In 155 Justin Martyr (100–65) appealed to Emperor Antoninu Pius, his sons, the Roman Senate and the entire Roman population, for justice on behalf of "those of all nations who are unjustly hated."

> But lest someone think this is an unreasonable and reckless utterance, we demand that the charges against the Christians be investigated, and that, if these be substantiated, they be punished as they deserve. . . . But if no one convict us of anything, true to reason forbid you, for the sake of a wicked rumor to wrong blameless men and indeed yourself, who think fit to direct affairs, not by judgement but by passion . . . it is your business, when you

> hear us, to be found, as reason demands, good judges. For if, when you have learned the truth, you do not do what is just, you will be before God without excuse. . . . And those among you who are accused, you do not punish before they are convicted; but in our case you receive the name as proof against us. . . . Again, if any of the accused deny the name, and say that he is not a Christian, you acquit him, as having no evidence against him as a wrongdoer; but if anyone acknowledges that he is a Christian, you punish him on account of this acknowledgement. Justice requires that you inquire into the life both of him who confesses and of him who denies, that by his deed it may become apparent what kind of man each is.[8]

Even when there was no persecution and imperial policy towards Christianity was not hostile, Christians did not always receive justice before the magistrates. Writing his apology in 197 Tertullian (160–225) made reference to Trajan's policy as given to Pliny some fifty years earlier and later followed by Hadrian.
Tertullian wrote:

> If it is certain that we are the most guilty of people, why do you treat us differently from our fellows, that is, from other criminals. Since it is only fair that the same guilt should meet with the same treatment. When others are accused on the charges which are brought against us they employ their own tongues and hired advocacy to plead their innocence. They have full opportunity or reply and cross-examination; for it is not permitted to condemn people undefended and unheard. Christians alone are not allowed to say anything to clear themselves, to defend truth, to save a judge from injustice. That alone is looked for, which the public hate requires—the confession of the name, not the investigation of the charge.[9]

(Note references to "the name" in the last two quotations). While they obeyed civic leaders and performed their civic duties, early Christians performed some passive resistance when civic duty went against Christian teaching and life, in particular, serving in the army and offering sacrifices to the emperor—this being idolatry. The reason for not taking up military service was best expressed by Tertullian (160–225). "We must first inquire whether warfare is proper at all for Christians. . . . Shall the son of peace take part in the battle when it is not fitting for him to sue at law? Shall he keep guard before temples which he has renounced? Then how many other offenses there are involved in the performance of camp offices?"[10] Tertullian maintained that when one converted to Christianity, there had to be an "immediate abandonment" of military service, for not doing so would be offending God. That applied, too, to official positions in the government in general: "Offices must be either refused, so that we may not fall into acts of sin, or martyrdoms endured that we may get quit of offices."[11]

The prohibition against serving in the military was lifted by the Council of Arles in 314 when Christians were also permitted to hold offices in the government. In general, Christians lived like anybody else except that they withdrew from certain practices and from society because of their status and circumstances, which often led them into persecution. From the time of emperor Nero to the reign of Trajan–Decius persecutions were local. It was Decius in 250 who started the first empire-wide assault on Christians, and these persecutions went on until the time of Constantine. Persecutions were not continuous; there were times of respite, like the early years of Valerian, 253–256, when the church partially recovered from the Decian persecutions. In 253 the church held a provincial synod where more than 66 African bishops were able to meet and discuss the issue of infant baptism; and in 255 another synod of 32 bishops met to deal with the validity of the baptism of heretics. Dionysius, the bishop of Alexandria, described the peace that the church enjoyed as the result of Valerian's benevolent attitude towards Christianity: "How mild and friendly he was to the men of God. For not a single one of the emperors before him was so kindly and favorably disposed towards them, not even those who were said to be openly Christians, as he manifestly was, when he received them at the beginning in the most intimate and friendly manner; indeed all his house had been filled with godly persons, and was a church of God."[12]

This good fortune of Christians did not continue, for in the summer of 257 Valerian suddenly reversed his policy of religious toleration and instituted persecutions, first directed at the leaders of the church, banishing to mines bishops, priests, and those believed to be rebellious individuals.[13] Cyprian, the bishop of Carthage, was exiled to the desert village of Curubis while Dionysius was sent to Cephro in Libya.[14] Valerian also prohibited, under the threat of capital punishment, assembly of Christians or the visiting of cemeteries. In the summer of 258, Valerian issued a rescript to the Senate for newer and harsher measures against Christians. The measures included the forfeit of property and execution for those who persisted in Christianity. It was during these persecutions that Pope Sixtus and four of his deacons were killed while visiting the catacombs of Callistus. Many Africans died in these persecutions, including bishops Theogenes, Agapius, Secundius, and Cyprian who was executed in September 258.[15] What caused the reversal of imperial religious policy? Misfortune and defeats befalling the empire were attributed to Christian leaders because they had abandoned worship of the gods and, secondly, that Christians refused to perform the *supplicatio*, that is, the kneeling and prostrating before the imperial statue.

Anyone who performed this religious rite to the gods, and before a designated Roman official received a certificate of sacrifice called *libellus*. The sacrifice was done in private as a declaration of religious loyalty to the gods of the empire, but the sacrifice was attested by an imperial official. In the strict sense, a *libellus* was a petition of residence of the empire addressed to the local authorities requesting them to countersign one's declaration of piety and loyalty. Anyone who could not show a *libellus* when so requested by a government official was arrested and executed if the individual refused to sacrifice. Below is a sample of a *libellus* from the time of the Decian persecution.

> *1st Hand.* To the commission chosen to superintend the sacrifices. From Aurelia Ammonarion of the village of Theadelphia. I and my children, Aurelius Didymus, Aurelius Nouphius, and Aurelius Taas, have always and without interruption sacrificed and shown piety to the gods, and now in your presence in accordance with the edict's decree we have poured libations, and made sacrifice, and partaken of the sacred victims. I request you to certify this for me below. Farewell.
> *2nd Hand.* We, Aurelius Serenus and Aurelius Hermas, saw you sacrificing.
> *3rd Hand.* I, Hermas, certify it.
> *1st Hand.* The year of one of the Emperor Caesar Gaius Messius Quintus Trajanus Decius Pius Felix Augustus, Payni 20 [20 June 250].[16]

Persecutions, on and off, and on again, became the general condition of the early Christians, the last wave of persecutions being from 303 to 312 ordered by emperor Diocletion (245–313). This persecution, known as the "Great" persecution, started with the edict of 23 February 303, which decreed that all churches were to be destroyed, scriptures and other liturgical books surrendered or burnt, church property confiscated, all meetings for worship banned, Christians denied legal action, and judicial privileges revoked, and those in the imperial service who were not soldiers reduced to slavery. In January 304, a further edict was decreed ordering all people of the empire to offer sacrifice to the gods or risk, death penalty. This wave of persecutions did not end until Emperor Galerius (emperor 307–11) on his deathbed issued the Edict of Tolerance in 311 which allowed "Christians to exist again and set up their places of worship; provided always that they do not offend against public order. . . . In return for this indulgence of ours it will be the duty of Christians to pray to God our [emperor's] recovery, for the public weal and for their own; that the state may be preserved from danger on every side, and that they themselves may dwell safely in their homes."[17] Galerius died five days later.

In spite of, and because of, the persecutions of the first two and half centuries, Christianity continued to increase, reaching practically all over the Roman empire. Tertullian (160–225), one of the early great north African theologians once said persecutions did not stop the advance of Christianity, rather the opposite, for "the blood of martyrs is seed."[18] Christianity grew rapidly during the persecutions for people fled to various places in the empire, where they spread their religious beliefs. By the third century it had become clear to any emperor that he would have to develop a policy of dealing with Christianity. The Edit of Tolerance by Galerius was the first recognition of that fact and a move towards imperial religious policy. It was emperor Constantine who changed the imperial attitude towards Christianity, having persuaded Licinius, emperor of the East, to issue (in February 313) an edict of religious toleration later to be known as the Edict of Milan. The edict offered universal religious toleration in the empire, and Christianity was recognized as a legal corporation, thereby permitting it to own property and restoring its confiscated church buildings. Although other religions were allowed the same privileges only Christianity was mentioned by name in the Edict of Milan. Events during the year before Constantine and Licinius signed the edict showed a serious change in the church-state relations. Towards the end of 312 Constantine sent two letters, one to Anulinus, proconsul of Africa, and the other to Caecillian, Bishop of Carthage, instructing Anulinus to restore to the church all property forfeited during the persecutions. The order included returning property now in the possession of private citizens. The bishop of Carthage, was granted funds from the imperial estates in North Africa for his use, as well as immunity from taxes and civic duties for the clergy.[19]

Constantine saw himself as a Christian emperor, therefore he took responsibility to end the Donatist controversy which was threatening to wreck the North African church. The controversy was over bishop Caecillian's consecration in 311 in which Felix Aptunga (a bishop who had surrendered the scriptures in a recent persecution) had participated. Although the consecration was recognized by the officials, the church was split; some bishops believed it was invalid because of the participation of Aptunga. Though Constantine had promised in a letter written in 312 the newly elected bishop support against his enemies, things did not improve. African bishops failed to mediate, they asked the emperor to intervene by sending impartial judges. In 314 Constantine called five bishops, among whom was the bishop of Rome, and they met in Arles in Gaul; this was the first council to meet in the West. A letter which Constantine wrote to his representative in Africa, the Christian Aelafus, concerning the resolution of the controversy, reveals his sense of himself as a Christian emperor: "Since I know that you also worship the Supreme, I advise Your Excellency that I do not consider it proper to make a secret of all these quarrels and wrangles. For they might well rouse God not only against the human race, but also against me, to whose rule and care His holy will has committed all earthly things, and provoke other measures. I shall never rest content nor expect prosperity and happiness from the Almighty's merciful power until I feel that all people offer to the All Holy the right worship of the Catholic religion in a common fellowship."[20]

Constantine believed himself to be a secular ruler and a spiritual guardian.

These dual roles of an absolute authority, secular and religious, are further revealed in his letter to Domitius Celsus, governor of Africa. The letter announced Constantine planed go to Africa to personally settle the Donatus controversy after the bishops' council in 314 at Arles had failed to resolve the differences. He wrote, "With the favor of the divine piety I shall come to Africa and shall fully demonstrate to all with an unequivocal verdict as much to Caecilian as to those who seem to be against him just how the Supreme Deity should be worshiped. . . . What more, can be done, more in accord with my constant practice and the very office of a prince, than after expelling error and destroying rash opinions to cause all people to agree together to follow true religion and simplicity of life and to render to Almighty God the worship that is his due."[21]

Constantine intended to use the powers of his two offices, emperor and vicar of God. In 316 he intervened using force, taking away the churches of the breakaway party and exiling all their bishops, including Donatus, their leader. The intervention did not bring peace, so in 321 Constantine stopped enforcing his decree and gave the Donatus up to the judgement of God. Enactments issued between 313 and 323 indicated that the direction imperial policy took towards religion was to make Christianity the religion of the empire. The laws reflected Christian morals and values: Constantine banned divination, sacrificing to idols, capital punishment, branding on the face, ordered a more humane treatment of slaves (21 March, 315),[22] and removed disabilities imposed by Augustus on celibacy (31 January, 320).[23] Constantine also ordered legislations concerning treatment of children and women, protecting family life, and concerning the punishment of creditors. He banned the writings of heretics, indeed eclipsing religious pluralism.[24] His intention to make Christianity the religion of the empire was expressed in the edict of 321, which declared Sun day the official day of rest in urban areas: "All judges, city people, and craftsmen shall rest on the venerable day of the Sun. But country people may without hindrance attend to agriculture, since it often happens that this is the most suitable day for sowing grain or planting vines, so that the opportunity afforded providence may not be lost, for the right season is of short duration."[25]

That Constantine intended to make Christianity the official religion of the empire was clear but it did not happen until he defeated Licinius in a civil war in 323–4. After the defeat of Licinius, Constantine became the sole ruler of the empire and he proceeded to elevate Christianity to the status of state religion. He ordered restitution to the heirs of those persecuted by emperor Licinius. He also ordered release from all the various forms of exile under Licinius; the clergy were released from civic duty but heretics were denied all privileges and immunities. Hence Christianity became the official religion of the empire and Constantine meant to use it as the cement of his empire. This vision was difficult to realize because, as he was to find once he moved his capital in 324 to Constantinople—a city he called the *Nova Roma* (New Rome)—the church itself was split over doctrinal issues. The churches in the eastern part of the empire—Egypt, Palestine, Syria, and Asia Minor—were outraged by the teaching of Arius, an excommunicated Egyptian priest who rejected the teaching that Jesus was of the same substance with the Father or *Homoousia* in Greek, the liturgical language of Eastern churches. (Churches in the Western part of the Empire used Latin as liturgical language.) Constantine's belief that the unity of the church would facilitate the unity of the empire, led him to convoke the first ecumenical synod at Nicea in 325.

Among the significant legislations Constantine passed was the one in 318 concerning incorporation of the church courts into the imperial judicial system. With this inclusion into one of the institutions of the state, the clergy achieved the corresponding status and were accorded the same respect as their counterparts in secular courts and civic society. The incorporation of episcopal courts into the imperial judicial system was not difficult since, as third century documents show, the episcopal courts had structured themselves along the style of the Roman senate. Bishop Cyprian of Carthage reveals this similarity when he describes in his letters the process of the meetings of the first African synods. The meeting of the Roman senate was called by the emperor; after the senate convened, the emperor read the outline of the discussion, the *relatio*, adding a few words of explanation, *verba facere*, followed by deliberation, the *interrogatio*, by all the senators present, each stating their *sententia* (point of view) without being verbose. The senate deliberated until they reached consensus, and this was what was announced as the *sententia* of the senate. Cyprian used the same procedure when he called a synod. He read the *relatio* followed by explanation and deliberation by all the bishops who had equal rights like the Roman senators. The *sententia* of the meeting was announced in a synodical letter to the parties concerned.[26] The same procedure was followed at the synod at Arles in Gaul, and according to the author of *Vita Constantini*, business was conducted in the same way at the first ecumenical council at Nicea.[27] As in the Roman senate, the council had been called by the emperor and the *relatio* was *Homoousios* (the unity of the Son, Jesus, with the Father being of one substance). As in the Roman senate, the emperor had no right to vote, and so it was at Nicea.

With the decree to consolidate the ecclesiastical and imperial courts, the church was brought fully into the state apparatus. Not only that, precedence had been set for the emperor to intervene in church matters, albeit with first consulting the concerned parties as was the procedure in the Roman senate. The first intervention was in the Donatist controversy; although the convocation at Arles was held by Constantine it had been at the petition of African bishops. This was not the first time that bishops had appealed to the emperor to settle their disputes; there was an earlier appeal in 272 to emperor Aurelian (215–75) petitioning him to arbitrate over the possession of a church building in Antioch. The argument was between the orthodox church and Paul of Samosota, a heretic who had been excommunicated but held on to a church building. Aurelian's reply to his petitioners was that the building would be "assigned to those with whom the bishops of the doctrine in Italy Rome should communicate in writing."[28]

The convocation at Nicea was initiated by Constantine himself after he had approached the principal parties concerned, bishop Arius and Alexander, the patriarch of Alexandria. The bishops' meeting at Antioch had agreed that the synod would meet and discuss the issue at Ancyra (Ankara), but Constantine transferred it to Nicea. About 230 bishops came to the council. As mentioned above, the meeting was conducted with the same protocol as the Roman senate. The element of the senatorial procedure establishing that the emperor did not vote, was in the church's favor; it allowed the church to maintain its independence from imperial decrees on matters of doctrine.

Constantine set precedence for intervening politically in church affairs and calling synods, and the church did not seem to mind. Considering himself the Christian emperor, therefore the protector of every Christian in the world, Constantine intervened in Persia on behalf of Christians there. In 326 Constantine wrote a letter to King Sapor (309–79) of Persia in praise of Christianity and commending Christians there to his protection.

The Christian position implied two institutional organizations which remained distinct, though each needed the other, and in normal case supported the other. History shows that the growth of world empires does indeed need religion for support, for the congeries of peoples, ethnicity, and those lacking strong ties, found no practical bond of union except a common religion. This is the reason Constantine legalized Christianity; but it is noteworthy that Constantine did not consider his authority above that of bishops. In his role as emperor at the Council of Nicea in 325, he understood the bishops "as gods and decreed that they should not be subject to his judgement but he should be dependent upon their will."[29] He considered it the function of the bishops to make decisions on matters of doctrine, so he wrote to the bishops who had not attended the council of Nicea, "Such being the case, be willing to accept this heavenly favor and an order so manifestly from God. For whatever is decided in the holy councils of the bishops must be attributed to the divine will."[30] This statement coming from someone who was not a Christian indicates a devotion and willingness to develop in the doctrines of church. It was not surprising that he granted the church many privileges.

Constantine emerged as an emperor who considered religion and the state as interrelated, politically and otherwise. Constantine embraced the church with all its teachings, and in turn the church enjoying the privileges the state provided, embraced Constantine. He carried out all these changes before he was baptized. He had planned to be baptized in Jerusalem (in the Jordan river) where he would go for the dedication of the church of the Holy Sepulcher. He did attend the dedication on 17 September 335, but he postponed his baptism until he was on his deathbed at Pentecost 337.

Constantine's religious policy was followed by succeeding emperors, beginning with his sons Constantine II, Constans, and Constantius who had staged a military coup on 9 September 334, and proclaimed themselves Augusti. The three sons divided the empire although Constantinople remained the capital: Constantine II became the Augustus of the West, Constans took Illyrium and Africa, while the youngest, Constantius was the ruler of the Eastern empire. Like their father they believed in the power of Christianity to unify the empire, but Constantius differed from the other two in his understanding of christology. He was inclined more to the teachings of Arius, who said the Son, Jesus, was just a mere creature; he was not of the same substance (*homoousia* in Greek) with the Father; or, that the Sonship of Jesus was not eternal but started when he was born to Mary. Having declared his belief openly, he wanted the rest of his subjects, that is, the whole Eastern Empire, to become Arian. He did not dictate his belief, but instead called for a synod to support his views. Although he convoked a council, which the Arians applauded and the orthodox protested, Constantius had not done right because his responsibility as Augustus was to defend the faith; he had shown partiality in siding with the minority whom the majority orthodox had condemned as heretics. All Constantine's sons accepted and respected the function of the synod in defining the faith, but they also maintained the right of the emperor to convoke synods. That explains why there were more synods under the reign of Constantius than any other emperor; the problem, however, was that his synods were filled with heretical bishops.

Constantine's sons retained the right to convoke synods and also to intervene politically in church affairs. Constantine II once in power ordered the return of Athanasius from exile resulting from his condemnation by the Synod of Tyre in 335, which was full of Arian bishops. Athanasius returned to Alexandria as patriarch on 23 November 337. The church, both East and West, continued to uphold the right of the emperor to convoke synods. On the other hand, Pope Julius (337–52) felt it was the task of the church to convoke synods, and to this end he convoked a synod of bishops in Rome for the purpose of rehabilitating Athanasius. Bishops of the East reminded Julius that he had the right to convoke synods, but that no decision made by a general council called by the emperor could be repealed by an ordinary Roman synod. Julius replied to the Eastern bishops that: (1) while the emperor convokes a synod, it was not his convocation; (2) that the recognition of the decision of the synod by the whole church gave a council its general and abiding character; (3) that in convoking a synod, he, Julius, invoked the customs and powers that were preserved in the church.

> Let us grant the "removal," as you write, of Athanasius and Marcellus [of Ancyra who had also been condemned with Athansius] from their places, yet what must one say of the case of other bishops and presbyters who, as I said before, came here from other places and complained that they had been forced away and had suffered the like injuries? O dearly beloved, the decisions of the church are no longer according to the Gospel, but tend furthermore to banishment and death. . . . And why was nothing written to us concerning the church of the Alexandrians in particular? Are you ignorant that the custom has been for word to be written first to us, and then for a just sentence to be passed from this place? . . . What I write is for the common good. What we have received from the blessed Apostle Peter, that I signify to you.[31]

This was the first conflict between imperial authority and ecclesiastical power and functions. Julius opposed the idea that the emperor's convocation of a synod implied he had authority over the functions of the church. Julius rejected the view by claiming the power of the papacy through the authority of Peter.

Emperors Theodosius I (347–95) and Justinian I (483–565) followed the precedence set by Constantine, and followed by his son. In 379 in Milan, Theodosius I issued a decree banning every heresy and in a second edict he authorized no other except Nicea:

> It is our desire that all the nations which are subject to our clemency and Moderation, should continue in the profession of that religion which was delivered to the Romans by the divine Apostle Peter, as it has been preserved by faithful tradition; and which is now professed by the Pontiff Damascus and by Peter, Bishop of Alexandria, a man of apostolic holiness. . . . We authorize the followers of this law to assume the title of Catholic Christians; but as for the others, since, in our judgement, they are foolish madmen, we decree that they shall be branded with the ignominious name of heretics, and shall not presume to give their venticles the name of churches.[32]

Theodosius, like Justinian, convoked councils for the church to settle theological differences. Theodosius called the Second Ecumenical Council that met in Constantinople in 381 to reach an agreement on the nature of Christ in relation to the Father, that is, to confirm Nicea and conclude the Arian controversy. When the 150 bishops gathered for the council announced their decision they made it clear to the emperor that matters of defining faith were their responsibility, and that his was to endorse the decisions of the bishops and defend the faith. In other words, the emperor had no authority over the bishops in matters of faith. "Our first duty in writing to Your Piety is to thank God for having established your empire for the common peace of the churches and for the confirmation of the true faith. Having rendered to God the thanks due to him, we must lay before Your Piety what has been decided in this council. . . . We therefore ask Your Clemency that a letter of Your Piety should ratify the decrees of this council. As you honored the church by your letter of convocation, so also lend your authority to our decision."[33] This, was not, however, a universal feeling for bishops in the West had submitted to imperial authority in matters of faith. An extract from the letter of the Roman Synod in 382 states that the bishops in the West wanted Roman civil officials and courts to be involved in the trial of religious leaders, metropolitans, and bishops.

> We request your Clemency, that your Piety would think fit to order if any shall have been condemned by the judgment either of Damascus [bishop of Rome 366–384] or of ourselves, who are Catholics, and shall unjustly wish to retain his church, or shall through contumacy refuse to attend when summoned by a synod of bishops, that he be brought to Rome either by those illustrious men, the Praetorium Prefects of your Italy or by the Vicar (of the city); or, if a question of this kind arises in more distant parts, that the examination be committed by the local courts to the Metropolitan; or, if the Metropolitan himself be the accused, that he should be ordered to go to Rome without delay, or to such judges as the Bishop of Rome may appoint.[34]

This attitude in the West also prevailed at the Synod of Carthage in June 404, when the synod petitioned imperial intervention in dealing with the Donantists and the synod itself was presided over by an imperial official.[35] This, too, was the imperial religious policy as indicated by Theodosius II in his letter to Cyril of Alexandria and the bishops of the East who were to meet at Ephesus in June 431 to address the Nestorian controversy. It is important to say something about this controversy because it eventually led to a lasting schism within the Eastern churches, or the Orthodox Tradition, between the Nestorians, monophysistes, and Chalcedonian churches. The final schism took place in May 451, at Chalcedon, the site of the Fourth Ecumenical Council, at which Nestorianism and Monophysitism were condemned; needless to say, the condemned churches do not acknowledge the Fourth Ecumenical Council.

Nestorius, the patriarch of Constantinople, disagreed with the teaching of the see of Alexandria as articulated by Athanasius, the patriarch of Alexandria (296–373) and later advanced by Cyril, patriarch of the same see (412–444). This teaching held that in Jesus two natures, divine and human, united into one indivisible union, but was dominated by the divine so that the human was in the background. The divine, called the *Logos* (reason or Word as in John 1:1), was united with human flesh. This was to claim that

Jesus was more of God than the human he appeared to be, for his body was an instrument of the divine. However, the union between the human and the divine was such that whatever is said of one side of the union can also be transferred to the other. There was a "communion of properties," or *communicatio idiomatum* as the Alexandrines put it. In expressing this idea Athanasius said, "For if the flesh is also in itself a part of the created world, yet it has become God's body. And we neither divide the body, being flesh, from the Word, and worship it by itself, nor when we wish to worship the Word do we set Him apart from the Flesh, but knowing, as we said, above, that the 'Word was made flesh,' we recognize Him as God also, after having come in flesh."[36]

Inheriting this tradition from Athanasius, Cyril's later followers were to state that the human side of Jesus was swallowed up by the divine. Alexandrines regarding Jesus of one divine nature started calling Mary, the mother of Jesus, "the mother of God," an idea called *theotokos* in Greek. While churches in Alexandria emphasized the divinity of Jesus, the church in Syria and Mesopotamia, areas under the See of Antioch, emphasized the humanity of Jesus, that is, seeing Jesus as a person with full human rational powers. In other words, he was not able to sin not because he was God, but because he was a human being who made rational choices. Accordingly, a Jesus whose rational human capacity was swallowed up by the divine would not be useful for human redemption. Therefore when the churches in the Antiochian patriarchy heard that the patriarchy of Alexandria advanced the idea that Mary was the mother of God, *theotokos*, they considered the teaching a heresy for Mary bore Jesus, a human being. Theodore of Mopsuestia (350–428) took exception to the idea of *theotokos*, maintaining with great vividness the full integrity of Jesus' human nature. Nestorius insisted on distinguishing between the humanity and divinity of Jesus, and he was so emphatic that he was in danger of ending up with two persons coexisting at the same time. With his strict distinction between the two natures, he saw *theotokos* as a confusion of the divine and the human in Jesus. His view was that Mary was a mother of a human being, Jesus, and at most one may call Mary "Bearer of Christ," since she is the mother of Christ's humanity but not of his divinity.

The disagreement on the natures of Jesus led to divisions within the Eastern churches, and it was because of this disagreement in doctrine that Theodore summoned the bishops to meet at what was to become the Third Ecumenical Council held at Ephesus in 413. In his letter to Cyril and the bishops who were to meet in Ephesus, Theodore wrote:

> The stability of the Republic depends on the religion by which we honor God. There is a close link between the two. They depend on each other and each thrives on the progress of the other. So that true religion will reveal itself in

> just dealing and the Republic will flourish supported by both. Since, then, God has handed us the reins of government and made us the link of piety and rectitude for all our subjects, we shall always keep undivided association between them and watch over the interests of both God and people. For we must minister to the prosperity of the Republic, and keeping, so to speak, a watchful eye on our subjects, we must see to it that they believe piously, lead lives worthy of pious believers, doing their best in both ways as far as in them lies. It cannot be that those who watch over one thing should neglect others. . . . We also are keenly interested in these matters and shall not easily allow anyone to absent himself. Anyone who will not be punctually present at the proposed place at the appointed time will have no excuse before God or ourselves.[37]

Clarifying the role of imperial representative at episcopal meetings he said the official was sent "With this injunction and on this condition that he shall have nothing to do with the problems and controversies regarding dogmas of faith, for it is not desirable that one who does not belong to the body of holy bishops should meddle with ecclesiastical questions and discussions. But he must use every means to remove from the city any monks or laymen who have gathered there for this council or will do so: those who are not required for the study of the sacred dogmas must not be allowed to create trouble or put obstacles in the way in matters which Your Holiness are there to settle and define."[38] To show his imperial authority over ecclesiastical leadership, Theodosius ordered the leaders of the two opposing parties—Cyril, Nestorius, and John—imprisoned. From Theodosius on, bishops developed an attitude that the emperor was infallible, and part of this was because of the church leaders' own weakness or dependence on emperors to settle doctrinal issues for them through banishment, imprisonment, or any other political measure. This situation was improved upon by the Acts of Chalcedon which defined the function of the General Councils. At Chalcedon, it was agreed that the imperial role was similar to that in the Roman senate, to convoke meetings and lead debates, ratify the *sententia*, and no more. This arrangement was followed by both parties for the last half of the fifth century, although Basiliscus (emperor 475–76) wanted to repeal the decision of Chalcedon. It was the right of priests to define doctrine, said Pope Felix III (483–92) in defending Chalcedon after emperor Zeno (474–91) had taken upon himself to establish a compromise between the orthodox and Monophysitists. Felix's position was clarified by pope Gelasius in 494 in writing to emperor Anastasius (491–518), who had succeeded Zeno in 491: "There are in fact two [powers], emperor Augustus, by which the world is sovereignly governed; the consecrated authority of the bishops and the royal power. Of these, the responsibility of the bishops is the more weighty, since even for the rulers of people they will have to give an account at the judgement seat of God."[39]

Justinian called the Fifth Ecumenical Council or the Second Council of

Constantinople in 553 to settle the Theodore/Nestorian Christological controversy. Justinian intruded too much into theological matters when he condemned the prominent Antiochian theologians known as the "Three Chapters" without convoking a synod and without consulting the bishops. African bishops revolted, and Pope Vigilius joined them, thus forcing the emperor to yield and call the ecumenical council.

Justinian gradually brought about the emergence of a phenomenon called "Christian Empire," and the ruler of that empire bore the official title of "faithful king in Christ-God." The government of such emperors became more and more permeated with Christian teachings and values. These emperors did not only grant extensive privileges of all kinds but also allowed the church to participate in the government's judicial authority and the control of public welfare. In doing this, Justinian and his immediate successors did not want to bring the state under the authority of the church; they sought a harmonious relationship. Justinian's own words in his Sixth Novella, dated 16 March 535, make this point clear: "The greatest gifts which God has granted to people are the priesthood and the empire, the priesthood concerns things divine, the empire presides over mortals."

The general tradition for church-state relations has been of two realms; spiritual and secular, with secular authorities subordinate to the former. Thus Ambrose (339–97), bishop of Milan, would say the emperor, "is within the church, not above it."[40] In a letter to Emperor Valentian II, he said, "bishops are wont to judge of Christian emperors, not emperors of bishops." Ambrose did not deny that it was Christian duty to obey civil authorities but he affirmed the right and duty of clergy to reprove secular rulers in matters of morals, a precept which he himself practiced. On one famous occasion he refused to celebrate the Eucharist in the presence of Emperor Theodosius because of the emperor's guilt in causing a massacre at Thessalonica in mid-September 390. "I, indeed, though a debtor to your kindness in all other things, for which I cannot be ungrateful, that kindness which has surpassed that of many emperors, and has been equaled by one only; I, I say, have no cause for a charge of contumacy against you, but have cause for fear; I dare not offer the sacrifice [Eucharist] if you intend to be present. Is that which is not allowed after shedding the blood on one innocent person, allowed after shedding the blood of many? I do not think so."[41] Using the example of King David in the Old Testament, Ambrose demanded that the emperor repent of his sin before the excommunication would be lifted. The emperor agreed to repent. In another instance, Ambrose steadfastly refused to surrender a church for the use of Arians upon the order of Emperor Valentinian II. Empress Justina, through her praetorian prefect in Italy, asked for the Portian basilica situated outside Milan as place for Arian Worship. Ambrose said:

> At last the command was given: surrender the Basilica. My reply was, it is not lawful for me to surrender it, nor advantageous for you. . . . It is asserted that everything is lawful for the emperor, that all things are his. My answer is: Do not, O Emperor, lay on yourself the burden of such a thought as that you have any imperial power over those things which belong to God. Exalt not yourself,

> but if you desire to reign long, submit yourself to God. It is written: The things which are God's to God, those which are Caesar's to Caesar. The palaces belong to the Emperor, the churches to the Bishop. Authority is committed to you over public, not sacred buildings.[42]

The court gave in. According to Ambrose, the secular ruler is subject to the church's instruction in spiritual matters and his authority over some ecclesiastical property is limited, but the church's right is to be maintained by spiritual means rather than resistance. In being defiant to the emperor Ambrose was following the tradition of John Chrysostom (347–407), the patriarch of Constantinople, who did not mince his words in addressing the imperial palace.

The obvious conflicts and ambiguities in the concept of two distinct yet complimentary organizations are apparent. In the course of the Christian tradition this position has presented difficulties to both the laity and leaders. The inconsistencies in Augustine (354–430), Bishop of Hippo (in Libya), one of Africa's greatest theologians of the early church, on the church-state relation typifies the problem Christianity has. Early in his life Augustine opposed the use of force against the Manicheans, but later, dealing with the Donatists, he reversed his position.[43] Sincerely believing that heresy was a deadly sin, Augustine could not contemplate its spread unopposed by those who were responsible for the earthly as well as the eternal welfare of their subjects.

Although Augustine had reluctantly moved towards the use of force to settle religious matters, that was not the case when he composed *The City of God*, a book written after the fall of Rome in 410 amidst charges that Christians were responsible for the end of the great historical city. In *The City of God* Augustine was definite on the distinction between the church and secular realms. Augustine approached the church and state relation from the understanding of the human as both spirit and body, and therefore, at once a citizen of the world and of the heavenly city. The fundamental fact of human life is the division of human interests—the worldly interests that center about the body and the otherworldly interests that belong specifically to the spirit. In *The City of God*, (Books XIV–XV and XVIII–XIX) Augustine made a key distinction in understanding human history, that it is always dominated by the contest of two societies, the earthly city founded on human impulses and the heavenly city of peace and spiritual salvation.

> Accordingly, two cities have been formed by two loves: the earthly by the love of self, even to the contempt of God; the heavenly by the love of God, even to the contempt of self. The former, in a word, glories in itself, the latter in the Lord. For one seeks glory from people; but the greatest glory of the other is God, the witness of conscience. . . . In the one, princes and the nations it

> subdues are ruled by the love of ruling, in the other, the princes and the subjects serve one another in love, the latter obeying, while the former takes thought for all. The one delights in its own strength, represented in the persons of its rulers; the other says to its God, "I will love, you, O Lord, my strength.[44]

According to Augustine, no matter how large earthly cities may become, they must all pass away for they are the kingdom of the devil—only the heavenly city will remain forever. This was to him the reason Rome fell. What is the relation between the two cities? The earthly city works on earthly peace which the heavenly city makes use of.

> The earthly city which does not live by faith seeks only an earthly peace, and limits the goal of its peace, of its harmony of authority and obedience among its citizens, to the voluntary and collective attainment of objectives necessary to moral existence. The heavenly city, meanwhile—or, rather, that part that is on pilgrimage in mortal life and lives by faith—must use this earthly peace until such time as our mortality which needs such peace has passed away. As a consequence, so as long as her life in the earthly city is that of a captive and an alien (although the church has the promise of ultimate delivery and the gift of the Spirit as a pledge), it has no hesitation about keeping in step with the civil law which governs matters pertaining to our existence here below.[45]

Augustine considered the heavenly city as on a pilgrimage in this world, it therefore collaborates with the earthly city, sometimes even enduring it. "Thus, the heavenly city, so long as it is wayfaring on earth, not only makes use of the earthly peace but fosters and actively pursues along with other human beings a common platform in regard to all that concerns our purely human life and does not interfere with faith and worship. Of course, though, the city of God subordinates this earthly peace to that of heaven. For this is not merely true peace, but, strictly speaking, for any rational creature, the only real peace, since it is, as I said, 'the perfectly ordered and harmonious communion of those who find their joy in God and in one another in God'."[46]

What we see emerging from the works of these two early church leaders, Ambrose and Augustine, is an emphasis on the concept of two authorities, a teaching which received authoritative statement at the close of the fifth century by Pope Gelasius I. Following Ambrose, he emphasized the independence and jurisdiction of ecclesial authorities in self-governing their institutions. Writing against subordination of ecclesiastical policy to the imperial court at Constantinople, he asserted that the priest's responsibility, being directed towards eternal salvation, was not superior to the king's power. He said, "The Omnipotent God has willed that the teachers and priests of the Christian religion shall not be governed by the civil law or secular authorities, but by bishops and priests."[47] He again wrote, "Christian emperors need bishops for the sake of eternal life, and bishops make use of imperial regulations to order the course of temporal affairs."[48] In sum, the king has power, but *authority* belongs to the Apostle Peter and his successors, and since the purpose of this life is to prepare people for the life to come, the function of the vicar of Peter is higher than that of the temporal ruler. This was not the original position of the early church. The attitude of the early Christians towards secular authorities was in many ways favorable since the Christians needed secular rulers for protection from mobs and others. After Christianity had become legalized by Constantine, the early church developed a dependence on the secular authorities, emperors, to define the faith.

NOTES

1. Everett Ferguson, *Backgrounds of Early Christianity* (Grand Rapids, MI: William Eerdmans, 1987), 480–1.81.
2. Ibid., 481.
3. Ibid.
4. Ibid., 482. As quoted from Eusebius.
5. Pliny to Trajan in Henry Bettenson *Documents of the Christian Church*, 2nd. ed. (London: Oxford University Press, 1963), 4.
6. Trajan to Pliny, Ibid.
7. James Stevenson, *A New Eusebius: Documents Illusrative of the History of the Church to A.D. 337* (London: SPCK, 1957), 16–17.
8. Justin, *Apology*.
9. Tertullian, "Apology," in Bettenson, *Documents*, 7.
10. Ibid.
11. Ibid.
12. Letter of Dionysius quoted in *Historia Ecclesistica* (designated *HE* hereafter), 7.5.1
13. *Act Proconsularia Sancti Cyprian* 1. 1.
14. Ibid., 1. 4.
15. Ibid., 2–5.
16. Papyri Hamburg in *Abhandlungen*, P. M. Meyer, ed. (Berlin: Berlin Academy, 1910), no. 2, 5.
17. Ibid., 15.
18. Tertullian, *Apology* 38. 3.
19. Eusebius, *HE*, X. 5, 15–17; X. 7, 2.
20. In Optatus, *De Schismate Donatistarum*, App. III, 204–6.
21. Constantine to Domitius Celcus. *Vicarius Africae* in Optutas, *De Schismate Donatistarum*, App. VII, 211–12.
22. *Codex Theodosianus*, IV. 40. 2.
23. Ibid., VIII. 16. 1.

24. *Vita Constantini*, in *Patrologiae series Graeca* (Hereafter PG), Migne, ed. (Paris, 1857–1866) 20, cols 1141, and following.

25. Constantine to Elpidius, in Bettenson, *Documents*, 18.

26. On the senatorial procedure see T. Monnsen, *Romisches Staatsrecht*, vol. III (Leipzing, 1888), 905–1003. For Cyprian letters see his *Epistles* 4, 7, 56, 64, 67, 70, 72.

27. Constantine, PG, vol. 20, cols. 1060–1080.

28. Eusebius, *HE*, VII. 30. 19.

29. Gregory VII to the bishop of Metz, in Bettenson, *Documents*, 106.

30. *Vita Constantini* in PG, vol. 20, col. 1080.

31. In James Stevenson, ed., *Creeds, Councils and Controversies* (London: SPCK, 1989), 5.

32. Theodosius on Catholic and Heretic. Cod. Theol. XVI, i. 2.

33. Mansi, Conciliorum, vol. III, col. 557. In *A History of Political Theory*. 4th. ed. George H. Sabine and Thoams L. Thorson (Hinsdale, IL: Dryden Press, 1973), 307.

34. An appeal from the Synod of Rome to Gratian and Valentianian II. In *Patrologiae cursus completus series Latina* (hereafter PL), Migne, ed. (Paris, 1844-1955), vol. XIII, 581.

35. The synod of Carthage petitioned the State to persecute Donatists, *PL*, LXVII, 212.

36. Athansius, *Epistle lx ad Adelp* 3. *Nicene and Post–Nicene Fathers* (Hereafter *NPNF*) 2nd. series, 4: 575).

37. Mansi, vol. IV, cols. 1112 ff.

38. Ibid. vol. IV. col. 1120.

39. Gelasius *Letter XII*, 2–3.

40. Quoted in Carlyle and Carlyle, *A History of Medieval Political Theory in the West*, 6 vols. (London: Blackwood, 1903–1906), vol. I, 180.

41. Ambrose secret letter to emperor Theodosius. Ambrose Letter LII. 17. in J. Stevenson, *Creeds, Councils and Controversies*, 139.

42. Ambrose, Epistle XX. *NPNF*, 19

43. The central teaching of Manichaeanism was the conflict between the eternal good and eternal evil. Donatists, followers of Donatus, were the indigenous Berbers in North Africa who believed that sacraments dispensed by fallen clergy were invalid.

44. Augustine, *NPNF*, 2:282–83.

45. Etiene Gilson, introduction St. Augustine, *City of God* (New York: Image Books, 1958), 464

46. Ibid., 465.

47. Quoted by Carlyle, *Leviathan*, 187, n.2.

48. Gelasius, *Tractatus*, IV, 11.

5

The Secularization of the State

In the last chapter we investigated the attitude of the early church to civil authorities. In this chapter we will continue to examine the concept of two governments advanced by the early church, well articulated by Gelasius and followed by later generations of church leaders. Of particular interest in this chapter will be to trace the development of the idea of the separation of church and state because the theory of two governments as presented by Gelasius did not draw the limits of power. From the historical survey of the separation of church and state and the practice of civil religion, I investigate the grounds upon which the church may speak on behalf of the people. I also explore areas of cooperation between church and state.

Up to the time of Gregory VII (1020-85), synods and church leaders followed the precedent of Ambrose of admonishing civil authorities and kings for their wrongs; and church leaders exercised great influence in electing and deposing rulers. It was Gregory who defined the limits of the power of both the church and secular authorities thus beginning the investiture controversy in which the pope and emperor maneuvered for supremacy. Gregory maintained that the church has power over secular authority. Like Ambrose, he practiced what he taught: he withdrew "the government of the whole kingdom of the Germans and of Italy from Henry the King, son of Henry the emperor. For he has risen against the church with unheard of arrogance. And I absolve all Christians from the bond of the oath which they have made to him or shall make. I forbid anyone to serve him as King."[1]

Gregory based his act and authority on theological grounds, arguing that the church has both moral and spiritual responsibilities given by God through "the power of binding and losing in heaven and on earth." His idea of the role church leaders ought to play in directing the affairs of Europe appears in his word to a council at Rome in 1080: "So act, I beg you, holy fathers and princes, that all the world may know that, if you have power to bind and lose in heaven, you have power on earth to take away or to grant empires, kingdoms, principalities, dukedoms, marches, counties, and the possession of all people according to their merits. . . . Let kings and all the princes of the world learn how great you are and what power you have and let these men fear to disobey the command of the church."[2] This authority amounted to the right to excommunicate which carried with it the power to depose. By implication, then, the power of the church diminishes but not nullify secular authority. The church does not take over the functions of secular government, but the church, the pope in particular, becomes the court of last resort on whose judgement a ruler's legitimacy depends.

We would be mistaken to believe that such a claim to power by the church would be taken lightly by a secular authority; Henry IV did not. He considered the act of Gregory not in line with the teaching of the Christian tradition. He argued that since his power derived from God directly and not through the church, he was responsible for its exercise solely to God. Hence he was to be judged by God alone, and could not be deposed, unless for heresy. "You have laid hands upon me also, though unworthy among Christians, I am anointed by kingship, and who, as the tradition of the Holy Fathers teaches, I am to be judged by God alone and to be deposed for any crime, unless I should wander from the faith, which God forbid."[3] Henry called councils at Mainz and Brixen to hear his case and both councils gave him sympathy and they declared Pope Gregory deposed.

In a letter to Bishop Hermann, Gregory explained to the fullest his view over the matter and he added that he was not the first to depose an emperor. "Many pontiffs have excommunicated kings or emperors. For, if particular examples of such princes are needed, the blessed Pope Innocent excommunicated the emperor Arcadius for consenting that St. John Chrysostom [347–407] be exiled from his see. Likewise Roman Pontiff, Zacchary, deposed king of the Franks. . . . And the blessed Ambrose—who, though a saint was still not a bishop over the whole church—excommunicated and excluded from the church the emperor Theodosius the Great for a fault which, by other priests, was not regarded as very grave."[4]

The early church did not hold the view that temporal authority derived from the spiritual; this was the belief of the Medieval church. It was first definitely maintained by Honorious of Augsburg in his *Summa Gloria*, which was written about 1123. He rested his case on the fact that in Jewish history there was no royal power till Saul was crowned, and that he was anointed by Samuel who was a priest, the Jews having been governed by priests from the time of Moses.

A great mind of the medieval period was Thomas Aquinas (1225–74). He explained his theory of government in *De Regimine Principum* (On Princely Government). He based his theory of social and political life on natural law, and following Aristotle, he perceived society as a mutual exchange of services to which many callings contribute, and with each group doing its proper work. The common good, according to Aquinas, requires that there be a ruling part, just as the body has the head, but leadership is a trust for the whole community, although the power of the ruler derives from God for the happy ordering of human life. "We must first have in mind that to govern is to guide what is governed to its appointed end. So we say a ship is under control when it is sailed on its right course to port by the skill of a sailor. . . . We believe, however, that it is the supreme power in temporal affairs which is the business of a king. Now government is of a higher order according to the importance of the ends it serves. For it is always the one how has the final ordering of affairs who directs those who carry out what pertains to the attainment of the final aim: just as the sailor who must navigate the ship advises the shipwright as to the type of ship which will suit his purpose."[5] It is therefore the duty of the ruler, hence the moral purpose of government, to direct the action of every class in the state that people may live a happy and virtuous life, which is the true end of persons in society, a thing that pleases God. "Thus the final aim of social life will be, not merely to live in virtue, but rather through virtuous life to attain to the enjoyment of God."[6] In light of the goal of government, Aquinas maintained that

> Only a divine rule, then, and not human government, can lead us to this end. Such government belongs only to the King who is both man, and also God: that is to Jesus Christ our Lord. . . . The ministry this kingdom is entrusted not to the rulers of the earth but to priests, so that temporal affairs may remain distinct from those spiritual: and, in particular, it is delegated to the High Priest, the successor of Peter and Vicar of Christ, the Roman Pontiff, to whom all kings in Christendom should be subjects, as to the Lord Jesus Christ Himself. For those who are concerned with the subordinate ends of life must be subject to him who is concerned with the supreme end and be directed by his command.[7]

The moral purpose for which political rule exists implies that authority ought to be limited, that it ought to be exercised only in accordance with law and to ensure material well-being. Furthermore, "in those matters . . . which concern the civil welfare, the temporal should be obeyed rather than the spiritual."[8] Prior to this comment, Aquinas said: "The temporal power is subject to the spiritual only to the extent that this is so ordered by God; namely, in those matters which affect the salvation of the soul. And in these matters the spiritual power is to be obeyed before the temporal." Aquinas sees the divinely designed and divinely desired harmony between temporal and spiritual authorities, the underlying principle being his dictum "*Gratia non tollit naturam, sed perficit*" (Grace does not destroy nature, but perfects it).

Aquinas was explicit about how the ruler's power was to be limited and he accepted resistance of the people to a tyrant. According to him, resistance is justifiable if it is a public act of a whole people, and the right is safeguarded by the moral condition that those who resist are responsible for ensuring that their action is less harmful to the general good than the abuse which they are trying to remove. He condemned sedition as a deadly sin. Aquinas was also convinced that there are circumstances in which it is lawful for the church to depose a ruler and absolve his subjects from their allegiance,[9] and as a matter of course, he regarded the *sacerdotium* as a higher kind of authority than the *imperium*.[10] But he still felt himself to be within the Gelasius tradition.

POLITICAL THEORY AND CIVIL RELIGION

The practice of endorsing state ideology, or using religious language to justify the state and unify the people occurred during the colonial era just as it can be seen in different historical periods of the Christian tradition. Civil religion has been a problem in the Western church; political theorists have throughout the ages maintained that it is the task of religion to unify a nation. From the works of great Western political theorists such as Marsilius of Padua, Machiavelli, Hobbes, and Rousseau one gets an insight into the development of the idea of civil religion in the West. We will not go into details concerning the development of civil religion, a few examples will do. The emergence of religion in political theory dates back to the Medieval period and it centered on the question of the theory of papal sovereignty. The power of the papacy over spiritual and temporal matters started to grow with the rise of a series of powerful popes beginning with Gregory VII and reached its height with Innocent III (1198–1216) but crumbled under Boniface VIII (1234–1303). Innocent reformed the curia, the whole Western church, and strengthened the power of the papacy in Western Europe. As Vicar of Christ—Innocent changed the title of the pope from Vicar of Peter—he intervened in the secular government where politics involved morality. As the representative of Christ, he was the pastor of the church and also had moral or spiritual authority over secular rulers. For him, the papacy had been established "above peoples and kingdoms," since he had "received the authority by which Samuel anointed David," and "by reason and in occasion of sin" he could depose a prince and give his title to another.[11] Innocent went on to claim: "As God the creator of the universe established two great lights in the heavens, the greater to preside over the day, and the smaller to preside over the night, thus did he also establish two great authorities in the heaven of the universal church. . . . The greater, that it might preside above souls as if they were days, and the lesser, that it might preside above bodies as if they were nights. These are the pontifical authority and royal power. On the other hand, just as the Moon receives its light from the Sun . . . so does the royal power receive the splendor of its dignity from pontifical authority.[12]

This claim to papal authority reached its end in the thirteenth century under the papacy of Innocent IV and Boniface VIII who was elected pope in 1294. Innocent IV (1243–54) with other canonists formulated the theory of papal power known as the Petrine doctrine. The doctrine asserts that the pope's authority or *plenitude potestatis*, is based on the fact that he is "the vicar of Christ." "Jesus Christ himself made Peter and Peter's successors his vicars when he gave them the keys of the heavenly kingdom and said, 'Feed my sheep.' Though there are many offices and governments in the world, there can always be an appeal to the pope when necessary, whether the need arises from the law, because the judge is uncertain what decision he ought legally to give, or from the fact, because there is no higher judge, or because inferior judges cannot execute their judgments, or are not willing to do justice they ought.[13]

The claim to Peter's authority was not new; it had been made as early as the third century by Bishop Stephen of Rome; Chrysostom described Peter as "the coyrphaeus of the choir, the mouthpiece of the apostolic company, the head of the band, the leader of the whole world, the foundation of the church, the ardent lover of Christ."[14] Cyril, the Patriarch of Alexandria (412–44) and Theodoret (393–460) of Cyrus said almost the same things about Peter and in the same language. They invoked Matthew 16:18, where it is recorded that on the road to Caesarea Philippi Peter confessed Jesus as the promised Messiah, and upon the confession Jesus declared, "Peter, you are a rock, and on this rock foundation I will build my church." To Stephen and other bishops, these words gave the bishop of Rome preeminence over all the rest of the bishoprics in the world. This was the first time to appeal to the Matthean text, but Rome had already been exercising influence over all the church for a long time. In his *Epistle to the Corinthians*, written about the year 96, Clement, the third bishop of Rome, intervened in the church of Corinth where divisions had occurred. Some young people had ejected the leadership, as Clement said, "the ignoble," rose up "against the honorable. . . . the young against elders, those of no reputation against those of repute, the foolish."[15] Clement apologized for not writing sooner.

This is the tradition that Stephen received from those before him. Not everyone in the early church or later generations agreed with this assertion; among those who opposed the supremacy of Rome in the church was Cyprian, the bishop of Carthage. While acknowledging the priority of Rome, this African bishop contended that in itself this did not grant authority over all the churches: "For neither did Peter, whom the Lord first chose, and upon whom he built his church, when Paul disputed with him afterwards about circumcision, claim anything to himself insolently, nor arrogantly assume anything; so as to say that he held the primacy and that he ought rather to be obeyed by novices and those lately come."[16] Cyprian was for episcopal autonomy within a federated episcopacy, and not Rome imposing its customs on Africa. "For neither does any of us set himself up as a bishop of bishops, nor by tyrannical terror does any compel his colleague to the necessity of obedience; since every bishop, according to the allowance of his liberty and power, has his own proper right of judgment, and cannot be judged by another than he himself can judge another. But let us all wait for the judgment of our Lord Jesus Christ, who is the only one that has the power both of preferring us in the government of His church, and of judging us in our conduct there."[17]

The Petrine doctrine that Innocent IV and other canonists formulated in the thirteenth century was long in the making; they merely restated an old position in the church. Boniface wanted to implement the doctrine but it led him into a clash with King Philip IV (the Fair) of France. The issue was that Philip attempted to raise revenue by imposing taxes on the French clergy. The pope believed such a move by a secular ruler to be illegal, and in 1296 he issued the bull, *Clericis laicos*, declaring taxation without papal permission illegal. To his surprise, Boniface found out that on the contrary, the French clergy considered that a matter of national concern over which the pope had no authority, forcing Boniface to rescind his position a few years later. Nonetheless, on 18 November 1302, Boniface issued a bull, *Unam Sanctam*, in which he asserted papal authority over secular rulers as the Vicar of Christ. He explained the authority of the papacy by using the metaphor of "two swords," a metaphor which was coined by Godfrey de la Vendôme and developed by Bernard. The two swords theory maintained that the swords, "the spiritual and the material, belong to the church, and one is handled by the church, by the hand of the priest, while the other is handled by the soldier, but upon the insinuation of the priest and the command of the king."[18] Through this metaphor Boniface asserted:

> But one sword must be under the other, and temporal authority must be subject to spiritual power. . . . Therefore we must clearly acknowledge that the spiritual power is superior in dignity and ability to the earthly one, just as spiritual things precede those which are temporal. . . . For taking truth as its witness, it behooves the spiritual authority to institute an earthly one, and to judge it if it is not good. . . . Therefore if the earthly power goes wayward, it shall be judged by the spiritual power. But if a lesser spiritual power abandons the right way, it shall be judged by a higher spiritual power. However if the supreme spiritual authority abandons the right way, it can only

> be judged by God, and not by men. . . . Therefore anyone who opposes this power resists the command of God. . . . On the other hand, we declare, affirm and define that it is absolutely necessary for the salvation of all human creatures that they be subject to the Roman Pontiff.[19]

This position was attacked by Philip, the university of Paris, and various factions in Italy itself. Many loyal Catholics, especially in France, felt the pope's claims of authority over the French monarchy violated their convictions about spiritual freedom within the church. Boniface followed this with an excommunication of Philip who replied by sending his minister, Nogaret, to arrest the pope at Anagni. Boniface was rescued by the townspeople; he died not long afterwards in 1303, and in 1309 the papacy was transferred to Avignon in what was to be a seventy-five period of "papal captivity."

This is the background of the events that led to writings of Marsilius. However, the immediate occasion took place in 1323 when pope John XXII (1245–1334) attempted to intervene from Avignon in a dispute over imperial election, that is over the authority of King Louis of Bavaria. John XXII and his successor Clement VI died without an agreement over the controversy, and it was not until the death of Louis in 1347 that a settlement was reached. Meantime, in Italy people were questioning the papal attempts to become the international arbiter of power. In 1338, the Imperial Electors issued the Declaration of Rense, which stated that an election did not require papal confirmation, thereby giving constitutional law independence, something that Henry IV (1050–1106) had claimed.

The controversy between John XXII and Louis the Bavarian produced a body of literature repudiating papal authority over secular rulers. Among the early individuals to contribute to the emerging literature which would be of interest to political theory were Marsilius of Padua (1275–1342) and William of Ockham (1280–1349). William was a theologian and philosopher whose treatises argued for the independence of the church by contending that civil authority is instituted by God as much as is the authority of the pope. In his writings, William raised questions concerning the rights of subjects against their rulers and the limitation of sovereign papal authority in matters of faith, and the right of a minority to resist coercion. In questioning papal absolutism, William was speaking on behalf of a branch of his Franciscan Order called the Spiritualists that had been excommunicated by John XXII for defending its vow of poverty. William sought a representative check upon what he considered the arbitrary exercise of papal power, although he did not object to the pope having huge discretionary power, provided the pope knew his legal limits so that he would not encroach on the jurisdiction of the sovereign and the rights of the people. William repudiated the pope's claim that the emperor's power derived from him; on the contrary, he argued, imperial power is from the consent of a corporate body of subjects expressed through their magistrates. Theologically, William considered papal sovereignty a heresy, and from a policy standpoint, a disastrous innovation that filled Europe with strife, destroyed Christian freedom, and had led to the invasion of the rights of secular rulers.

The writings of Marsilius on the theory of secular government, or the theory of the separation between church and state, are more systematic than those of William of Ockham. An Italian by birth, an Aristotelian scholar in Avignon, Marsilius wrote *Defensor Pacis*, a book he addressed to Louis the Bavarian. After the publication of *Defensor pacis*, Marsilius obtained protection in Germany, where he lived most of his life. Scholars are not sure why he sought refuge in Germany for the book was not against Louis the Bavarian, and it was based on the city-states of his native land, Italy. Moreover, the book was about his bitterness towards the papacy which he considered the cause of disunity in Italy, a subject that was advanced two centuries later by another Italian, Machiavelli. In *Defensor pacis*, Marsilius defended the empire but expressed his bitterness towards the papal imperial system as developed by Pope Innocent III and the theory of Canon Law. Defining the meaning of law—in *Defensor pacis* he gives four kinds of law—he drew, directly or indirectly, the limits of spiritual authority and control, and he expanded the power of secular government.

The basis of his political theory was the philosophy of Aristotle in *Politics*, especially the part dealing with revolution and civil disorder. Aristotle's principle, which Marsilius focused on, was the concept of community, the self-sufficing community capable of supplying both its physical and moral needs. In Aristotle, a self-sufficing community is one with each part performing its own function for the perfection of the whole. The basis of a perfect community is the family, in other words, the city is the extension of the family—Aristotle had in mind Ionian city-states. Following these ideas, Marsilius defined the state as a "living being" with various parts performing their necessary functions for the good or "health" of the whole.[20] The idea of parts and functions was important for Marsilius because he wanted to argue that the clergy were just another class among other classes of society, such as farmers, artisans and soldiers. The function of the other three classes is to supply material goods and needed revenue for the state while "The function of clergy is to know and teach those things which, according to Scripture, it is necessary to believe, to do, or to avoid, in order to obtain eternal salvation and escape woe."[21] The conclusion from this idea of classes and their function is that the clergy are like any other class but that their function concerns otherworldly things and not the temporal order. Therefore their control of the social order is without basis.

For him, religion was a social phenomenon which uses material agencies and produces social consequences. In this respect religion is subject to social regulation like other human interests, for whatever its effects, the life to come is better left to the future. Spiritual interests, being otherworldly, are logically irrelevant to this life and those religious or moral concerns that do affect this life are all within the control of the human community, and by extension the state. Accordingly, the church is part of the secular state in every respect in which it affects temporal matters. There is no frontal attack on spiritual interests which the church teaches and which Christians believe to be the ultimate interests of humanity. As for its truth claims, Marsilius believed religion was something that any rational or reasonable person could not dispute. Here, then, we have the separation of reason from faith, a direct result of religious skepticism whose consequences amount to a secularism which is both anti-religious and anti-Christian.

Concerning law, Marsilius said there are two kinds of law, divine and human, distinguished by the kind of their punishments. "Divine law is a command of God directly, without human deliberation, about voluntary acts of human beings to be done or avoided in this world but for the sake of attaining the best end, or some condition desirable for people, in the world to come."[22] Turning to human law he said: "Human law is a command of the whole body of citizens, or of its prevailing part, arising directly from the deliberation of those empowered to make law, about voluntary acts of human beings to be done or avoided in this world, for the sake of attaining the best end, or some condition desirable for humans, in this world. I mean a command the transgression of which is enforced in this world by a penalty or punishment on the aggressor."[23] In these definitions of law, penalty is a critical word along with command and sanction. For Marsilius, the one who issues the command also sanctions and enforces it, and therefore determines who has authority. Punishment for divine law will be given by God in the hereafter while penalties for human law are in this life. From this, Marsilius concludes that the clergy have no real power or authority since they are unable to enforce their law in this life through coercive means, in contrast to the legislator who is able to impose his will in this life. This is the heart of Marsilius' political theory. "The legislator, or first and proper efficient cause of law, is the people or whole body of citizens, or a prevailing part of it, commanding and deciding by its own choice or will in a general assembly and in set terms that something among the civil acts of human beings be done or omitted, on pain of a penalty or temporal punishment."[24]

It follows from this that canon law is useless in this life since it is not binding to the people because the source of legal authority is the people, or its prevailing part, the state; canon law lacks that authority over the people. Once again, the emphasis is that the church has no authority over the people's lives or property except for what happens after this life, and that is to be left to the future. As to property in the form of tithes, the church (or the clergy) cannot be said to own wealth because it is like a grant or subsidy by the people in support of public worship. Furthermore, ecclesiastical offices are gifts from civil officers, therefore any ecclesiastical officer, from the pope down, as long as he receives benefices, is subject to civil society which can depose him. Given the arguments of Marsilius in *Defensor pacis*, it comes as no surprise that the pope condemned it; the condemnation also named John of Jandun, a professor at Paris as a co-author with Marsilius, a claim that scholars then, and now, have not been able to establish. In Marsilius's works, *Defensor pacis* and *Defensor Minor*, the separation of church and state is complete and remains for generations to elaborate and apply it.

In his political theory, Machiavelli stressed the need for religion in the nation because it greatly assists in keeping the army in obedience, the nation in unity, and the populace in contentment. Since Machiavelli considered religion useful for the state, he brought it under the control of the prince, should act as an autonomous politician unimpeded by any moral considerations. Thus Machiavelli, as Marsilius, paved the way for the infamous post-Reformation saying: "*cuius regio, eius religio*" (religion of the ruler is the religion of the nation), implying state-established religion. Henry VIII of England (1491–1547), followed by the king of France, personified this idea of nationalization of the church. Here starts the process which would set in motion the secularization of Western society.

The process took root with the political writings of succeeding generations of thinkers; here we will consider the contribution of Hobbes and Rousseau to the secularization of society or the development of civil religion. Hobbes' theory of sovereignty, which brought to a completion the process of subordinating the church to civil power, carried Marsilius's theory to its logical conclusion of the separation of the spiritual and the temporal authorities. A church was for Hobbes merely a corporation, and like any other corporation it has a head, the sovereign. Along with other corporations and institutions in society, it is subject to the sovereign of the state. Hence in *De Civitate*, Hobbes recommended that "The state has the absolute right to command which names and titles of God should be used."[25]

Hobbes carried his ideas of the subordination of the church to the sovereign to dangerous proportions. While he considered belief as something that cannot be forced, he maintained that the profession of faith is an overt act and therefore falls within the province of the law. He carried this further, adding that observances and professions, the canon of religious texts, the creed and the government of the church all get their authority from the sovereign. Since there is no objective standard for religious truth, establishment of any belief or form of worship must be an act of the sovereign. Like Marsilius, Hobbes maintains that the church has a duty to teach, but he adds that no teaching is lawful unless authorized by sovereign. Hobbes concludes that there cannot be any conflict between divine and human law, therefore in every sense that counts religion is completely under the sway of law and government. In the late 1980s when the African church began to voice God's displeasure at the suffering of the people, heads of state reacted in purely a Hobbesian manner: they argued that the church was under the state law, so it must behave itself within the limits of the law or it would forfeit its freedom of worship.

Rousseau explained the reasons for the separation between civil and religious institutions. According to him, Jesus founded on earth a spiritual kingdom based on the separation of the theological from political systems, thereby separating religious and civil institutions. Rousseau maintained that Jesus introduced two forms of religion: a "religion of the man" and a "religion of citizens," the former being the inner veneration or worship of God presented in the gospels, while the latter was confined to a particular country and its divinities and reverence to the native land—call it a religious patriotism or religious ethnicity. In the evangelization of Africa, one sees both forms of Rousseau's religion being planted. Missionary Christianity being denominational was a religion of independent states: Presbyterians of Scotland, Lutherans of Germany, Methodists of England, Dutch, Irish, Portuguese and Spanish Catholics. Missionaries therefore propagated Christianity of the gospels but also that of their native lands, which supported the ideology of the government of their homeland. Very rarely did missionaries oppose the policies of their national governments; if anything, they proclaimed justification for those policies and urged African Christians to obey them. Church theology was not critical theology but theology of the status quo; it was political theology or civil religion.

THE REFORMERS AND CIVIL AUTHORITY

Martin Luther (1483–1546)

The early reformers, Luther and Calvin, like the medieval theologians, did not produce a political theory. Their attitude to civil authorities was conditioned by the fact that they depended on princes and magistrates for the success of their reforms, they therefore held the view that resistance to rulers is in all circumstances wicked. Luther's political writings and views on temporal authority developed during his own struggle with temporal authorities. In 1521 he was commanded by the highest temporal authority, the emperor, to recant his theses and his works; he refused and as a consequence several rulers burned the works and imprisoned his followers. In 1522 he preached sermons on temporal authority before Duke John of Saxony and others. The people urged him to publish his ideas on the subject, the first of his writings in 1523, *Temporal Authority, to What Extent it*

Should be Obeyed. This was followed by three other writings published in 1525, all being his responses to the discontent and revolt of farmers in Swabia (1524–1525). These were followed by writings on war in 1526 (*Whether Soldiers, too, Can be Saved)*; in 1529 on the Turkish invasion of Europe (*On War Against the Turk*); and in 1531 he expressed his fear that civil war might break out as an attempt by Emperor Charles V to eliminate Lutherans in Germany.

Luther, as the other reformers, advocated passive obedience to civil authorities as a Christian duty since all authority comes from God, and God alone assigns offices to subjects according to divine will. Luther said: "Now no individual ought to set himself against the community or attract the support of the community to himself, for in doing so he is chopping over his head, and the chips will surely fall in his eyes. From this you can see that [those] who resist their rulers resist the ordinance of God as Paul teaches us in Romans 13." He also quoted I Peter 2:13–14: "Be subject to every kind of human ordinance, whether it be to the king as supreme, or to governors, as those who have been sent by him [God] to punish the wicked and to praise the righteous." It is from this understanding that Luther opposed sedition: "It is no wise proper for everyone who would be a Christian to set himself up against his government, whether it act justly or unjustly." He further asserted: "There are no better works than to obey and serve all those who are set over us as superiors. For this reason also disobedience is a greater sin than murder, unchastity, theft, and dishonesty, and all that these may include."[26]

Luther's view on passive obedience was based on what he called "orders of creation," which are part of God's creative design. These orders are represented by three social institutions: the parents, the state, and the church. Each of them has a function to fulfill for the harmony of the order of creation: parents are to enforce strict discipline "when ruling domestics and the children"; state officials "bear the sword for the sake of coercing the obstinate and remiss by their power of discipline"; and "the church governs by the word of God."[27] Luther saw each of the orders as primarily an effective instrument for curbing sin and it was for this reason that God "ordained two governments: the spiritual, by which the Holy spirit produces Christians and the righteous people under Christ; and the temporal, which restrains the un-Christian and wicked so that—no thanks to them—they are obliged to keep still and to maintain an outward peace."[28] For this reason, "these two governments must be permitted to remain; the one to produce righteousness, the other to bring about external peace and prevent evil deeds. Neither is sufficient in the world without the other. . . . Because the sword is most beneficial and necessary for the whole world in order to preserve peace, punish sin, and restrain the wicked, the Christian submits most willingly to the rule of the sword, pays taxes, honors those in authority, serves, helps, and does all he can to assist the governing authority, that it may continue to function and be held in honor and fear."[29]

The two governments have two different laws: temporal laws concern life, property, and affairs of this world, while the spiritual laws concern affairs of the soul. "Therefore, where the temporal authority presumes to prescribe laws for the soul, it encroaches upon God's government and only misleads souls and destroys them. We want to make this clear that everyone will grasp it, and that our fine gentlemen, the princes and bishops, will see what fools they are when they seek to coerce the people with their laws and commandments into believing this or that."[30] While enjoining the people to be obedient to princes, Luther did not approve obeying a prince who is wrong. "No, for it is no one's duty to do wrong; we must obey God (who desires the right) than men [Acts 5:29]. . . . a prince's duty is fourfold: first, towards God there must be true confidence and earnest prayer; second, towards his subjects there must be love and Christian service; third, with respect to his counselors and officials he must maintain an untrammeled reason and fettered judgement; fourth, with respect to evil doers he must manifest a restrained severity and firmness."[31] Although not stated in this quotation, the prince's duty to keep peace runs through the political writings of Luther. For the sake of maintaining peace, therefore, the prince may go to war even though no Christian acting as an individual would be right in doing so. "Every lord and prince is bound to protect his people and get peace for them. That is his office; it is for that he has the sword (Romans 13). This should be for him a matter of conscience and he should so depend upon it as to know that this work is right in the eyes of God and is commanded by him."[32]

Unlike the theologians of the medieval period, Luther recognized the reality of being under rulers who may not be Christian; to those, too, a Christian is duty bound to obey them. "To be sure it would be good if he [the prince] were a Christian besides and believed in God; then he would be happy; but it is not princely to be a Christian and therefore few princes can be Christian, as they say, 'A Prince is a rare bird in heaven.' Now even if they are not Christians, nevertheless they ought to do what is right and good according to God's outward ordinance. He will have this of them."[33]

Let us end the section on Luther with the words of a contemporary eminent German theologian, Jürgen Moltmann, who commented on Luther's two governments or two kingdom doctrine by saying:

> Luther's two kingdom doctrine is in truth a critical-polemical separation between God and Caesar. It permits neither a Caesaro-papalism nor a clerical theocracy. It intended to teach that the world and politics may not be deified, nor may they be religiously administered. One should give to Caesar what belongs to Caesar—no more and no less—and to give to God, that which is

> God's. One should turn the self deified world into world, and let God be God. One should deal rationally with the world, with the law and with force. The world is not and it will never become the kingdom of God; rather it is a good earthly order against evil chaos. One should deal spiritually—which means with faith—with God and his gospel. The gospel does not create a new world but saves people through faith.[34]

John Calvin (1509–64)

Calvin's political theory appears in a chapter called "On Civil Government," which is the last chapter of the most famous of his writings, the *Institutes of Christian Religion*. The issues raised in "On Civil Government" were matters that he struggled with throughout his career in Geneva as he sought independence of the church from the civil authorities of the city. The situation in Geneva—as in Bern, a city from which the former had received its reformation—was that the triumphant bourgeoisie controlled all the affairs, political and religious. Calvin went into exile in 1538 because he could not accept the city council's ruling that communion should be offered to all in the city regardless of their commitment to Christian teachings and life. On his return, Calvin insisted on ordinances that would give the church some independence from the authorities, thus the beginning of the Consistory, also called "Session" in Scottish Presbyterianism. Calvin's starting point is

> that there is a twofold government in man: one in revering God; the second is political, whereby the human is educated for the duties of humanity and citizenship that must be maintained among people. These are usually called the "spiritual" and the "temporal" jurisdiction (not improper terms) by which is meant that the former sort of government pertains to the life of the soul, while the latter has to do with the concerns of the present life—not only with food and clothing but with laying down laws whereby one may live one's life among other people holly, honorably, and temperately. For the former resides in the inner mind, while the latter regulates only outward behavior. The one may call the spiritual kingdom, the other, the political kingdom.[35]

Calvin's view on church and state did not differ very much from that of Luther; he also taught passive obedience to civil authorities, since secular power is the external means to salvation. A secular government is sacred and legitimate, "Wherefore no doubt ought now to be entertained by any person that civil magistracy is a calling not only holy and legitimate, but far the most sacred and honorable in human life. . . . For if it be his [God's] pleasure to appoint kings over kingdoms, and senators or other magistrates over free cities, it is our duty to be obedient to any governors whom God has established over the places in which we reside."[36] People are to obey the magistrate because "the magistrate is 'the minister of God to us for good,' we understand from this that he is divinely appointed, in order that we may be defended by his power and protection against malice and injuries of wicked people and may lead peaceful and secure lives."[37]

It is from this perspective that Calvin considered the work of the elected official most honorable, for the official is the vicar of God. Like Luther, he advised judges not to be partial or inflict severe punishment. "Yet it behooves the magistrate to be on his guard against both errors—that he do not, by excessive severity, would rather than heal, or through a superstitious affectation of clemency, fall into a mistaken humanity, which is the worse kind of cruelty, by indulging a weak and ill-judged lenity to the detriment of multitudes."[38] Like Luther, he insisted that the bad ruler is a divine visitation on the people for their sins, therefore such a ruler deserves unconditional obedience from the people, for submission is not to the ruler but the office the ruler holds. Calvin adduced Old Testament passages in favor of his point: Jeremiah represents God as calling Nebuchadnezzar "my servant" and commanding the people to serve him and live, although in fact he was a "pestilent and cruel tyrant." Therefore Calvin maintained that "Whatever be their characters, they have their government only from God; that those who govern for the public good are true specimens and mirrors of God's beneficence; and that those who rule in unjust and tyrannical manner are raised up by him to punish the iniquity of the people; that all possess that sacred majesty with which God has invested the legitimate authority."[39] Calvin did not want to create the impression that all is well with bad rulers. Believing that the immutable law of God is binding to both rulers and subjects, Calvin saw the evil ruler as guilty of sedition against God. Although he admonished people in obeying rulers, he made one exception, that is, a commandment by a ruler against God. "If they command anything against God, it ought not have the least attention, nor, in this case, it ought to pay any regard to all that dignity attached to magistrates, to which no injury is done when it is subjected to the unrivalled and supreme power of God."[40]

Concerning civil law, Calvin maintained that it derived from natural law, which all people know because God endows it to all people and its task is merely to fix penalty for what is intrinsically wrong. John Locke, the English social philosopher, was to follow this position centuries later. Calvin followed the traditional distinction of the three forms of law: moral, ceremonial, and judicial. The first is the perpetual authority, the second is to aide in piety, while judicial law is the basis of the constitution with rule of equity and justice for all to live in peace. In sum, natural law is the basis of equity.

Calvin believed the first duty of government is to maintain pure worship of God and to uproot idolatry, sacrilege, blasphemy and heresy. "It is the purpose of temporal rule," wrote Calvin, "so long as we live among men, to foster and support the external worship of God, to defend pure doctrine and the standing of the church, to conform our lives to human society, to mould our conduct to civil justice, to harmonize it with each other, and to preserve the common peace."[41] Here Calvin shared the same views with Aquinas on the function of the state, but Calvin gives the state a larger sphere of action than Aquinas.

Calvin diverged from Luther at two points: first, he did not deprive subjects of all resistance, but made specific provision for the overthrow of a tyrant. In a classical passage in the *Institutes of Christian Religion*, Calvin admonishes Christians as private persons to obedience and says to leave resistance to magistrates who would act in their capacity as representatives of the people. "I am so far from forbidding them to withstand, in accordance with their duty, the fierce licentiousness of kings, that, if they wink at kings who violently fall upon and assault the lowly common folk, I declare that their dissimulation involves nefarious perfidy, because they dishonestly betray the freedom of the people, of which they know that they have been appointed protectors by God's ordinance."[42] When Calvin says magistrates are to act, he is presupposing that these are elected officials, something like representatives in a national assembly.

The second point at which he differed with Luther was that Calvin considered morals and religion under the protection of the sovereignty of magistrates, implying that the responsibility of civil government includes maintaining tranquility of the church and restraining theological heresy.

In these two points we note that Calvin disagreed with those who held the view that in the prince is the substitute for divine rule and also those who felt that the freedom of the Gospel eliminates the need for civil government. Calvin's position was that the church had a fundamental right to declare pure doctrine and exercise universal censorship with the support of civil authority. A Calvinist church, therefore, would drop obedience and assert the right to resist if civil authorities would refuse to admit the truth of its teachings. This is the situation in which John Knox and his fellow Calvinists found themselves in Scotland. Calvinists in France had the same experience.

Calvin's view of the state mirrors in some ways the work of Marsilius in *Defensor Pacis*. The state is God given and sacred, and to regard it as incompatible with the Christian faith, was, in Calvin's view, to insult God. In saying this Calvin had in mind the Anabaptists and other religious groups who maintained that the state is the embodiment of evil and therefore Christians must refrain from any sort of participation in it. For him magistrates are guardians of the laws and their making and enforcing is presided over by God. Calvin enlarged the responsibility of the state to more than promotion of justice and peace to include social responsibilities, specifically emphasizing education and health as the common goods. For Calvin, the state being God-given, it is under divine mandate to deliver "legitimate and just government and this includes meeting the people's basic needs.[43]

John Knox (1513–72)

In order to appreciate John Knox's position on the relation between the church and civil authorities, it is helpful to outline the historical events surrounding the beginnings of the Scottish reformation. The reformation in Scotland is associated with John Knox, although he was not the one who started it. A number of Scots brought home the ideas and writings of Luther from their studies in Germany. These people seem to have made a noticeable impact, enough to cause the Scottish Parliament to pass laws against those writings and the spread of Protestant preaching. The first executions against itinerant preachers took place in 1528. In general, the reformation in Scotland took place amidst internal and foreign political instability as the country sought its independence from England and France. The internal problems were caused by the struggle between Protestant Scottish nobles who were supported by England—a country many Scots had always been suspicious of—and the Catholics supported by France. The conflict concerned royalty: whether the infant Mary Stuart, daughter of James V (who had died in 1542), would marry Edward, son of Henry VIII. Scottish Catholics wished her to go and have her education in France, thus defeating the plan of Scottish Protestant nobles that would have led to a united kingdom with Protestant England. The Catholics won, Mary went to France where she married a French prince.

Reacting to this, a group of Protestants took over the Castle at St. Andrews and killed the archbishop. The government sent an army but failed to retake the castle. It was at this time that John Knox came into the picture of the Scottish reformation. After his ordination, John Knox became a tutor to two sons of a Scottish noble. After the conspirators had taken St. Andrews, Knox was ordered to take the two boys to the castle at St. Andrews, although his plan was to go to Germany and study Protestant theology. Things changed once he got to St. Andrews, for he was made a preacher, against his will, for the Protestant community. From then on, the story of the Scottish reformation became identified with his name, for he became its spokesperson. The Protestant siege of St. Andrews did not last because France, having settled its internal conflicts, sent reinforcements to Scotland to help the Scottish army defeat the Protestants. In violation of the terms of the surrender, Knox and several other leaders were sentenced to the galleys, where Knox spent thirteen months of cruel labor. He was released at the intervention of England, where he then went and pastored.

It is not necessary to belabor the history of Scotland, but let it be enough to say that political events in Scotland were not in favor of the Scottish Protestants, and the situation still continued to revolve around the English, Mary Stuart, and France. Knox returned to Scotland before the lords decided to invite Mary Stuart to return to Scotland and reclaim her throne. She returned, but she alienated Protestants despite the advice of her half brother, James Stuart, who was himself a Protestant leader. Tension grew between the Protestants and the queen so that a clash was inevitable. By being a Catholic, the queen refused what Knox considered true faith (Catholicism was idolatry to him). With Protestant lords and followers, Knox organized the Reformed Church of Scotland.

This is the background to understanding the position of John Knox on the relation of the church and the civil authorities. Knox essentially believed the principles of Calvin: freedom of the church and its duty to enforce its discipline against all who do not willingly accept it. The situation discussed above, forced Knox to abandon Calvin's principle that resistance to civil authorities is always wrong. Actually, Knox defended resistance as part of the duty to sustain religious freedom. "For now the common song of all men is, we must obey our kings, be they good or be they bad; for God hath so commanded. But horrible shall the vengeance be, that shall be poured forth such blasphemers of God his Holy name and ordinance. For it is no less blasphemy to say that God has commanded kings to be obeyed when they command impiety, than to say God by his precept is author and maintainer of all iniquity."[44]

Knox believed that the punishment of idolatry, blasphemy, and other crimes that touch the majesty of God would not be left to kings and chief rulers only, but also to the whole society, to each member according to the vocation and possibility to resist. Knox believed that the reformation would fail in Scotland without resisting the queen.

THE ORTHODOX TRADITION

My focus thus far has been on one part of the Christian tradition, the Western or Roman Church. We will now examine the church-state relation in the Orthodox tradition or the Eastern Church. The attitude of Orthodox churches towards secular authorities differs from that of their counterparts in the West. The reason for this attitude is to be found in history and culture. It is important to give a brief account of the separation of the Eastern and Western churches in order to see the conditions or circumstances that shaped the attitudes of Eastern churches to civil authorities.

The Great Schism

Up to the fifth century, the church was one, but that unity did not survive. The seeds of disunity emerged with the Nestorian controversy, which was about the two natures—divine and human—as they related to Mary, the *theotokos* debate. Depending on which nature was emphasized, Mary was either the mother of God (as Cyril and the Egyptian Church maintained) or the bearer of God (according to Nestorius and Antiochene Church which stressed the human side of Jesus). To settle this dispute, emperors Valentian III and Theodore convoked a general council to meet in Ephesus on 7 June 431. This was the Third Ecumenical Council. The proponents of *theotokos* argued that to deny Mary this title was to break the unity of the person of Jesus, since person who Mary bore was a single and undivided person, human and divine at the same time. This was to contend that *theotokos* safeguarded the unity of the incarnation, and this was the position the Council of Ephesus took. Nestorius was condemned as a heretic and retired to a monastery, but his followers remained active, carrying missionary work to China in the fifth century.

The disagreement between the followers of Nestorius and Cyril made it necessary to have a synodical meeting in 433 at which another formula was worked out, to recognize the two natures of Jesus without stressing one over the other. The delicate balance between the two natures was to be the cause of another fight between the churches fifteen years later. In 448 Eutyches, an abbot at a monastery at Constantinople, started teaching that Jesus had the two natures before the union, but one only after the union. His point was that at the incarnation, or birth, the two natures became united into one divine-human nature. At a synod in Constantinople, Eutyches was condemned for teaching that Jesus had only one nature after the incarnation. He and Flavian, the patriarch of Constantinople who had presided over the synod, appealed to Pope Leo I (400–61), who responded by writing his *Tome* (a large book) explaining the Western view that Jesus had two natures. Meanwhile, Cyril had died (in 444) in Egypt and Discorous had replaced him as the patriarch of Alexandria. Wanting to advance the idea of one nature, "monophysite"—from Greek *mono*, one, and *phusis*, nature or substance—he requested the emperor to call a council. The council met in 449 in Ephesus: the decision of Constantinople was reversed and Leo's *Tome* was not even read.

In 450 emperor Theodosius died, and he was succeeded by Marcian and his wife whose sympathies were with Leo, who requested a new council. The council met in 451 at Chalcedon, near Nicea, and about 520 bishops, along with an eighteen member imperial legate, gathered at the Basilica of Saint Euphemia. This was the Fourth Ecumenical Council. In settling the controversy, the council decided on the side of Leo who insisted that Jesus had two natures, without confusion, change, division, or separation, and that the difference in natures was not taken away by the union, but that the properties of each nature were preserved in one person. The terms, "confusion" (or unmixed) and "unchanged" were directed against Alexandria, which tended to unite the two natures into one by mixing and changing them. The second set of words, "without division and without separation," were against Antioch with its tendency to disunite the nature by dividing and separating them.

By declaring one nature, monophysite, a heresy in the *Definition* of Chalcedon (as the Chalcedon agreement was called), the churches of Egypt, Ethiopia, Armenian, Syria, and Palestine felt excluded from the Christian community. By condemning division and separation, the *Definition* made Nestorians also feel left out of the world-wide Christian communion. Thus Chalcedon produced three churches: monophysite, Nestorian, and Chalcedonian, the latter being those who accepted the *Definition* of Chalcedon. The meeting at Chalcedon was not only a theological defeat for Alexandria but also a political one for Alexandria had aspired to be the New Rome after the fall of Rome; Canon XXVIII of Chalcedon confirmed Canon III of Constantinople assigning the latter city the honor of the Old Rome.

These divisions within the Christian tradition remained until the seventh century when another rift developed between the churches of East and West. The rift was precipitated by several factors: political, geographic, cultural, and theological. The division between the East and West began in the third century when the empire was divided in two parts, each with its own emperor. Constantine furthered the division by moving the imperial capital to Constantinople. European invasions continued the separation of the two parts of the Christian church. Cultural and economic contacts became even more difficult when Islam rose to power and took control of areas of the West. These were the external factors for the rift, but the cause of schism between the East and West, or Rome and Constantinople, came from within. The first stage of the schism came in 800 when the pope crowned Charles the Great, King of the Franks, as emperor. The East, upholding the idea of imperial unity, regarded Charlemagne's coronation as an act of schism within the empire, therefore the east refused Charlemagne's requests to recognize him as ruler of the empire.

The political problems led to theological issues. Having been refused recognition, Charlemagne accused the east of not using certain words concerning the Holy Spirit in the Creed. The Nicene-Constantinople creed stated, "I believe . . . in the Holy Spirit, the Lord, the Giver of Life, *who proceeds from the Father*, who with the Father and the Son is worship." Around the sixth century, the churches in the West started interpolating in the creed the formula, "and from the Son," thus identifying the Holy Spirit as one "who proceeds from the Father and from the Son." This was known as the *filioque*. The idea was to affirm the dual procession of the Holy Spirit. The East objected to *filioque* because (1) ecumenical councils forbade making any changes in the creed and if changes were to be done a general council was to be convened for the purpose. On the contrary, the West had taken the liberty to make changes on its own on what was the common possession of the church. (2) The East considered *filioque* a heresy that destroyed the balance of the trinity and led to a misunderstanding of the work of the Holy Spirit in the world.

The *filioque* issue did not become a major controversy until the middle of the ninth century, although Spanish churches had interpolated it as early as 589 at the third council of Toledo. The occasion for the rise of *filioque* to center stage came as part of a dispute between Pope Nicholas I (819–67) and a newly appointed patriarch of Constantinople, Photius. He had ascended to the patriarchy while the previous patriarch, Ignatius, was in exile. The supporters of Ignatius considered Photius a usurper. When Photius sent a letter to Nicholas announcing his accession to the high office, the pope decided to investigate the claims of the Ignatius party. He sent his legates to the East in 861, and they returned and reported to him that at the council held in Constantinople they had agreed that Photius was the legitimate patriarch. Nicholas rejected their decision, claiming that they had no right to come to conclusion on the matter. He took the matter himself and a council presided by him in Rome in 863 recognized Ignatius as the legitimate patriarch and deposed Photius. The churches took note of the council's action but felt that the pope had overstepped his authority. Photius called a council at Constantinople which declared Nicholas a heretic and excommunicated him. In 867 Photius was deposed by the emperor and Ignatius restored to the patriarchy, but Photius returned again in 877 after the death of Ignatius. To cut a long story short, the schism between East and West took place for two major reasons; papal claim to authority and *filioque*. While there were other disagreements in 1009, the final stage of the schism came in 1054 over the demand in Latin churches in Constantinople to adopt Greek practices and for Greek churches to use Latin customs in Byzantine Italy. To this were added other factors, the main one being that the pope's legation to settle the dispute between the East and the West ended in excommunicating the patriarch of Constantinople. Attempts to reconcile the two proved impossible.

ORTHODOXY AND SECULAR AUTHORITY

The theory of state according to the Byzantine (Orthodox) Church from the time of Justinian I, was that there was only one Christian emperor on earth, that of Constantinople (the capital of the Eastern empire), the Protector of the universal church and the Chosen of God. In this theory, neither state (emperor) nor the church (pope) claimed superior power, they sought a balance in their powers. This pragmatic balance was broken only by the iconoclastic emperors Leo III (717–741) and Constantine V (741–775), who formally claimed plenitude of both powers, spiritual and secular. Although there were only two iconoclastic emperors, the iconoclastic party itself remained well and alive till its defeat in 843. After this crisis, a balance was once again achieved between church and state, this time with a clear distinction between the limits and rights of the emperor and the patriarch. It was Patriarch Photius (810–95) who drew the distinctions in a legal document called *Epanagoge*. The document states that "the constitution consists like a human person of parts and members and of these the greatest and most necessary are the emperor and the patriarchy. Thus the peace and felicity of subjects, in body and soul, depends on the agreement and concord of the kingship and priesthood in all things."[45]

This harmonious relationship changed with the creation of autocephalous churches within the boundaries of nation-state. Autocephaly means more than independence but also acts as an authentication of Christian culture, national identity, and an assurance of the removal or exclusion of foreign clergy. This last act gives the church political influence in the nation. In addition, autocephaly creates an arena in which church-state issues or conflicts may arise. It is not necessary to give accounts of the relation between the patriarch and the crown in each country where there is an orthodox church, a few examples will do. The earliest break from the Byzantine theory of state took place when the Bulgarians and Serbs, each in turn, sought to secede from Constantinople. Bulgarian and Serb churches tried but failed to get the imperial crown for their rulers; the only political goal they achieved was to force Constantinople to recognize their autonomy for national churches.

The first real church-state conflict within the orthodox tradition emerged when Patriarch Nikon (1672–1725) of Russia sought to dominate the czar. Such efforts were not to be accepted by the young Peter the Great. Nonetheless, it was not until after the death of Patriarch Hadrian (1700), that Peter the Great forbade the church to hold elections for a new patriarch for twenty-one years. In 1721 he declared his *Spiritual Regulation*. The *Regulation*, compiled by Theophanes Prokopovich, Bishop of Pskov, abolished the patriarchate and in its stead placed a collegiate body, the holy synod, at the head of the church. The Holy Synod consisted of two bishops and three priests. In addition, a lay procurator, appointed by the czar, was required to take part in all discussions (without being a member of the Synod) and gradually became the head of the administrative organization of the church. When asked to approve the new arrangement, all Eastern patriarchs consented except Dositheus, the Patriarch of Jerusalem, who, speaking on behalf of Orthodoxy, tried in vain to reject the whole of the czar's social and ecclesiastical reforms. From 1721 to the time of the Russian revolution of 1917 the church was virtually enslaved by the state; it fared no better during the 70 years of Communist rule. Here is a classical example of what can happen to a church when it allows itself to be domesticated by the powers that be.

The Rumanian Orthodox Church, formed by the act of ecumenical patriarch in 1885, is the second largest, behind Russian orthodox church. The Rumanian Church was closely tied to the old monarchy and one of its patriarchs, Myron, once presided over the Council of Ministers. With the fall of the monarchy, came the end of the power of the church, but the Marxist regime recognized the "general regime of religion" in 1948, the regime adopted to pay salaries of clergy and church-run schools on the condition that bishops had to take an oath of allegiance to the state before the minister of religion when they were installed. Part of the oath read: "As a servant of God, as a man and citizen, I swear to be faithful to the People and to defend the Popular Rumanian Republic against its enemies both internal and external . . . so help me God."

The Rumanian arrangement was not typical of all Communist regimes. The situation of the church in Communist countries was that it came under the control of the state. The state took over the government, finances, and running of the church. The general tendency of orthodox churches, once autocephalous, is to align themselves with the state. Of course this causes problems for them whenever the crown is deposed; they lose their status as a state church and with it goes the privileges the clergy—mainly patriarchs and bishops—enjoy. There are a few cases where the orthodox churches have not suffered as the result of its connection to secular authorities. The most well known example is the Greek Orthodox Church, which remains a state church, and is the only orthodox state church in modern times.

Let us end with examples from Africa: the Ethiopian Orthodox and Coptic churches both of which are monophysite. From the time of its recognition by the Patriarch of Alexandria in 328, the sovereign in Ethiopia has played a critical role. It is important to underscore that it was the sovereign, King Ezana, who initiated contact with Alexandria by sending Frumentius to Alexandria to learn at the feet of Patriarch Athanasius the Pillar of Orthodoxy.[46] Until the overthrow of Emperor Haile Selassie I, the Ethiopian Orthodox Church was a state church. Concerning this church-state relationship, article 126 of the revised constitution of Ethiopia of 1955, states: "The Ethiopian Orthodox Church, founded in the fourth century on the doctrine of St. Mark, is the Established Church of the Empire and is as such, supported by the state. The Emperor shall always profess the Ethiopian Orthodox Faith. The name of the Emperor shall be mentioned in all religious services." Article 127 adds: "The secular administration of the Established Church shall be governed by law." The constitution left the monastic and spiritual life in the hands of the church to be administered according to canon law and with the approval of the emperor. It is noteworthy that these two articles in the 1955 Constitution reflect most of the things carried out during the reform legislation of 30 November 1942, when the church became the state church. The legislation concerned regulation of church property, the administration of the clergy, church finances, and the status of the church courts. These regulations aimed at limiting the church's temporal and independent power base. The revised constitution of 1955 continued to make church holidays state holidays, supported church activities with public funds, and paid salaries of church officials. Orthodoxy was taught in schools as part of moral education.

In 1967 the government took another step in its control of the church. An order was issued in the official government organ, *Negarit Gazette*, defining the responsibilities of the church council. According to the order, the council was to consist of the patriarch, the chairman, and eight bishops who were to be appointed by the emperor on the recommendation of the patriarch. The council was charged with the responsibility to "establish such rules and procedures as it may deem appropriate for the conduct of its affairs and generally for secular administration."

It is with this background that we should understand the latest crises, that is, the election and appointment of Abune Paulos Gebrehiwot as the fifth patriarch in July 1992. The appointment caused a scandal within the church for it was alleged that the election violated the church's tradition and canon law which precludes election of a new patriarch while an existing patriarch is still alive. It was alleged that the existing patriarch, Abune Merkorios, was forced to resign by the Ethiopian Progressive Revolutionary Democratic Front (EPRDF) when it seized power in May 1991. It was also further alleged that the second patriarch, Abune Teoflos, was murdered by the Derg (military junta) in July 1979, after three years of imprisonment as part of Lieutenant Colonel Mengistu Haile Mariaum's ruthless elimination of those associated with Haile Selassie's regime.[47]

When we examine the history of church-state relation within the Orthodox tradition since the time of Justinian I, we see that the tradition has not produced a political theory or theology. The churches have often allied with imperial power and that has led to the domestication and greatly undermined efforts towards a political theology and ethics. Churches in the tradition have certainly produced a theology of survival during a hostile regime, but that does not exculpate their acquiescence to the imperial authorities in the first place. The Cyprus Orthodox Church is an exception; its leadership has played a very critical role in national politics, particularly in the Cypriot struggle for union. Archbishop Makarios, who was elected in 1950, took a leading role in this; he later became the president of Cyprus.

We also see that Orthodox churches tend to be nationalistic. The establishment of national patriarchs in Bulgaria and Serbia was part of the state building process that was closely associated with the assertion of national identity. The Russian church has identified nationality with the Orthodox tradition. Nationalism was seen in the short-lived Coptic National Movement (1952–54) which had its own flag and uniform. The Movement promoted learning of Coptic language. The nationalism of the Coptic Church was an opposition to Islamic nationalism. Coptic nationalism again emerged in the 1970s when there were moves to make civil law conform to Islamic law (*Shar`ia*) in Egypt. In the summer of 1977, the Coptic patriarch, Shenouda, ordered Copts to observe a fast as protest against the draft legislation for Islamic law. Violent clashes between Muslims and Christians took place in two provinces, Assiut and Minya.[48] These clashes sharpened in 1981, causing the Egyptian president, Anwar Sadat, to arrest many Islamic fundamentalists as well as patriarch Shenouda III, along with eight bishops, thirty priests, and one hundred and thirty lay Copts. Responding to the arrests, the Coptic Board in the Near East, issued a statement on September 7, 1981, asking President Sadat to end religious discrimination and to release the patriarch because the president, being a secular authority, had no right to banish the Coptic patriarch. The Coptic Board demanded constitutional guarantees to the Copts recognizing their ethnicity, the right to form their own political party, establish a Coptic university, end of censorship of Coptic publications and revelation of the "real" population of Egyptian Copts.[49] Hosni Mubarak, Sadat's successor, was the one who eventually released the patriarch from his banishment from a monastery.

In closing the discussion on the Coptic church, let it be mentioned that the Copts have always seen themselves as dissenters, with monophystism as a symbol of their opposition to the emperor and to the government of Constantinople. They consider monophystism a symbol of opposition to the emperor since it was he who convoked the council but also protected the *Definition* of Chalcedon.

From ecclesiastical nationalism seen in the Orthodox churches seems to emerge the understanding that if a church is deeply rooted in national ethos, then national ethos and culture, even the nation itself, cannot survive without the church. The words of Antony, the patriarch of Constantinople to Grand Prince Vasilii of Russia in 1395 seem to be true: "The holy emperor has a great place in the church. He is not as other rulers and governors of other regions are; and this is because the emperors, from the beginning, established and confirmed true religion in all the inhabited world. . . . It is not possible for Christians to have a church and not to have an empire. Church and empire have a great unity and community; nor can they be separated from each other."[50] But this attitude leads the church to being co-opted, as happened with the Russian Orthodox whose hierarchy was closely supervised by the state's council for Religious Affairs. The Council could tell state officials that

> The council controls the synod. The question of selection and appointment of its permanent members used to be, and still is, completely in the hands of the Council; candidacy of special members is also determined upon previous agreement by appropriate official of the Council. All topics to be presented for discussion at the Synod are first submitted by Patriarch Pimen and the permanent members of the Synod to the executive committee of the Council and its departments. Furthermore, the Council approves the final "Decision of the Holy Synod."
>
> Exercising its constant and unrelenting control over the activities of the Synod, appropriate officials of the Council conduct systematic work to educate and enlighten the members of the Synod, maintain confidential contacts with them, shape their patriotic views and attitudes, and exert necessary influence on the entire episcopate through the members of the Synod with their help.
>
> The Council and its commissioners in various locations are paying constant and relenting attention to the study of the system and activity not only of the members of the Synod but also of the episcopate in general. There is no consecration of a bishop, no transfer without thorough investigation of the candidate by appropriate officials of the Council in close cooperation with the commissioner, local organs and corresponding interested organization.[51]

This secret report smuggled out of Russia during the time of the Soviet Union, reveals how much the Russian Orthodox Church had been infiltrated, co-opted, and how powerless it had become.

To conclude the discussion on the attitude of Orthodox churches to the state, we observe several different patterns: autocephaly (Rumania, Serbia), ecclesiastical nationalism which may lead to autocephaly (Ethiopia) or opposition to the state (Coptic), and domestication or co-option (Russian). Co-option has always been the price the churches had to pay for survival, but this has been survival at the expense of legal helplessness and institutional weakness. In terms of church-state relation, Orthodox churches tend towards a symphony than a Caesaro-papism, that is, subordinating the church to the state. Orthodox churches tend to seek a situation where neither party exercises absolute control over the other. Common to all Orthodox churches is that they consider themselves the vehicle for and custodian of, national culture and ethos. It is for this reason that Orthodox churches have successfully integrated cultural values into Christianity to such an extent that culture and Christianity are inseparable, and the people are unable to imagine themselves without either their religion or their culture. For example, to be Greek is to belong to the Greek Orthodox Church. Although this cannot be said of the Ethiopian and Coptic churches, still we see that these are the most indigenized on the continent. Before the overthrow of Haile Selassie, to be Ethiopian was to belong to Telewhodo (Ehtiopian Orthodox Church), and it is still true with most Amhara.

In this section of the chapter we have briefly sketched the development of the church's understanding about the limits of civil authorities and the obligation of the clergy to the church and civil law. It is indeed true that since the time of Constantine church leaders dealt mostly with Christian rulers. That is not the case in contemporary Africa where most states are secular. Although political leaders in Africa may not have a commitment to a particular religion, it remains an obligation and duty of religious leaders, Christian or Muslim, to strive for the autonomy of their institutions and teachings.

THE MISSION OF THE CHURCH

While the state is mainly concerned with protecting private interests, it also has a duty towards preservation and quality of human life. In this respect, the state shares the same concern with the church. Unlike the state, the power of the church is not from the people within the church. There are no contending interests among its members, for which the church is the arbitrator. The power of the church is from the ONE who established it—God—and the church's duty is to provide people with possibilities for the self-transcendence of life. In other words, the commission of the church is for fullness of life in concrete historical situations. Given this commission, the church is, or should be, concerned with the human condition in the present historical context. This means that the church, on behalf of God, is to denounce all powers and principalities which prevent fullness of life.

This is where the tension between the church and state emerges, the question then is: on what grounds or right has the church to speak on behalf of the people in a secular state? On 10 December, 1948, the General Assembly of the United Nations adopted and declared the Universal Declaration of Human Rights, which stipulates human freedoms and the obligation of nation-states to uphold and maintain those freedoms (rights). These include freedom of religion, opinion and expression, peaceful assembly and association, and taking part in the government of one's country, among others. Nation-states which are member states of United Nations ascribe to this charter of human freedoms and they are included in their constitutions. Based on this charter and on the constitution, the church is recognized as having freedom of association, freedom of its members to organize, and have religious belief and worship without interference from the state.

These rights have also been declared by various churches. Affirming the United Nations *Universal Declaration of Human Rights*, the Anglican Communion gathered at the 1948 Lambeth Conference said, "The Conference declares that all people, irrespective of race or color, are equally the objects of God's love and are called to love and save him. All people are made in God's own image: for all Christ died; and to all there is made the offer of eternal life. Every individual is therefore bound by duties towards God and towards other people, and has certain rights without the enjoyment of which the individual cannot freely perform those duties. These rights should be declared by the church, recognized by the State and safeguarded by international law."[52]

In the Catholic Church human rights have been a major social concern since 1961 when pope John XXIII said the church was "dominated by one basic theme—an unshakable affirmation and vigorous defence of the dignity and rights of the human person."[53] This view has been reiterated by a number of publications of the church including one published at the last session of the Second Vatican Council in 1965, *The Pastoral Constitution on the Church in the Modern World.* When the Synod of Bishops met in 1974 they issued their publication on human rights: *Message Concerning Human Rights and Reconciliation.* The issue was taken up by a papal commission, *Justitia et Pax*, which published a paper in 1975 entitled, *The Church and Human Rights.* Drawing from the teachings of Thomas Aquinas on natural law, the paper said: "The teaching of the *Magisterium* on fundamental human rights is based in the first place or is suggested by the inherent requirements of human nature . . . within the sphere of Natural Law."

Many other churches, ecumenical organizations, and other religious bodies affirm human rights and they have developed biblical and theological basis for human dignity. At its meeting in 1970 in Nairobi, the World Alliance of Reformed Churches (WARC), initiated a study towards an ecumenical "Christian Declaration on Human Rights." In its statement the WARC said: "Human beings in the fullness of their life and in all life's relationships—economic, social, political, and personal—are destined to live 'before the face of God,' to respond to the Word of God, and responsibility to carry out their task in the world implied in their being created in the image of God. They are persons before God and as such capable of acting on God's behalf and responsible to him. As a consequence of this, a person's rights and duties as a human being are inalienable and indivisible."[54]

It is to be observed from the quotations above that the church understands these freedoms to be grounded in the freedom of God, and of God's own freedom in the face of any human institution. The church's freedom granted by the constitution implies that it is free to organize its own institutions and govern itself without interference by the state or the ruling party. From the freedom of God, the church also understands that it is outside the power of the state, it is universal and yet through its members, who are citizens of the local state, it participates in affairs pertaining to the common good. Through the work of its members the church participates in politics, but it is not a political party for it is above the body politic. A clear distinction between the church and body politic is neither possible, nor desirable, since the same person is simultaneously a citizen, a member of the body politic or party, and a church member. A clear division would only be possible by cutting the person in two. The point is that what affects the person as a citizen becomes the concern of the church as well. The church as an association of those whose freedoms are protected by the constitution, has responsibility, a moral obligation towards the well-being of its members. Above all, the church has a higher calling, a divine mandate, to minister to the needs of God's people.

As it hearkens to the divine command in its ministry, the church influences and quickens people with its moral and spiritual power. In carrying out divine purpose, in ministering to the world, the church promotes the common good, thereby contributing to the work of the state. The church does not dictate its will to the state, for it recognizes the autonomy of the body politic and towards state, but the church uses its power of moral persuasion to influence the state into things that make for good life and dignity of persons. In calling the state to the common good, the church does not act as an "opposition party," but calls the state to accountability and reminds it that it draws its power from its citizens, or rather, that it has an obligation to the well-being of the people. Malawian Presbyterians made this point clear in their letter titled, "The Nation of Malawi in Crisis: The Church's Concern." The letter, written in support of the Catholic bishops' letter for reforms which was issued at the beginning of Holy Week (8 March 1992), was presented to Dr. Kamuzu Banda, then life president of Malawi. The Presbyterians said: "Our desire in writing to Your Excellency in this way is to promote the glory of God and the good of the people of Malawi. *We neither represent nor desire any political power: we are simply trying to 'seek the kingdom of God and His justice' (Matthew 6:33).*"[55] The Second Vatican Council also emphasizes the same point: "It is of supreme importance, especially in a pluralistic society, to work out a proper vision of the relation between the political community and the church, and to distinguish clearly between the activities of Christians, individually or collectively in their own name as citizens guided by the dictates of a Christian conscience, and their activity acting long with their pastors in the name of the church. *The church by reason of her role and competence, is not identified with any political community nor bound by ties to any political system.* It is at once the sign and the safeguard of the transcendental dimension of the human. "[56]

Recognizing its twofold nature, that it is in the world yet not of the world, the church condemns structures, practices, and abuses of power not as an enemy of the state, but as a responsibility to its members and to the state for the privileges it enjoys. In fact, the church wishes the state well and feels it has an obligation to pray for blessings and prosperity of the state, but it also has an obligation to bring to the attention of the secular authorities things of concern to the people. Maintaining that the church should speak on issues of the welfare of the people does not mean that the church should devise a plan or the precise means of promoting the common good. There are no specific "Christian solutions" to social or economic problems. Although church cannot give the remedy, it must still speak out for it can tell when there is disease in society. It would be wrong in a secular state for the church even to think of giving a sketch of an ideal or perfect social order; that would be utopia.

The church should take its mission seriously. Its calling is to provide people with the possibility of fullness of life. God's concern is for all creation to have life. God wants all life to be preserved and give human life the possibility for full realization. For God, the task does not end with creation; preservation is part of divine creativity. This means the church is called to continue God's work of creation and preservation. The church is therefore obliged to speak against forces, ideologies, and powers which destroy life and prevent personhood. The church must announce divine disapproval of the actions of those distorting the divine image in people. Silence makes the church an accomplice to the forces of evil seeking to destroy people.

CHURCH AND STATE COOPERATION

Since the church does not act in opposition to the state but seeks to promote the common good, there is a need for cooperation between the two institutions. The church does not consider the state a profane institution for as far as it performs its duties and responsibilities well, that is, promotes prosperity and equitable distribution of material things which support good life and dignity of persons, it performs a sacred function to which the church itself has also been commissioned. Again, the state's sacred functions include creating favorable conditions for political, social, and cultural development and well-being, that is, enforce the freedoms in the constitution which resonate with the freedoms God gives to people. By guaranteeing judicial order or regulating society according to the demands of justice, the state properly contributes to the spiritual interests and welfare of the church. When the state fails in its sacred function, the church cannot keep quiet.

This mutual cooperation extends into the quest for truth. The church is committed to (revealed) truth; the state, too, is obligated to the truth to which the people themselves, the citizens, adhere and expect from the state. The state does not know another truth than that which the people know. Truth is one and comes from God, as Clement of Alexandria (130–215) said. This truth inspires and enlightens the people to higher moral standards in social as well as political life. Even in places where there is rampant corruption in social and political life, people expect high moral standards from the state in its exercise of justice and enforcement of law, and in supervising the conditions for good life of the people. The church's truth is eternal while that of the state is intermediate, but grounded in the eternal. The church plays a very important role when it calls both the people and the state to higher moral standards. The quest for truth, then, should promote mutual cooperation between the state and the church.

In this mutual cooperation, the state must take care not to encroach on religious matters for it cannot do so without violating the constitutional freedoms of the church. The state has neither power nor authority to impose faith nor the practice of it, although it must supervise the conditions and means in society for good human life. The curse of a state church is that the state interferes and even dictates its will on matters of faith and practice, including organization and government of the church.

When I insist that the state should not encroach on religious matters, this nevertheless, does not mean that the state must stand aloof in the face of religious strife or in case of practices that may endanger the life of its members or the basis of common good. This is of course a very slippery area on which Augustine fell. What is meant is that the state may get involved only when it has established beyond doubt that the common good is in jeopardy, that religious or doctrinal differences and practices produce strife or threaten the welfare of followers and society. There are certain issues here which are indeed very difficult. For instance, should the state abrogate the freedom of belief of those who believe in faith healing? If faith healing does not seem to initiate healing, and the life of the patient is in danger, and especially if the disease the patient is suffering is contagious—say tuberculosis or cholera—the government should use all its persuasive power to initiate treatment. Why? Life and the common welfare are threatened and it is the duty of the state to preserve both. The point being emphasized here is that in protecting the civil liberties of the church, the state opens possibilities for the church to engage in works of common good, such as moral development, health, education, and relief. Through this protection and enforcement of the law, the state helps the church in its spiritual work; it helps Christians in the exercise of their duty and practice of piety which enables them to live a full and integrated life.

In the Catholic Church, Vatican Council II expressed very well the need for cooperation between the church and body politic, while yet recognizing the distinctiveness of each institution: "The political community and the church are autonomous and independent of each other in their own fields. Nevertheless both are devoted to the personal vocation of man, though under different titles. This service will rebound the more effectively to the welfare of all insofar as both institution practice better co-operation to the local and prevailing situation. For man's horizons are bound only by the temporal order; living on the level of human history he preserves the integrity of his eternal destiny."[57] The church cannot dispense with the temporal order for this is where people fulfill their human destiny, that is, fullness of life. On the other hand, the church cannot have its destiny tied to that of the temporal order which passes. The church must work with the temporal order and yet transcend it.

NOTES

1. "Deposition of Henry IV by Gregory VII, 4, 31 February 1076," in *Documents of the Christian Church*, Bettenson, ed., 146.
2. Gregory in *Bibliotheca rerum Germanicarum*, P. Jaffé, vol. II, Monumenta Gregorian, 404.
3. Quoted by Carlyle, *Leviathan*, vol. IV, 186, n. 1.
4. *Gregory VII's Letter to the Bishop of Metz, 1081* in Bettenson, *Documents of the Christian Church*, 105–106.
5. Quoted in Robin Gill, *A Textbook of Christian Ethics* (Edinburgh: T. & T. Clark, 1985), 200, 202.
6. Ibid., 202.
7. Ibid., 202–203.
8. Aquinas, commentary on the sentences of Peter Lombard, *Summa Theologica*, Book II, Dist. 44, Q. 3.
9. Thomas Aquinas, *Summa Theologica*, 1a, 2ae, question 90, 4.
10. Thomas Aquinas, *De regimine principum*, 1, 14.
11. Quoted by Justo L. González, *A History of Christian Thought*. Vol. 2, *From Augustine to the Eve of the Reformation* (Nashville, TN: Abingdon, 1988), 223.
12. Ibid., 223–24.
13. Quoted in Carlyle, Vol. 5, 323, n. 1.
14. J. N. D. Kelly, *Early Christian Doctrines* (New York: Harper and Row, 1978), 408.
15. Bettenson, *Documents*, 8–9.
16. Ibid.; *The Ante-Nicene Fathers* (hereafter *ANF*) 5:377.
17. *ANF* 5:565.
18. Ibid., 224–25.
19. Ibid., 226.
20. See "The Theory of the Household" in Book I of *The Politics of Aristotle*, beginning section X. Ernest Barker, trans. *The Politics of Aristotle* (London: Oxford University Press, 1958).
21. Marsilius, *Defensor Pacis*, vol I, section 6, 8.
22. Marsilius, *Defensor Pacis*, vol. 1, 2.
23. Ibid., vol. I, 4.
24. Marsilius, *Defensor Pacis*, vol. I, section 12, 3.
25. Hobbes, *De Civitate*, 15.

26. Martin Luther, "On Good Works," in *Werke*, W.A. Lambert, trans., vol. VI, 250. Quoted in *A History of Political Theory*, George H. Sabine and Thomas L. Thorson, 4th ed. (Hinsdale, IL: Dryden Press, 1973), 338.

27. Martin Luther, "Lectures on Genesis, Chapters 15–20," in *Luther's Works*, vol. III, Jaraslov Pelican, ed. (St. Louis, Missouri: Concordia Publishing House, 1961), 279.

28. Martin Luther, "Temporal Authority: To what extent it should be obeyed," *Luther: Selected Political Writings*, J. M. Porter, ed. and introduction (Philadelphia: Fortress Press, 1974), 55–56.

29. Ibid., 56–57.

30. Ibid., 61.

31. Ibid., 66, 67.

32. Ibid.

33. Martin Luther, "Whether soldiers, too, can be saved," in *Works of Martin Luther*, vol. V. (Philadelphia, Fortress Press, 1931), 59ff.

34. Jürgen Moltmann, *On Human Dignity: Political Theology and Ethics* (Philadelphia: Fortress Press, 1984), 70–71.

35. John Calvin, *Institutes of the Christian Religion*, vol. 3, sect. 19, 15.

36. "Calvin on Civil Government," in *Calvin On God and Political Duty*, John T. MacNeill (Indianapolis, IN: Bobbs-Merrill Education Publishing, 1980), 49, 54.

37. Ibid., 67.

38. Ibid., 59.

39. Ibid., 74.

40. Ibid., 90.

41. John Calvin, *Institutes of the Christian Religion*, John T. McNeill, ed., and Ford Lewis Battles, trans. (Philadelphia: Westminster, 1960)., IV, xx 2.

42. Ibid., IV, Chap. xx, par. xxxi.

43. John Calvin, *Commentaries on the Epistle of Paul, the Apostle to the Romans* (Grand Rapids, MI: Eerdmans, 1948), 469.

44. John Knox, *Appellation: Works*, vol. IV. David Laing, ed. (Edinburgh: Bannatyne Society, 1846–64), 496.

45. Quoted in John McManners, ed. *The Oxford History of Christianity* (New York: Oxford University Press, 1993), 133.

46. Concerning the origin and development of the Ethiopian church see Harvey J. Sindima, "Africa's Christian Heritage: Notes on Ethiopian Christianity," *Africa Theological Journal* 20, 2 (1991):108–122.

47. *Ethiopian Review* (August 1992): 8.

48. J. D. Pennington, "The Copts in Modern Egypt," *Middle Eastern Studies* 18, 2 (April 1982):171–72.

49. *Al-'Amal* (Beirut), 8 September, 1981, 10.

50. McManners, *History of Christianity*, 133–34.

51. Pedro Ramet, "Autocephaly and National Identity in Church-State Relations in Eastern Christianity: An Introduction," in *Eastern Christianity and Politics in the Twentieth Century*, Pedro Ramet, ed. (Durham, NC: Duke University Press, 1988), 12.

52. Philip Russell and Arthur Gosling, *Resolutions of the Lambeth Conference, 1867–1978* (Published by the Secretary General of the Anglican Consultative Council for the Lambeth Conference, 1988).

53. Quoted in David Hollenbach, *Claims in Conflict: Retrieving and Renewing the Catholic Human Rights Tradition* (New York: Paulist Press, 1979), 63.

54. Jürgen Moltmann, "The Original Study Paper," in *A Christian Declaration of Human Rights*, A. O. Miller, ed. (Grand Rapids, MI: Eerdmans, 1978), 132.

55. Letter dated 2 June, 1992, but presented to the president on 5 June. The bishops pastoral letter was read in churches throughout Malawi on 8 March, 1992.

56. Vatican Council II, "Gaudium et Spes," Part II, chap. 4, Section 76.

57. Ibid. My emphasis.

6

Power and Authority in the Bible

In the previous chapter we inquired how the Christian tradition has dealt with the issue of civil religion; we now turn to the scriptures to note what they say about religion and civil authorities. Numerous references to scriptures have already been made throughout the book but in this chapter we want to make a short but systematic biblical exploration of the church and state relation, focusing on the concept of power and authority, or the church's responsibility to the world. The usual way of studying scripture is to keep its harmony, that is, to begin with the Old Testament; here we will begin with the New Testament so as to end with the prophetic tradition of the Old Testament.

THE NEW TESTAMENT CONCEPT OF POWER

In studying how the New Testament addressed the question of power, attention is on symbolizations of power within the church. Key passages dealing with power are: Mark 12:13–17 (compare Matthew 22:15–22; Luke 20:20–16); Romans 13:1–7; I Timothy 2:1–8; I Peter 2:11–17; Titus 3:1–2 and Revelation 13. Other passages in the New Testament speak about the exercise of power by appointed authorities. The texts include the following passages: the murder of all male children by Herod (Matthew 2:1–19); the imprisonment and murder of John the baptist by Herod the Tetrarch (Matthew 14:1–12; Luke 3:18–20) and the trial of Jesus by Pilate (Matthew 27:2, 11–26; Mark 15:1–15; Luke 23:1–25; John 18:28–40). Before his condemnation by Pilate, Jesus was also taken before Herod (Luke 23:6–12).

The early church's concept of power is implicit in the notion of Jesus the king. In his prologue, Matthew introduces Jesus as of the lineage of King David (Matthew 1:16). By doing so, Matthew proclaims Jesus king of Israel. Matthew supports his claim concerning the kingship of Jesus with the story of the wise men who travel from the east to worship "he who has been born king of the Jews" (Matthew 2:2). With this story, Matthew further shows his readers that the kingship of Jesus is known beyond the boundaries of Israel. In other words, Jesus is the universally proclaimed king. Almost immediately after proclaiming the universality of the kingship of Jesus, Matthew shows how kings react to the kingship of Jesus. According to Matthew, earthly authorities react with anger when told there is a higher authority than their own, that is, the kingship of Jesus. Herod in his fury launches an all-out murder of male children in Israel. Herod's anger gives a clue to the nature of the conflict that is to follow the assertion that Jesus is king. The hostility of earthly rulers against the kingship of Jesus brings out the worst in human nature. The charge that the accusers of Jesus make against him before the Sanhendrin and Pilate is based on the claim to kingship by Jesus. Soldiers beat and mock him by giving false homage to him as king (Mark 15). His cross bears the inscription "King of the Jews" (Mark 15:26).

It is not only Matthew who has proclaimed Jesus a universal king; all the New Testament writers affirm this view. John says, Jesus as king, has the authority to execute judgment (John 5:27). For Paul, Jesus has power and authority and will rule until all his enemies are defeated (I Corinthians 15:24–27). Again in Colossians 2:10, Paul asserts that Jesus is "the head of all rule and authority" (compare Revelation 13). The New Testament in general, ascribes power and authority on earth to Jesus.

In his statements, Jesus himself affirms having authority and power from God (Matthew 9:6; Mark 2:10). He has been given power and authority to bring all creation, powers and principalities under God's rule. Thus he commands the sea, heals the sick, and raises the dead. He gives his disciples this authority as he commissions them to do the same (Mark 10:1; Mark 6:7; Luke 9:8). Jesus does not say this is his own authority; he says it is of God who sent him (John 12:49; compare John 14:10).

Along with the concept of king, the New Testament writers also developed the concept of the kingdom of God. This concept figures in many places in the New Testament: John the Baptist, the forerunner of Jesus, begins his ministry by announcing that "the kingdom of God is at hand" (Matthew 3:2; 4:17); before he begins his ministry, Jesus must decide whether or not his kingship will be of this world; in the third temptation Jesus states that he seeks to inaugurate the authority of God—the kingdom of heaven—for God is the only king to be worshiped and served. We get this point from his rebuke of Satan. Jesus says: "Begone Satan . . . you shall worship the Lord your God and him only shall you serve" (Matthew 4:10; compare Luke 4:12). Jesus later refers to divine authority when he commissions his disciples, "All authority in heaven and on earth has been given to me" (Matthew 28:18; compare Luke 10:22; John 3:35).

The symbol of the kingdom is central in the parables and other teachings of Jesus (Matthew 5:13, 1–52; 16:19; Mark 3:24, 4:26). The gospel itself is the good news of God's kingdom (of God's rule) as Jesus states in his sermon on the mount (Matthew 5:3, 10). In another place, Jesus tells people to seek first the kingdom and righteousness of God (Matthew 6:33); and also to pray for fulfillment of the kingdom on earth (Matthew 6:10). Concerning this kingdom, Jesus teaches his disciples to pray for its coming: "Your kingdom come." The Protestant version of the Lord's prayer goes further, it asserts God's power saying: "Yours is the kingdom, the power, and the glory."

A brief overview of the concept of power and authority in the New Testament reveals several important points. The first and foremost point is that New Testament writers affirm the Old Testament belief and assertion that all power and authority belong to God (compare II Corinthians 4:7). This is to say, God is the supreme ruler of the world. Paul states it succinctly: "There is no authority except from God" (Romans 13:1). It is in light of this view that New Testament writers develop the symbol of king—Jesus the king of the world. He is king for he is "the power of God." (I Corinthians 1:24). The implication of this understanding is that all rulers are under God's power. To be more precise, rulers are given power by God as Jesus told Pilate: "You would have no power over me unless it had been given you from above" (John 19:1; also John 3:27).

Since all power is from God, the early church urged Christians to submit to the rulers. They took submission to the authorities as obedience to God, the giver of all power and authority (Romans 13:17; I Peter 2:17). This was not a new teaching, any Jew knew this teaching; it was clear and familiar. It had its roots in the Old Testament. The teaching was so familiar in Old Testament times that it became one of the precepts parents told their children. For example, the poet of Proverbs writes, "My son, fear the Lord and the King and do not disobey either of them" (Proverbs 24:22).

Besides the symbol of king, the New Testament also invokes the symbol of kingdom. This symbol has been appropriated to emphasize that the whole world is in God's hands. The New Testament like, the Old Testament, seeks to emphasize that there is nothing that is not within the sphere of God's power and authority. All departments of life, all institutions in society, everyone and everything, is under God's control. In short, there is no division between the secular and the sacred or politics and religion. It is within this context that Peter can put the following ideas in a single verse: "Honor all people. Love fellowship. Fear God. Honor the King" (I Peter 2:17).

Peter does not equate earthly kings with God but describes Christian attitude and relation towards people, God, and civil authorities. According to Peter, the Christian seeks fellowship of love, a community in which all people are honored for the simple reason that they are made in the image of God. A Christian honors rulers for they, too, are within God's plan of salvation. Similarly, Paul urges Christians to pray "for all people, for kings and all who are in high positions" (I Timothy 2:1). Paul gives several reasons for praying for kings, namely; "that we may lead a quiet and peaceable life, godly and respectful in every way" (verse 2) but above all, it is within God's plan of salvation; God "desires all people to be saved" (I Timothy 2:4). Here, we are once again shown that civil power is within the domain of God.

This idea is implicit in the words of Jesus about paying taxes. When Jesus says, "render therefore to Caesar the things that are Caesar's, and to God the things that are God's" (Matthew 22:21), he does not want to imply that there are two kingdoms or powers—the kingdom of God and that of Caesar. That would be putting Caesar on par with God. *All* power is from God, therefore people have a moral obligation to pay taxes (compare Romans 13:6-7). Paying taxes is not doing something outside the kingdom of God.

Although the New Testament urges people to obey rulers it is not blind to the fact that earthly authorities can be mean and inhumane. The early Christian community was all too aware of persecutions. Matthew, more than all the gospel writers, clearly shows how nasty and vicious earthly authorities can be. With the story of the two Herods, Matthew shows opposition of earthly rulers to the kingship of Jesus. All the writers of the first three gospels speak of persecutions awaiting the disciples (Matthew 10:17–18; Mark 13:9–13; Luke 21:12–19). Persecutions occurred when the early Christians refused to engage in civil religion. Sometimes persecutions arose because of proclamation of faith itself (see Acts of the Apostles 17:7, for example).

The writer of the Book of Revelation depicts a much worse picture of what happens when earthly rulers forget or ignore the fact that all power belongs to God and that they are merely servants within the kingdom of God. Revelation 13 says whenever this happens rulers, have regard neither for God nor people; they usurp the place of God. They assert themselves as gods and demand worship. Here we see a picture of the idolatry of the state. When a state becomes idolatrous, it instills fear and creates a sense of powerlessness among its subjects ("Who is like the beast, and who can fight against it" Revelation 13:4b). An idolatrous state goes still further: it demands obedience of everybody at all times and in all places, that is to say, it demands to be worshipped. Persecution of Christians follows (Revelation 13:7a).

It is important to note that when a state becomes idolatrous it moves towards the church to assimilate, conquer, and domesticate it (Revelation

13:11–18). It attempts to assimilate and conquer the church through false prophets. The state finds these false prophets within the membership of the clergy. These are the type of prophets who no longer speak for God, either for fear of their life or because of complete misconception of the nature of the office to which they are called. These prophets use the power of the holy office for the service of the idolatrous state and use symbols of the church or religious language to justify the status quo. The function of these prophets is to lead people in the worship of the state or civil (political) religion. These prophets priests perform tricks to lure people away from true faith and worship to uncritical endorsement and worship of the state. These prophets "performs miracles" (verse 13) arousing misplaced faith (contrast Matthew 4:3–6 with Luke 4:2–4, 9–11); "builds deceitful 'image' of the 'immortal' beast (the idolatrous state) verses 14–15, and makes worship of the image a test of religious and political loyalty. The last thing the corrupt prophets do is to put religious belief under public control (verses 16–17)."[1]

What should Christians do with rulers who abuse their power? The Book of Revelation offers Christians guidance beyond prayer for authorities. The writer of Revelation knows that the price for resisting authorities can be high; nonetheless, he introduces the teaching of non-cooperation. The teaching says the church should not cooperate with authorities when they usurp the place of God (Revelation 13), that is to say, the church should not engage in political religion. The church cannot identify itself with authorities who disregard their divinely appointed task (which is to preserve human life made in the image of God) and demand obedience due God. Since those who refuse to give obedience to corrupt authorities will be persecuted, the church must go underground. Going underground is not keeping silent or behaving as if nothing is wrong; it is to demonstrate non-cooperation with corrupt authorities, the forces of evil in society. The Book of Revelation is the story of a church that refuses to support corrupt authorities, thus it goes underground. By going underground, the church chooses to be unpopular, thereby risking being considered revolutionary by uncritical Christians and their leadership, which uses the powers of the sacred office to advance justification and glorification of the state. Anytime Christians disassociate themselves with the powers that be they are considered subversive, their actions are called seditious and revolutionary; they disturb the prevailing peace and calm. For the writer of Revelation it is better to be called subversive than offer uncritical endorsement of authorities who disregard the human condition, seek self-interests, and take the place of God.

While making the assertion that all power is from God, New Testament writers realize that their concept of power differs from that of earthly authorities. For these authorities, power is used towards one's ends and to oppress others. It is with this in mind that Jesus speaks about power among gentiles. He says that outside the people of *Yahweh*, power is control, or as he puts it, gentile "rulers lord it over them" (Matthew 20:25; Mark 10:42–45; Luke 22:25–27). In other words, outside the knowledge of God, power is corrupt and has no regard for the welfare, dignity, and respect of others. Jesus reinterprets the concept of power by explaining how power is to be understood among those under the authority of God. According to Jesus, those who know God realize that the power they have is not their own. They are aware that power is given from above for the purpose of building God's kingdom.

Jesus says power is service, by which he means that power should not be used for self-aggrandizement or fulfillment but to enable others. Anyone who perceives power as something entrusted to her or him by God through the people, gets a new self-understanding and a new understanding of the office to which one is called. The person perceives herself or himself as a servant of God, therefore a servant of the people. Power then is conceived as that which enables others to live fully. Power in the New Testament is for enhancing or building community life. This is a way of life that lets others live fully by setting free their creative energies.

ROMANS 13

Romans 13:1–7 has been mentioned numerous times in this book for through the centuries the passage has been taken as a text offering guidance on general principles of Christian faith and practice in society. As we have observed, great theologians and other people of faith refer to the passage. At some points in history, the passage has also been wrongly appropriated. The text has been used to demand uncritical and unconditional submission to authorities. There are many instances in history which indicate that the passage was invoked to further the interests of powerful and dominant groups in church and society. During the Reformation, for example, church authorities invoked Romans 13:1–7 to suppress Baptists and other "radical" groups.[2] Modern examples are too many to list and it has already been indicated that in postcolonial Africa, as it was in the missionary era, the church invoked the text to admonish people to give the government unconditional submission. Evangelicals in Africa have often invoked Romans 13 to support their lack of political involvement. Until the late 1980s, evangelicals in South Africa were not part of the Christian opposition to the system of *apartheid*; they justified their indifference by citing Romans 13. They have since reconsidered their position and made a turn around.[3]

Why is it that people draw from the text whatever they want to get out of it? The concrete social, political, economic, and historical circumstances surrounding the text usually do not form part of its interpretation. A text or story has its roots in a specific historical reality. If interpretation is to be faithful to the original event(s), then the reality in which the story arose has to be examined. Failure to understand the historical context leads to the wrong interpretation of the text.

In the case of Romans 13:1–7, historical background is plentiful. Scholars have produced a great deal of biblical and extra-biblical data on the contextual situation surrounding the creation of the text.[4] The apostle Luke has furnished his readers with some background information concerning the state of affairs prior to Paul's writing of the letter to the Romans. Luke, in his list of nationalities present in Jerusalem at Pentecost, includes people from Rome (Acts 2:5, 10). These visitors may have related their experience to others in Rome and in so doing sowed the seeds of Christianity. According to the evidence given in Acts 28:21, the Jews in Rome seem to have maintained some correspondence with Palestine. The words spoken by the leaders of the Jews in Rome, "none of the brethren coming here has reported or spoken any evil about you," suggest that some religious authorities, probably rabbis, came to Rome frequently either for instruction or some other religious functions. Brown and Meier argue that the movement of the temple tax was involved in the correspondence, so these rabbis may have come to Rome to collect the temple tax raised by local Jewish leaders.[5]

Luke also says that some of the Jews in Rome converted to Christianity (Acts 18) and a few of them seem to have been engaged in trade and commerce. Luke mentions two of them by name: Aquila and Priscilla. Extra-biblical evidence supports Luke's suggestion that Jews in Rome were involved in trade and commerce. Josephus, a distinguished Jewish historian of the first century, says Jews in Rome formed an influential minority. Their influence was the result of their involvement in trade and commerce.[6] He further states that Jews in Rome enjoyed special privileges because of their support for Julius Caesar. They had religious freedom: they could "assemble and feast in accordance with their native customs and ordinances."[7] Judaism reaped a handsome reward from Jewish political maneuvers with Julius Caesar. Political freedom yielded popularity and attraction to Judaism. Its popularity reached the royal court, even attracting some there: Poppaea, Emperor Nero's wife, became attracted to Judaism.[8] This popularity also attracted hostility to the Jews from the citizens and other residents of Rome whose religion did not enjoy such privileges. Bammel and Moule in their study of "Romans 13," note that the Jews in Rome were not only a minority, but they also lacked organization to give them the same political influence as their fellow Jews in Alexandria. Jews in Alexandria had considerable political influence.

From internal evidence we also learn that the political climate in Rome was not favorable to Jews. In introducing Aquila, Luke says Aquila "had lately come from Italy with his wife Priscilla, because Claudius had commanded Jews to leave Rome" (Acts 18:2). This expulsion is believed to have taken place in the year 49. From extra-biblical evidence we know that this was not the first expulsion in the memory of either Luke or Paul. There was an earlier deportation in the year 19 when emperor Tiberius shipped thousands of them to Sardinia.[9] Since the Christian community in Rome had grown from the Jewish population, the expulsion of Jews directly affected Christian communities there. The Jewish-Christian connection, Gentile-Jewish tension to be specific, is a subject of importance to Paul (Romans 11:17–21). This is because in the absence of a Jewish leadership of the church, the Gentiles took over and they were beginning to think they were better leaders than the Jews; further that, some of the Gentiles saw Jewish expulsion as a form of divine judgment on them for their rejection of Jesus.

What does this evidence, biblical and extra-biblical, say about the writing and interpretation of Romans 13:1–7? When Paul writes, "Let every person be subject to the governing authorities," he is not reminding the Christian community in Rome of some common old precept, but is being realistic about the political situation in Rome. When he sits down to dictate his letter, he is fully aware of the religious and political climate in Rome. From people like Aquila and Priscilla and other sources he has learned that people in Rome are generally suspicious of cults. Christianity is one of the new cults appearing in Rome through Jews and traders of other nationalities. The Christian situation is compounded by the fact that some members of Christian communities are Jews. It is not a hidden fact that Jews are not well favored by the majority of people in Rome. In the light of the Jewish-Roman conflict and also the political climate, Paul finds it sensible to tell the Christian communities to keep a low profile.

Paul explains why Christians in Rome should submit to authorities; writing that "there is no authority except from God" (verse 2). Here Paul goes to the scriptures to support his assertion on submission. He quotes Proverbs 8:15–16, "By me kings reign, and rulers decree what is just; by me princes rule, and nobles govern the earth." Perhaps he also has in mind Jeremiah 25:9 where *Yahweh* called Nebuchadnezzar "my servant," a verse which was later quoted by Calvin.

There is another reason for giving general principles of Christian conduct to the Christians in Rome. Paul is aware of the fact that the government in Rome is a democratic one. He knows, too, like all people in Rome and even today, that even in a democratic system, political power comes through birth, connection, wealth, or through cunning ways. Sometimes political power is achieved through ruthless self-advancement. Since political power in a democratic Roman empire came through these channels, it was not feasible for most people to achieve it. Why then should Christians hope or strive for it? Why bother at all? Paul, therefore, exhorts Christians to live within the given structures. This is a practical advice. Paul, like all New Testament writers, is a political realist. He does not want to raise hope where there is none.

Paul has to be careful about what he tells Christian communities in Rome. He must be as clear as possible, avoiding all political misinterpretation. Like all Jews, he knows all too well how swift the government in Rome crushes movements. After explaining why people should submit, he feels obliged to speak on a very sensitive political issue in Rome: taxes and revenues (Romans 13:6–7). He knows that there is bitterness in Rome concerning indirect taxation and that Nero has proposed a tax reform. According to Nero's proposed tax reform, all indirect taxation is to be abolished. His senators argue against the tax reform, saying there will be a fall in revenue should the reform be carried through. Moreover, this might lead people to demand abolition of taxes altogether.

Much of the anger in society towards Jews grew from the fact that from the time of Julius Caesar they were exempted from taxes on the grounds that they paid taxes to the Temple in Jerusalem. The general population accused Jews of tax evasion. Revenue collectors too, were angry at the Jews because they did not pay any revenue. Since Christians were identified with Jews, these charges were likely to be leveled against Christians should they not pay taxes and revenue. Unlike the Jews, Christians could be taken to the court of law for they had no tax exempt status. Christians were very vulnerable, that is why they must exercise all caution. Therefore Paul advised they should pay taxes and revenues to avoid the hostility of Rome on the Christian community.

Here, in brief, is the background and explanation of the most misinterpreted and misappropriated text of the New Testament. The text does not urge Christians to unconditional submission to civil authorities, but calls for a careful assessment of their political situation making sure that they do not unduly provoke the authorities into actions which may be detrimental to the church. This position does not mean condoning evil, for that would be sinning against God. The text is in no way a mandate for political non-involvement; it is a gross misinterpretation to understand it that way.

THE PROPHETIC CHALLENGE

The prophetic tradition in the Old Testament sets an example of what the church should do and say when life and human dignity, or the moral fabric of society, are destroyed. In order to understand how Jews perceived the nature and role of the prophetic tradition, it will be helpful to grasp Israel's concept of self and of the world. Israel was first and foremost the identity of people who traced their ancestry to Jacob, Isaac, and Abraham. Genesis 15:18–20 says that Abraham made a covenant with his God, *Yahweh*. The covenant relationship between Abraham and *Yahweh* made the descendants of Abraham a special people; thus the first meaning of Israel was in reference to belonging to a particular religious community—a covenant people. Consequently, the descendants of Abraham went to war identifying themselves as the "people of *Yahweh*."

The Israelites did not have a king for they belonged to *Yahweh*. It was *Yahweh* who led them out of captivity in Egypt and won them victories in battles with other nations. *Yahweh* saved them from natural catastrophes as well as defeats in war; *Yahweh* was their leader and was represented in the community by priests through whom he spoke to people. Thus, priests "ruled" Israel on behalf of *Yahweh*. Samuel was the last of the priests to have "ruled" Israel. He ruled Israel his entire life (I Samuel 7:15). Since Israel meant "a covenant people," or the "people of *Yahweh*," there was no separation of civil and religious powers. All powers, as all spheres of life, belonged to *Yahweh*, their leader. The form of government Israel had up to the time of Samuel was a theocracy, a government in which the deity is recognized as the civil ruler but a priest(s) administers functions of government on behalf of the deity.

During the period of the theocracy, priests combined offices of priesthood and "political leadership" of Israel. This changed when the monarchy emerged. With the anointing of Saul as the first king, political and religious division appeared. The political became the domain of the king while the priesthood was responsible for religious affairs. This division was to produce tension between the king and the priests in the future. There were two areas in which this tension surfaced. Troubles arose whenever a priest spoke out on the shortcomings or evils prevailing in the social and political realms. Another source of tension came when priests raised questions concerning the moral life of the king. Many times when the king sinned priests did not condemn the evil. Three reasons account for their silence: (1) fear for their life; (2) misunderstanding concerning the duties of their office; and (3) corruption of the priests themselves. When priests condoned evil, *Yahweh* raised a prophet to announce divine criticism of the political order and of the king's way of life. Thus the prophetic tradition emerged to announce divine abhorrence and criticism of the political structure and moral life of the king. We might say prophecy emerged as check for the social and political systems symbolized by the king.[10]

Prophets spoke on a wide range of local and international subjects. Here are some examples of prophets speaking about international issues: Isaiah told Ahaz that the defense agreement signed between Judah and the Assyrian king, Tilglath Pileser III, was an ill-advised plan, for Judah would not win the Syro-Ephraimite war (Isaiah 7). The war took place in 734–733 B.C.E. (Before the Common Era) and Judah lost. Isaiah also told Hezekiah that his move against Senncherib was wrong—it would be disastrous to the nation.

Hosea also brought unwelcome news to the people of Ephraim: he told them that a defense treaty with Egypt and Assyria was worthless (Hosea 5:8–6:6; 7:11–12).

A very important point about the ministry of the prophets is that as divine checks on the sociopolitical system, they concerned themselves primarily with the affairs of the royal court—the king's administration and way of life (his behavior and conduct).[11] The following prophets are those whose main focus was on the royal court: Samuel, Nathan, Gad, Ahijah, Micah, Elijah, and Elisha. During the exile, we find Haggai doing the same (Hagai 1:1). Reactions to divine criticism differed from king to king. In general, the early kings (Saul and David) accepted divine criticism and punishment (I Samuel 15:24–31; II Samuel 12:7–5). The kings who followed Saul and David not only accepted the prophetic condemnation but they also sought divine guidance through the prophets. Those kings were Jehossaphat (I Kings 22:5, 7), Hezekiah (II Kings 19–20) and Josiah (II Kings 14–20).

The situation was different with the kings after Josiah. Divine discontent with the social and political life was met with harsh treatment of prophets by kings. The first rejection of a prophetic voice is recorded in I Kings 3:4. The text says that Jeroboam I tried to imprison the unnamed prophet who had condemned the king for building the altar at Bethel. Yet the same king asked the prophet to pray for the cure of his hand, which had suddenly withered. The fate of the unknown prophet was to be experienced by Elijah, Isaiah, and Jeremiah. King Ahab called Elijah "troubler of Israel" (I Kings 18:17) and "my enemy" (I Kings 21:20). Ahaz refused to hear the prophetic words of Isaiah (Isaiah 7). Perhaps the king who showed the most contempt for divine discontent was Jehoiakim. Concerning his attitude towards the prophetic words of Jeremiah the Bible describes Jehoiakim as not "afraid" and this attitude prevailed in the royal court for his servants did not "rend their garments" when the prophetic message was read to him and his servants. With his penknife, the king cut off the scrolls and threw "them into the fire . . . until the entire scroll was consumed in the fire in the brazier" (Jeremiah 36:23). As if that were not enough, Jehoiakim sought to arrest Jeremiah and his secretary, Baruch, "but the Lord hid them" (Jeremiah 36:26). The last king of Judah, Zedekiah, accepted Jeremiah's condemnation but he also delivered him to the princes for execution.

This brief discussion of prophets in Israel shows that they addressed kings on a wide range of issues, the most common ones being the moral conduct of kings (for example, David's adultery with Bathsheba, Uriah's wife; Ahab's corruption of the legal system to execute Naboth), abuse of power, lack of provisions for justice and security for the people, and international affairs. A closer look at the ministry of the prophets reveals that their task was primarily to call the king to divine obedience. The king had to be reminded that there was a higher power and authority. As a sign of his obedience to the higher authority, his leadership, administration of law, justice, and his handling of the economy and international affairs were to be above reproach. His personal life was to be exemplary to the whole nation. In short, the whole of the king's life was to be brought to the obedience of God, a failure of which invoked divine criticism and condemnation.

In our study we have also observed that there was no dimension of life which could be called "non-religious." All departments of life were religious,[12] and accordingly, subject to divine criticism. Above all, the "people of *Yahweh*," Israel, understood all power to be from God and that kings were appointed by God. Divine appointment was symbolized by the priest's act of anointing the king. The evolution from theocracy to monarchy itself was through a priest—Samuel. That kings were chosen by *Yahweh* is loud and clear in the Wisdom literature. Proverbs 8:15–16 is perhaps a good example: "By me kings reign and rulers decree what is just; by me princes rule, and nobles govern the earth." The concept is also present in the prophetic literature, although there the emphasis is on the power of *Yahweh* to choose kings even outside Israel in order to carry out a divine mission. We get this also in Jeremiah 27:5–7: "It is I [*Yahweh*] who by my great power and my out stretched arm have made the earth, with men and animals that are on earth, and I give it to whomever it seems right to me." Similarly, Isaiah says God has raised and appointed Cyrus to punish the people (Isaiah 41:2–4). In the apocalyptic literature we find the same assertion that all power and authority belongs to "the Most High" and that God gives power to whom he will (Daniel 2:21; 3:7–8; 4:17, 25, 31; 5:21).

What all these writers sought to emphasize was that kings or rulers were responsible before *Yahweh* and therefore constrained to obey *Yahweh* or disobey and invoke judgement upon themselves. The implication was that bad kings or rulers would certainly be punished by God. By the time the New Testament was written this notion had become a dominant view among all Jews.

The biblical tradition is emphatic and constant in its assertion that the priesthood has a responsibility to denounce the evils committed by rulers. Corrupt rulers can only force people to worship them. This is a very real danger in any form of personal rule because it creates a propensity for people to pay homage to their leader. Rulers ought to be respected but not worshipped in any sense. The church should not stand still when such things happen. Biblical evidence is clear: God hates corrupt rulers and their priests.

NOTES

1. H. Schlier, "Die Beurteilung des states in Neuen Testament," *Die der Kirche* (Freiburg: Herder, 1956), 24.

2. U. Wilckens shows how Romans 13:1–7 has been used in history. See his book *Romer* (EKK VI/3; Zürich: Benzier/Neukirche: Neukirchener, 1982), 43–66.

3. For more information concerning this new attitude see their self-critical document "Evangelical Witness in South Africa," *Transformation* (1987).

4. See E. M. Smallwood, *The Jews under Roman Rule* (Leiden: Brill, 1981); *The Romans Debate*, K. P. Donfried, ed. (Minneapolis: Augsburg, 1977), 101–105; F. Cumont, *Oriental Religions in Roman Paganism* (New York: Dover, 1956).

5. R. E. Brown and J. P. Meier, *Antioch and Rome* (London: Chapman, 1983), 96.

6. See E. Bammel and C. F. D. Moule, eds. *Jesus and the Politics of His Day* (London: Cambridge University Press, 1984), 368.

7. Josephus, *Ant* 14, 214–216.

8. Ibid. 20, 195.

9. See Tacitus, Ann, 2. 85. 4.

10. G. E. Wright, discusses this point at length in his article, "The Nations in Israel's Prophecy," *Encounter* 26 (1965): 225–237.

11. I am here informed by Patrick Miller's "The Prophetic Critique of Kings," *Ex Auditu* 2 (1986):82–95.

12. Brevard Childs, *Old Testament Theology in Canonical Context* (Philadelphia, PA: Fortress, 1986), 178.

7

Christianity, Islam, and Politics

A BACKGROUND TO THE CONFLICT

This chapter explores the relation between Christians and Muslims because a substantial population of Africa is Muslim; consequently, Islam is a political, economic, and religious force in Africa. Islam's presence in Africa is widespread; it covers the whole of North Africa and Sahel regions (Egypt, Libya, Tunisia, Algeria, Mauritania, Morocco, Mali, Niger, Chad, Senegal), the Sahara (Gambia, Guinea-Bissau, Guinea Conakry, Nigeria), the Horn of Africa (Ethiopia, Eritrea, Somalia, and Sudan), and East Africa (Tanzania). These countries on the mainland, along with the Comoro Islands in the Indian Ocean, either have a majority Muslim population or is almost half muslim. Other countries have a recognizable following of Islam: Benin, Cameroon, Burkina Faso, Gabon, Kenya, Uganda, Malawi, Democratic Republic of Congo, and South Africa. From this list we see that from North Africa through Saharan West Africa to the Horn of Africa, Islam is very strong.

There are, and have been, Muslim presidents elsewhere in Africa besides North Africa. At independence, Mali, Guinea Conakry, and Niger elected Muslims as their first presidents, and at the time of this writing there are a few presidents who profess Islam: the presidents of Senegal (Abdou Diouf), Sudan (Omar Hassan Al-Bashir), and Malawi (Bakili Muluzi). There have been others in the past in Cameroon (Ahmadou Ahidji), Nigeria (Tafawa Balewa, Shagari, and Ibrahim Babangida), Gabon (Omar Bongo), Niger (Seyni Kountche), Sudan (Nimeiri), Tanzania (Ali Hassan Mwinyi), Zanzibar (Abeid Karume, before the union with Tanganyika), and Uganda (Idi Amin Dada).

Some of these countries belong to the Organization of Islamic Conference and/or League of Arab States, organizations whose aim is to promote Islamic solidarity. Twenty-three African countries are members of the Organization of Islamic Conference (OIC), which was formed on 21 August 1969 at Rabat, Morocco. Heads of state from Islamic countries gathered to find security measures to safeguard holy places such as the Al-Asqu (Jerusalem) Mosque, which had experienced a Jewish arson attack in 1969. The leaders decided to go beyond security issues to find ways to express their cooperation in economic, sociocultural, scientific, and other spheres of common concern. The meeting organized various institutions to address the issues of common interests and concern. Among those is the Islamic Development Bank (IDB), which was established in December 1973. The purpose of the Bank is to stimulate economic development and social progress of member-states and Muslim communities in non-member countries. Many nations in Africa, Muslim and non-Muslim, have become beneficiaries of the IDB programs which include technical assistance, foreign trade financing, and scholarship, among others. In 1989, IDB's assistance to non-member countries in the fields of education, health, and other social programs totaled 18.9 million U.S. dollars, while its scholarship program had helped 293 students in non-member states to study agriculture, medicine, pharmacy, dentistry, and engineering.

Membership in these organizations brings Muslims together, but sometimes it also becomes the source of political divisions, especially when it comes to African-Arab relations such as in the case of Eritrea. In the Eritrian struggle for independence from Ethiopia, African Muslims took the position that current boundaries drawn by Europeans should be kept for fear of the problems that could arise if they were to be redrawn. Arab-Africa, especially Libya, supported Eritrea for it considered the problem to be religious, that is, Muslim Eritrea against Christian Ethiopia. The same positions were taken when Libya claimed Chad as an Arab country. Gaddafy made this point clear at the Arab Peoples Congress held in Tripoli on 20 January, 1981: "There is a large proportion of Arabs among the Chadian people. Eastern and south-eastern Chad is entirely Arab and a large section of the Chadian people are Arab by origin and race, while the overwhelming number are Muslim, and Arab culture is the prevailing culture in Chad. The Chadian people have a specificity very different from all Black African peoples."[1] It was on Muslim-Arab grounds that Libya justified its military intervention in Chad, and its call to mobilize the "Islamic Legion" to do the same in a number of West African states.

The picture of Islam in Africa presented here reveals the political strength of Islam, and economic power, too, for among all the countries that are members of the Organization of Islamic Conference (OIC), only Sudan and Somalia are poor. Given this picture of the presence of Islam in Africa, it will be understood that some political problems in these countries have been caused, or exacerbated by confrontations between Christians and Muslims.

Disagreements over religion are alien to Africa, for religious toleration is a way of life in traditional society, but Christianity and Islam have not learned this important lesson.

There are a number of factors that prevent mutual coexistence between the followers of these religions. Historically, Christians and Muslims have considered each other infidels to be conquered and controlled. Although Islam respects Christianity as a "religion of the book," that is, revealed religion, it nevertheless considers some of the teachings of Christianity false. From the very beginning of Islam, Christianity characterized Islam as a religion of the sword and superstition. Later slave trade was added, a depiction which Christian missionaries in Africa emphasized as they downplayed or ignored the Atlantic slave trade in which Europeans forced thousands of Africans from their homes. The holy wars of Christianity (the Crusades) and Islam *(Jihad)* were rooted in the idea that the other was not a true religion.

In modern Africa, Muslims see Christianity as a bearer of materialism and other negative elements working against society, and especially against *umma*, the community of faith. It is for this reason that Muslims in some African countries want to institutionalize *Shar`ia*, Islamic law, as the law of the land. It must be understood that in Islam law is not negative; it is not prohibition, compulsion, or force, but a guide necessary to life for anyone who willingly submits to the commands and injunctions of Allah (God). These divine injunctions, divinely designed, regulate all aspects of life, from the routine to the philosophical. These injunctions and precepts were followed by Muhammed and his companions. Therefore, to lead a of life of obedience to Allah (God), one must follow the example of the Prophet and his companions. Thus *Shar`ia* includes divine commands, injunctions, and precepts. One of the arguments in favor of instituting *Shar`ia* as the law of the land is that this is the only power that will heal society of the moral bankruptcy resulting from the failure of Christianity and Western Law to provide moral guidance. Christianity has failed to provide the needed moral guidance because it accepts secularism, which by its very nature is anti-faith, and Western law has failed because it is not rooted in faith. Muslims also assert that secularism is part of the Christian heritage and tends to take an anti-Muslim attitude where *Shar`ia* is proposed, such as in Nigeria.

THE SPREAD OF CHRISTIANITY AND ISLAM

Christianity and Islam are now "African" religions in the sense that they have been in Africa since their early days. Some of the first converts to these religions were Africans, and incidently they were from Ethiopia. I have discussed the beginning and growth of Christianity in Africa in another book,[2] therefore I will just make a brief outline of the first centuries. Acts of the Apostles, 2:5 and 10 mention Africans from Libya and Egypt as among the "devout people" present in Jerusalem on the day of Pentecost; and it is recorded in Acts 8:26–40 that first persons to be converted outside Jerusalem were from Ethiopia, an entourage of an Ethiopian royal court official, a treasurer, who was baptized by Philip the Deacon on the latter's way to Gaza. The Coptic Church tradition maintains that Christianity was planted in Egypt by John Mark, the author of the first Gospel, the Gospel According to Mark. He established a church in Alexandria in 42 C.E. (Common Era). From Egypt Christianity expanded west into Libya and beyond. Two centers of learning known as catechetical schools were established in Alexandria and Carthage, and it was from these schools that great contributions were made to Christian doctrine. The southward expansion of the church brought it into Nubia (Sudan) and Aksum (Ethiopia). Although Christianity became a powerful force in Roman Africa, the fall of the empire and the rise of Islam effectively eliminated the Christian presence except for pockets of Coptic Christians in the Nile Valley.

In Islam, it is known that Bilal Ibn Rahab, a freed slave from Ethiopian was not only an early convert but also the first *mu'adhdhin*. Ibn Isaq (704–761) and Ibn Hisham (828 or 833), biographers of the Prophet Muhammad, recorded that when persecution was high in Mecca under the Quarayshite oligarchy, the Prophet sent some of his early converts to Aksum (Ethiopia), on a *hijra* (flight). After the death of Muhammad in 622, and under the caliphate of 'Umar, the second successor of Muhammed, Muslim generals conquered Misr (Egypt) in 642. From Egypt, Islam went west, and in 675 Muslims founded Kairouan, a city in Ifriqiya (part of today's Tunisia), which became a great military and naval base. Kairouan also became a center of Islamic learning and missionary activity into the Western Sahara, the land of the Berbers, an ethnic group comprised of three major groupings, namely, the Lowata, Sanhaji, and Zanata. Through a series of raids and wars, Muslims went from Misr through *al-Maghrib Al-Aqsa* (the west) into Europe, and all the way to France, overrunning Christian institutions on its march.

Islam spread to west Africa, then known as Western Sudan through the trans-Sahara trade which the indigenous Berber had began long before Muslim conquests. In the seventh century, however, Muslim caravan traders, some of whom were Berber, increased the trade by building more commercial centers between north Africa and the regions of ancient Ghana and Kanem-Bornu. Muslim merchants were the missionaries who carried Islam to large areas of west Africa and their missionary work was expanded by Almoravids (a Muslim movement whose aim was to purify Islam) forces who conquered ancient Ghana in 1054, a victory that "led to the political triumph of Islam throughout the Sahel region between Senegal and Niger [rivers]." With this victory, "The Soninke of Ghana were compelled to adopt Islam and they not only did so *en masse* but began to spread it among the many people over whom they still ruled."[3] The fall of ancient Ghana opened the way for Islam to reach Mali, Songhai, Hausa, and Kernem-Bornu on Lake Chad. Muslims not only taught Islam to the conquered but they also introduced Arab culture and civilization, which in time, was integrated into indigenous culture. The Islamization of Western Sudan was possible because among the Muslims who entered the area were Arabs who came with their families to settle as immigrants.

In northeast Africa—Nubia (Sudan), Ethiopia, and Somalia—Islam came earlier on than in West Africa, but its growth was considerably slower. Islam first came to Ethiopia within the lifetime of the Prophet, but the religion did not have an impact in the land till the seventh century when there was penetration into the region from the Red Sea coast through the Dahlak Islands and from Zeila further south. The settlement of Arab traders, teachers, and political refugees along the coast in the neighborhood of Zeila took Islam into the interior where they established some Muslim communities along the Awash River and further south, a process which culminated in the founding of the Sultanate of Shawa, whose founders claimed to be the descendants of the Makhuzumi ethnic group of Mecca.[4] But the earliest centralized state seems to have been Ifat;[5] later states included Dawaro, Futajar, Hadya, and Bali. Three of the four Islamic schools of law called *madhahib*—the Shafi'i, Hanafi, and Maliki—have been represented in Ethiopia from the early days of the religion in that land. The growth of Islam in Ethiopia has been checked because of the strong presence of Christianity, especially since the fourth century when monophysite Christianity became the organized religion of the empire.

Islam came to Ethiopia with Arabs from Mecca, Hijaz, and Yemen, but also from Nubia (or eastern Sudan, roughly the area of modern day Sudan). In Nubia itself, which was Christian, Islam came from Misr (Egypt) but also from western Sudan with Muslims passing through the Nubian territory on their *Hajj* (piligrim to Mecca). For centuries, the relation between Christian Nubia and Muslims was peaceful, but this ended with the increasing number of Muslims from upper Egypt entering the area, settling, and intermarrying with the locals. The real end of Nubia came when general 'Abd All ibn Sa'd ibn Ali Sarh, going south from Egypt, launched an invasion on Nubia. He failed to subdue the Nubians and had to content himself with a treaty of mutual toleration, which he signed with the Nubians in 652.[6] According to the treaty, Nubians would give Arabs 360 slaves a year, in exchange for grain which the latter would give Nubians. While travel was allowed between the two, settlement in each other's territories was prohibited.

Arabs had been in touch with East Africa long before the birth of Islam. The Indian Ocean and Red Sea trade brought Arabs and Africans in contact with each other. The spread of Islam in this region was mostly by Arab traders who had settlements along the coast, and who maintained strong communities on the islands of Zanzibar, Kilwa, and Pemba in the Indian Ocean. For the purposes of trade in slaves and Africa's resources—timber, tortoiseshell, leopard skins, and gold—Arabs from the Persian Gulf and South Arabia settled along the coastal regions of East Africa, from the Somali coast to Lamu, Mombasa, Kilwa, and down to Malindi, and Sofala (land of gold). The Arabs went onto the islands of Zanzibar, Kilwa, and Pemba from where they controlled the lucrative trade of gold, slaves, and ivory until the 1600s when the Portuguese gained control of the area. The Arabs got slaves and African resources from the interior and exported them to Persia, Arabia, and the East to such places as India, Indonesia, and China.

The Portuguese stay in East Africa did not put the Arabs out of business. In spite of Portuguese presence, Arabs continued to make some gains in economic and religious terms, for the propagation of Islam into the interior continued with Arab traders, the Swahili, and their agents, the Yao and Nyawmwezi. When Persians and Arabs settled on the East African coast, they intermarried between themselves but also with the indigenous populations of the coast. From these people came the Swahili, Afro-Arabs who played a critical role in spreading Islam and Arabian culture. The term *sawāhili*, was originally used by the Arabs to refer to coast dwellers, but eventually it became a way of distinguishing non-Arab Muslims from *washezi* (non-Muslims). These Afro-Arab-Persian coastal people developed a cross-bred culture and a new language, Kiswahili, a 40 percent Persian-Arab synthesis with African languages. Swahili became the language of the "civilized" and in the independence era, Swahili was to become the *lingua-franca* of East Africa. It was the Swahili and their agents, the Yao, who carried the religion into the interior, southward to the areas of Lake Malawi. To the west, it was the Nyamwezi who responded to Islam and became trade agents of the Swahili as well as missionaries of Islam.

This brief discussion of the planting of Islam in Africa shows that Islam grew through caravan and ocean trade but also as a result of political forces, particularly in West Africa. In both regions, converts to Islam were mostly town dwellers, residents of commercial centers, and the aristocracy. In West and East Africa, Islam came as a religion of class and power—economic and political. After its victory over Christianity in North Africa, Islam became the dominant foreign religion in Africa; Christianity and Judaism confined to Ethiopia and pockets in the Nile valley. In West Africa, Arab culture blended into indigenous life so much so that Arab food, clothes, family, and social life became part of the daily life of the people. Arabic became widely used throughout the region as the medium of instruction at major centers of learning: Timbuktu, Timbu, Birr, and Gunjur. Arabic was also used in administrative and business transactions. Arab culture was transmitted through Qur'anic schools which were numerous in the region. In East Africa, the Swahili introduced Islam and Arab culture along the coast and also into the interior.

ISLAM UNDER COLONIAL RULE

When Christianity and colonialism came to Africa, Islam and Arabic culture had been well established for centuries. In West Africa, leaders of famous empires had converted to Islam between the thirteenth and fifteenth centuries, with the consequence that their people had become Muslims and part of Arab culture. The Fulani and Hausa are the best examples of those who integrated themselves fully into Arab culture. The Fulani carried out *Jihads* which continued to propagate Islam, and which resulted in the creation of the Sokoto Caliphate, the largest political unit in nineteenth-century West Africa. Under the leadership of Usman dan Fordio, the Fulani in Hausaland carried out a reformist movement to purify the faith which they believed had been corrupted by non-practicing Muslims. The goal of the Fulani was to recreate an Islamic *umma* such as the one that existed during the "Golden Age of Islam," the period of the first four caliphs. With this vision, they established in what was to be Nigeria, "an Islamic world-view as the dominant ideology in the north and the formation of a political and religious governmental system based in emirates during the 19th century were perhaps the most important events. This Sokoto Caliphate came to be seen as part of a sacred history, 'God's Act'."[7] The Caliphate was a confederacy of Muslim *emirates* (states) with religious allegiance to the Amir al-Muminin: "the effective source of all authority and certainly, the common bond which held the components as one polity."[8] The Fulani failed to carry their *Jihad* into Yorubaland and to establish their caliphate there. Nonetheless, by the time the British came to Nigeria, they found a strong African-Islamic social and political culture. In East Africa, too, Europeans found that the Arabs had ruled Zanzibar long before their arrival. In both East and West Africa, Christianity and colonialism found that they had to work with powerful rulers whose subjects had built on strong economic blocks established by Muslims.

The British and the French adopted almost the same policy towards the political and economic powers they had found. French colonial administrators took the attitude that the Arabs were a little bit enlightened, not like Christians, but nonetheless better than Africans still clinging to their indigenous religions. The following quotation drawn from a doctoral dissertation presented at Sorbonne University, France, expresses very well the ideas that might have reinforced the French attitude towards indigenous people of West Africa: "Muslim propaganda is a step forward towards civilization in West Africa, and it is universally recognized that Muslim peoples are superior to those who had remained fetishist, in social organization, intellectual culture, commerce, industry, well being, style of life and education."[9] Knowing also that Islam had already unified the people of West Africa, French colonial administrators wanted to use the religion to consolidate their territorial gains in West Africa. For these two reasons, the French preferred to work with Arabs and Muslims, wherever Muslims cooperated and French interests were not jeopardized. Wherever Muslims showed cooperation, the French gave donations towards building mosques and even financially helped some make the *hajj*. The French also built Médersas, French-Arab colleges to foster cultural exchange through the teaching of French language and culture along with Islamic sciences. The French wanted to create an Islamic elite that would be loyal to them. In most places the French seemed to favor Muslims since they were literate; they could therefore be hired to work in lower ranks of French administration. In cases where the French had Western educated Africans and Muslims, they preferred to work with latter because they considered the non-Muslim a troublemaker. While they preferred to work with Muslims, the French were harsh wherever their interests were threatened, and such is seen in their repressive measures towards the marabouts, whom the officials believed were against them.

Although the British did not have much regard for Muslims as the French, they too seemed to favor the literate Muslims over Africans practicing indigenous religions. The British attitude towards Islam was expressed by Frederick Lugard when he said, "Islam as a militant creed which teaches contempt for those who are not its votaries, panders to the weakness of the African character—self-conceit and vanity."[10] In Nigeria, the British decided that Muslims would be left alone to run their affairs without the interference of the British as long as they administered their areas well. This exemplifies the so called in-direct rule policy advanced by Lugard, the British colonial administrator in Nigeria who served as British High Commissioner for Northern Nigeria 1900–1906. He served as governor of both North and South Nigeria from 1912 to 1914, then became governor-general as the two regions were amalgamated. He retired in 1919. The policy of indirect rule, or as Lugard put it, "direct rule by indirect means,"[11] was a system in which the British used local authorities and institutions for administrative and judicial purposes. British policy was necessitated by two facts: (1) the British did not have enough personnel to carry out administrative work in large areas of the north; and (2) the recognition of the power of the highly stratified Muslim culture in the region. In the system of indirect rule, the emirate was controlled by the emir, who was himself under British supervision.

It was in light of the idea of mutual relationship that the British did not allow Christian missionaries to go into emirates, but let the emirs decide to accept them or not. Defending this policy, Lugard stated: "I hold it that it would be a misuse of power and authority of the Government if that power were used to compel natives of the country to accept a mission which they resented and which they could not accept unless compelled by superior power. I myself am of the opinion that it is unwise and unjust to force missions upon the Muslim population for it must be remembered that without the moral support of the Government the people have some cause to disbelieve the emphatic pledges I have given that their religion shall in no way be interfered with."[12] This policy remained in effect during the first thirty years of colonialism. Except for the regions Christian missionaries had reached before the establishment of colonial rule, Christian missionary progress in the north was slow, so slow that until 1914 there were only 45 churches and 650 students in mission schools.[13] Few emirs who allowed Christian missionaries into their areas, and missionaries blamed the government for the emirs' religious intolerance, a charge which was inaccurate.

Lugard's colonial policy in some ways helped the expansion of Islam, for smaller and weaker non-Muslim traditional rulers were placed under emirs, thus weakening and undermining traditional authority and social organizations. The British idea in prohibiting Christian missionaries was to prevent hostile reaction from Muslim rulers, which they feared could end in an uprising against their rule. In other words, the policy was a concession by the British to the leaders in the north. British policy limited Christian missionaries since they could only work in non-missionary areas or in those few areas where the emir would allow.

This policy was to have an adverse effect on the future of the nation because those who filled junior positions in the colonial government were the Christian mission-trained southerners, for it was the south which had embraced Christianity and Western education and values. Since these southerners controlled the internal affairs of all Nigeria, they were able to channel development projects to their region. The difference between north and south were not just that the north used Arabic and Hausa for business while the south had English, but that colonialism had established a system which underdeveloped the north, and weakened the power and authority of northern rulers by placing them under British control. These grievances did not make for a mutual relationship between the two regions: the north feared the growing economic and political power of the south, which had submitted to white supremacy and religion instead of Allah. Islam came to be viewed as a religion of resistance to submission to colonialism and Christianity; hence the emergence of the north-south or Muslim-Christian tension in Nigeria.

In Sudan, the British reversed their policy of "protecting" the Muslim north; there it was the Christian south which was closed off to Muslims. Technically, Sudan was not a British territory like Nigeria since the control of the land was in the hands of England and Egypt according an agreement signed between the two in January 1899. Despite the agreement, Britain administered the country. Fearing the expansion of Islam as the result of its revival by the Madhi movent, the British prohibited Muslim traders in the south. They established schools and made Sunday a day of rest for the south and Friday for the north.

In East Africa, Tanganyika and Zanzibar to be specific, the Germans followed a different policy. In 1891, Germany took control of East Africa coastal settlements after defeating the Muslims who were ruled by the sultan of Zanzibar. The Germans extended their control to all of Tanganyika by 1898. In their administration of the colony, the Germans appointed local Muslim leaders known as the *alkali* and the *akida*, coastal Swahili speakers. In Zanzibar, the Germans gave preferential treatment to Arabs to whom they offered administrative positions and jobs governing Africans. Initially, the Germans, like the French, considered Islamic culture superior and thought that it could be used to improve the social, moral, and religious condition of Africans. This attitude and German favoritism produced the Arab-African conflict which threatened, stability of German rule. The Germans changed their attitude towards Islam during the Maji-Maji uprising 1905–7, a resistance movement against forced labor on German cotton growing farms. The movement was against German economic imperialism as experienced in Indian, Arab, and Swahili communities but the Germans saw it as Muslim resistance. In 1909, the Germans outlawed *dhikr* (remembrance) ceremonies because they believed that *Qadiriyya tariqa*, a Mulsim brotherhood or order, was fanning Islamic revival on the coast. The ban was rescinded in 1911. The Germans did not last in East Africa for after World War I the administration of the area was given to Britain. The British followed indirect rule, but in place of working with Muslims, they sought those educated in mission schools.

During the brief period the Germans were in East Africa, Islam and Arabic culture made significant gains because of German policy which favored the Swahili (whom they employed as clerks and other positions). The favored status allowed Muslims to carry *da'wa* (mission or invitation, as Muslims would prefer) into the interior, a task that was carried out by Swahili and Arab traders, and the *mwalimu* (Qur'anic teachers). Islamic expansion continued with the work of the brotherhood orders, the *tariqa*, who started coming to East Africa by the turn of the century. Four orders were common in Tanganyika: the *Rifa'yya*, with its roots in Aden, was the oldest and most popular during German occupation; the *Qadiriyya*, was the most popular of the orders—it arrived in Tanganyika in 1929; the *Shadhiliyya*, which originated in the Comoro Islands, was second in popularity, and came towards the end of German colonization; and the *Askariyya* was organized in Dar es Salaam.

CHRISTIANS AND MUSLIMS IN CONTEMPORARY AFRICA

In order to get a better picture of Christian-Muslim relations in postcolonial Africa, we will use two countries, Nigeria and Sudan, as case studies for analyzing the religious factor in national politics. In Sudan and Nigeria religion has been a factor in serious political issues and conflicts. In Sudan, Muslims are the majority, but in the absence of available statistics (due to the sensitivity of demographies in Nigeria) one cannot be unequivocal concerning the claim of a Muslim majority in that country.

Religion in Postcolonial Nigeria

The exploration of political issues in Christian-Muslim relations will begin with a study of the Nigerian situation. Nigeria, the most populated country in Africa, became independent on October 1, 1960, and became a republic in 1963. When the country became independent the new government was modeled on the Westminster parliamentary system. The road to independence began in the north, which had been forced into a union with the south by the British. It is important to recall that when the British came to the north, they had found a well established Muslim confederacy, with an Islamic form of government and judicial system under Islamic culture. There also existed an elaborate Islamic system of education so that most of the people in the Sokoto Caliphate were literate and had reduced Hausa and Fulani in Arabic script. This literacy was to be considered illiteracy once the British came, for even though they knew nothing about Arabic, the British treated the people as uneducated since they had not received British education. Accordingly, the British had more southerners in their administration since there were only a few northerners who had received Western education through Christian mission schools. Mission schools in the north were few because of the British policy of limiting Christian missionaries to non-Muslim areas. The north seemed to have lost a great deal with the British conquest of the north and the subsequent establishment of colonial administration. The north lost sovereignty, for the emirs were supervised by the British and most positions in the new administration were filled by southerners, thus further marginalizing the north; Islamic civilization was threatened with the introduction of Christianity and Western education.

Throughout the colonial era, political power in Nigeria was in the south; not only were the Christian-educated elites in government, but they were also in nationalist movements because opposition to British rule brought the south together. The south's solidarity was not based on common identity but on opposition to colonialism, while union in the north was an outcome of many common elements between the people. Northern opposition was in fact a reaction to political marginalization, which seemed to increase with the rise of nationalist movements in the south. These nationalist movements, formed themselves into political parties in the 1950s, but they were parties established along regional lines. In the north the religious factor came in. The Northern People's Congress (NPC), mostly a Hausa-Fulani party, was dominated by Muslims and supported by emirs and it sought to unite northerners to resist southern domination in government both at the state and federal levels. This party was followed by the Northern Elements Progressive Union (NEPU), again a Hausa-Fulani dominated party, but one which was critical of the NPC and the power elites in the north. Other parties opposing NPC were formed in the non-Muslim south and they were Christian: the Middle Zone League (MZL) and the Middle Belt People's Party, which later changed to the United Middle Belt Congress (UMBC). The MZL was led by a trained pastor and both the MZL and UMBC were supported by Christians in other areas of the north.

With the formation of political parties along regional and religious lines, Nigerian politics began to appear as a Christian-Muslim conflict. Of concern to the northern Muslims was that the educated elite in the south would take over from the British at independence since southerners were already in power. The northerners feared that if such were to happen, resources would be directed to the south, thus further underdeveloping the north. There were fears in the south that they would be persecuted under the leadership of a majority north, and also that there would be massive Islamization of society. Missionaries shared this fear, and this was the major reason for their quick transfer of power and property to African leadership because they believed that in case of a Muslim domination, the churches would have a better chance of survival in African hands. Many political leaders, north and south, feared that religion would be a divisive element in new the political order and it was for this reason that they appealed for unity among all Nigerians. The Sardauma of Sokoto, Ahmadu Bello, made many such appeals during the struggle to independence. In 1959, the Sardauma, who was in the habit of delivering a Christmas message to Christians in the north, thanked Christians for the contribution their schools had made in the north, but he also went on to say: "Families of all creeds and color can rely on these assurances; we have no intention of favoring one religion at the expense of another. Subject to the overriding need to preserve lasting peace and order, it is our determination that everyone should have absolute liberty to practice his beliefs according the dictates of his conscience. . . . Let us forget the difference in our religions and, remembering the common brotherhood before

God, dedicate ourselves to the great tasks which lie before us."[14] Words such as these, repeated in different contexts did manage to ease some anxiety in the south, but the fear of persecution by Muslims did not die out and religion became a major factor in the general elections before independence. The Muslim north aligned itself with the Christian east, leaving the Yoruba in the opposition. The new government shifted power from the Christian south to the Muslim north since it was the NPC which formed the government under the leadership of Ahmadu Bello. The fears Christians had that there would be an Islamization of the country under the leadership of the Muslim north began to be realized. Bello started promoting Islamic identity, and also established relations with Egypt, Kuwait, and Saudi Arabia.

Bello's government lasted only five years, but political reasons rather than religious problems led to its overthrow by the military in 1965. General Nzeogu's coup was "hijacked" in 1966 by Major-General Johnson Aguiyi-Ironsi, whose Unification Decree was interpreted by the north as plan for southern, Igbo Christians, to achieve domination over the Muslim north. Viewed as a southern conspiracy, Ironsi's Unification Decree triggered a series of attacks on the Igbo who were driven out of the north. The Decree did not last, for in the same year another coup took place and brought to power General Yakubu Gowon, a northern Christian from the Middle Belt; a fact Muslims found hard to take, and which in some ways led to the division of the country into twelve states (six in the north) for equal representation in a federal form of government. This did not ease tensions between the north and the Igbo; a civil war ensued in 1967 and it lasted three years under the leadership of Colonel Odumegwu Ojukwu who wanted Biafra to secede. The civil war was not over religion but the south described it as such.

Since the Biafran war, Nigeria has gone through a number of governments, military and civilian, and with more leaders coming from the Muslim north than from the Christian south. That has been a point of concern for the south because of the tendency of northern leaders to attempt to Islamize the nation. Two issues that have emerged in this regard are secularism and *Shar'ia* courts, the latter perceived by Muslims as a solution to the former. The issue that has raised controversy and a heated debate between Christians and Muslims has centered on the nature of the modern state. Secularism as discussed within the Nigerian context does not refer to the positivist or sociological understanding according to which religion or the sacred is gradually relegated to the private sphere so that it no longer dictates activities in the political realm. This view is based on evolutionary theory in religion first proposed by Comte, the French philosopher, and advanced by James Frazer, of the British school of anthropologists. Comte, followed by Frazer, believed that religion was midway between superstition and science, with science being the highest form of human cognition. Comte believed that superstition is the first step in finding answers concerning human existence, but as human cognition and knowledge develops, this level is superseded by religion. However religion fails to provide answers, therefore people turn to science, a higher level of knowledge. Once science replaces religion, then religion no longer serves as the glue that holds society together—as Emile Durkheim would say—it is therefore relegated to private life.

In Nigeria secularism has little relation to this theory whereby religion is replaced by science; the debate is whether religion should be private in the sense that it should not be allowed to influence the running of the state—this is the idea of the separation of religion and politics. This is the bone of contention between Muslims and Christians, for Muslims feel that secularism has serious political implications. The Christian-Muslim debate on the secular state has a long history in Nigeria, but let us just point out that article 11 of the Constitution of 1979 says that Nigeria is a secular state. Muslims have political and theological problems with the idea of a secular state. To begin with, Muslims consider secularism as a Christian attempt to control them, a continuation of the European rule since colonialists and Christian missionaries had an agenda which was almost identical. It cannot be denied, so Muslims maintain, that the colonial government was informed and guided by Christian principles. The colonial government was Christian: the calendar it followed was Christian, and its education system was based on Christian principles. Thus to argue, as Christians do, that secularism refers to neutrality of the government, is not at all true; secularist neutrality is a myth, for Christianity in Africa worked hand in hand with Western imperial power. Therefore, they see the secularist argument as necessary to maintain European-Christian hegemony in countries with a Muslim majority. Muslims contend that the idea of separation of religion (church) and state, is itself rooted in the Christian/Western heritage, but it does not work in a religiously pluralistic society for it tends to be prejudicial, as attested by the fact that the colonial government attacked Muslim social and political institutions including law and education.

Muslims believe the separation of religion and state leads to moral decadence in society, therefore only *Shar`ia*, divine injunctions and positive law, can curb the moral decline. The failure of national governments and their political and legal institutions, modeled on Western political paradigms, sharpens the need for a government based on *Shar`ia*. The Muslim agenda for resisting secularism is twofold: (1) to increase the number of adherents through mass or wide-scale conversion; (2) to close ranks within the *Umma* (faith community) by raising consciousness of Islamic life so as to show what is at stake in the secularist debate, and strategize accordingly on religious and political approaches to the controversy. Christians reject the accusation that the secularist debate is necessary for Western-Christian superiority and dominance in political, economic, and social organization. On the contrary, Christians perceive the call for *Shar`ia* as an attempt to subordinate non-Muslims and to Arabize society and culture.

The debate over *Shar`ia* came to a head during the rule of General Obasanjo, when a proposal was made for an Islamic judicial system to be applied throughout the country. It is to be recalled that *Shar`ia* had been enforced in the Muslim north since the fourteenth century, going back to the time of dan Fordio who introduced *Shar`ia* in accordance with the teachings of the Prophet. According to the Prophet, the head of an Islamic community, *umma*, was to be an imam, caliph or emir, who was both a religious and civil leader. Below him would be: *waziri*, head of justice and an advisor to the caliph; next would be the *kadi*, a person with impeccable character, versed in *Shar`ia*, but a man knowledgeable in worldly wisdom; the *nazir al-mazalim* would be the last level. Dan Fordio set his caliphate on a strict and firm *Shar`ia* path so that the Caliphate of Sokoto was second only to Saudi Arabia and Afghanistan.

When the British reached Hausaland, they found *Shar`ia* being widely used, so when they defeated the Hausa-Fulani Muslim rule in 1902, they decided not to abolish *Shar`ia* and the judicial system of the north, instead they introduced some reforms in 1947 and 1958.[15] The first two constitutions of independent Nigeria (1960 and 1963) included *Shar`ia* court of appeal and Islamic law. The Constitutional Assembly of 1976-78 upheld the idea of maintaining *Shar`ia* courts of appeal in states which required them, but that did not sit well with either Christians or Muslims. For Christians, the Assembly did not take into account the presence of Christians in the south. There were some Muslims, especially members of the Muslim Committee for a Progressive Nigeria (MCPN) who agreed with the Christian opposition. These were socialists, Marxists to be specific, led by Yusuf Bala Usman, and they saw religion as divisive and as an instrument of minority feudal emirs to oppress the powerless. The *Shar`ia* debate was about more than courts, it also included other issues, the most important of which were: the separation of religion and state, the nature of the Nigerian federation, and freedom of both Muslims and Christians to practice their religions. Underlying these problems were other deeper issues, namely, political and economic, for whichever religion controlled the courts also controlled the government, thus controlling the bureaucracy that decides the distribution of national wealth. A compromise was then worked out which stated that a Chamber would be provided in the Federal Courts of Appeal for appeals from *Shar`ia* state courts. The compromise did not please Muslims who demanded that *Shar'ia* be on the federal level. Ninety-three Muslim members of the Constituent Assembly withdrew when the Assembly endorsed the compromise on *Shar`ia*. The members returned only after President Obasanjo intervened, appealing for peace since there were protests in the north against the compromise.

Another issue that produced a heated debate between Christians and Muslims was enshrined in Decree 6, which set up the Nigerian Pilgrims Commission. Decree 6, passed by the military government in 1975 authorized subsidizing the *Hajj* and also handling transportation and accommodation of pilgrims. The *Hajj* is a big event in Nigeria; in 1977 there were more than 100,000 pilgrims to Mecca. When the military government handed power to civilians, and Shehu Shagari, a northerner candidate of the NPN (successor of NPC), formed government of the Second Republic, he chose Alexander Ekweueme, a Christian from the south, as vice president. Shagari, who had entered the presidency with a promise of religious neutrality found himself faced with religious lobbyists and pressure groups. He extended Decree 6 to subsidize Christian pilgrims, and his government gave Christians and Muslims 10 million Naira each to build a national cathedral and mosque in Abuja, the capital. Shagari invited the pope to visit, and the pontiff came to Nigeria in February 1982; and in April, Runcie, the Archbishop of Canterbury, visited Nigeria.

Shagari was elected to a second term of office amid voting irregularities. To the Muslim north, Shagari had failed to advance Islam but instead had shown favoritism to Christians, but his attempt to establish a Department of Islamic Affairs made Christians charge him with favoritism, too. He dropped the idea of forming the Department of Islamic Affairs and instead introduced National Guidance. Religious unrest, attributed to Islamic revivalism of the Maitastine Movement appeared in the north in 1983. Thousands of people died in these unrests and some statistics put the number of dead at Kano to as high as 6,000. The army and air force were sent to put down the unrest, which ended with its leader Muhammed Marwa being killed. The rioters claimed to have rebelled because the state had become corrupt. Shagari was overthrown on 3 December, 1983, in a military coup led by General Muhammadu Buhari, a Muslim from the north. One of the priorities of Buhari's government was to pay compensation to victims of religious disturbances but also to set a tribunal of inquiry to investigate the causes of those disturbances. Shagari before him, had also a called tribunal of inquiry to investigate Kano disturbances of 1980; under Major-General Ibrahim Babanginda a tribunal of similar nature was also set to investigate religious disturbances that took place in March 1987, in Kafanchan, Kaduna state. Buhari introduced economic austerity policies. To reduce government spending and to control foreign exchange reserves, he decided to cut down the number of pilgrims to Mecca from 70,000 to 10,000, and to limit the amount of money taken out for the *Hajj* to 800 Naira, while other citizens were allowed only 100 Naira. Heavy criticism of the "Presidential Allocation" as the measure was called, came from Muslims who saw Buhari as against the *Hajj*, a very important religious experience required for Muslims who can afford it. Christians did not say much about the allocation, but soon Buhari introduced a measure that was to make Christians angry too: his Supreme Military Council carried out a suggestion that had been made by Shagari's government, namely, abolishing Easter Monday as a public holiday. Christians opposed the measure with sufficient force that the action was rescinded.[16]

By 1986, Buhari's government had become unpopular because it had failed to carry out the reforms that it had promised, and it failed to satisfy Christians as well as Muslims. The stage was set for another coup. Major-General Ibrahim Babanginda, a Muslim, took the reins of power and promised neutrality of the state. Babanginda's regime was dominated by political issues with religious roots. In January 1986, Babanginda set up a political bureau to study political possibilities for the future of the country. After consulting with Nigerians on *Shar'ia*, the bureau recommended to Babanginda's government that the existing system be retained. The current arrangement was that a state could establish *Shar'ia* court of appeal and that appeals could be from a state *Shar'ia* court of appeal to the Federal Court of Appeal. The issue was not closed when the military government accepted the recommendation from the new Constituent Assembly sitting in Abuja, the federal capital, to set up a state Judicature Committee. The "*Shar'ia* Committee," as it was popularly known, became a forum for Christian and Muslim extremists who argued strongly for and against *Shar'ia*. Christians invoked Section 11 of the 1979 Constitution which stated that Nigeria was a secular state, but Muslims asked whether it was proper to impose on unwilling Muslims a legal system based on Western Judeo-Christian principles. For Christians on the other hand, the question was whether *Shar'ia* is compatible with democracy. Muslims in the forum were supported by the Council of Ulama of Nigeria. The debate was getting nowhere; Babanginda set up an Elders Committee to settle matters, but the Elders failed. Fearing a religious crisis, Babanginda sent Augustus Aikhomo, Vice-Admiral and Chief of General Staff, to Abuja to intervene.

Nigeria had been an observer in the Organization of Islamic Conference (OIC) since 1970, but in 1986 Nigeria secretly changed its observer status to full membership. The matter had been carried out with such secrecy that even the Chief of General Staff did not know anything about it. Nigerians learned of their membership in OIC through the press, first through a French news agency and then the domestic press. When the matter was known, there was confusion among government officials about the admission. Christians were enraged that the matter was never announced and that the people had never been given an opportunity to debate the issue. Christians denounced the government's move arguing that it had no right to take Nigeria into any religious organization. Muslims saw the secret application for membership in the OIC as the Babanginda government's move back into the Muslim fold after having leaned too much towards Christians. Muslims also saw the economic benefits that would derive from the organization as the result of the membership. Politically, the secret membership to OIC poisoned what had seemed like a religious tolerance of sorts since the 1976 *Shar`ia* debate in the Constituent Assembly, which had threatened a division of the country along religious lines. As in 1976, extremists on both sides marshalled arguments for withdrawal from the federation. Realizing that the move had aroused strong feelings on both sides, Babanginda in February 1986, appointed a twenty-four member panel with equal numbers of Muslims and Christians to study the implications of the membership and to further explore how the government could best assist the country in religious and spiritual development. Increasing pressure on the government made Babanginda establish an Advisory Council on religious affairs. The function of the Religious Affairs Council, formed in January 1987, was to seek ways of understanding for people of various religions and "to regulate activities of all religious groups and promote dialogue among them."[17]

This is a brief discussion of political problems caused or exacerbated by religious factors. There were more incidents of religious crisis in Nigeria in the 1980s than in the 1970s. There was only one notable religious crisis in the 1970s; it occurred at a girls secondary school in the north, and that seemed to have opened the door for more in the 1980s. In December 1980, there was a religious crisis caused by activities of the Maitatsine or Yan Tatsine sect which organized systematic riots. Other religious disturbances happened at Maiduguri in 1982, at Yola in 1984, Gombe in 1985, and the largest one occurred in Kaduna state in March 1987. Except for the 1987 crisis, disturbances were caused by Islamic revivalists led by Maitastine. The reports of the tribunal of inquiries set to investigate the causes of these disturbances came to the conclusion that except for the 1987 crisis, the rest had been motivated by the idea of purging Islam from the corrupt state into which it had degenerated in Nigeria. The reports said students were involved in all these religious upheavals, and they and the Maitatsine movement, were inspired by the revolutionary theology of Iran. The 1987 crisis was ignited by Christian extremists who disparaged the *Qur'an* while proselytizing at Teachers Training College, Kafanchan. The riots that ensued quickly spread to other areas, and in Zaria alone, over forty churches were destroyed. All these religious disturbances took place in the north, a point which shows that the religious issue is not just the north versus the south but two Semitic religions against each other.

It would be interesting to discuss the revivalist or fundamentalist movements in Islam and Christianity in Nigeria, but that is outside the scope of the present work, I will simply mention that the resurgence of such movements (and Muslim brotherhoods) partly accounted for the rise in religious intolerance in Nigeria in the 1980s. Even in the *Shar`ia* crisis, it was extremists on both sides who threatened to bring the country to civil war. During the impasse on the debate on *Shar`ia*, and after a compromise had been reached, members of the Muslim Students Society in the north, and especially at Ahmadu Bello University, Zaria, continued to demonstrate and shout "No *Shar`ia*, no peace! No *Shar`ia*, no constitution! *Shar`ia* is the only answer!" They saw the question of *Shar'ia* as a way to establish an Islamic state, but also as a form of *Jihad*, after the manner of dan Fordio. Christian militants on the other hand, called it a crime to impose *Shar`ia* on people who did not want to submit to it. To mention religious extremists is not, however, to charge them as the sole cause of religious upheavals in Nigeria. On the contrary, the religious issue has always been latent, waiting for a trigger to erupt. Given this situation, a whole range of reasons, including discontent of the young with the deteriorating moral, political, and economic situation, has given vent to the pressure in society; the weak lines along which it has exploded have been religion.

Before concluding this section, let us go back to the question whether *Shar`ia* is compatible with democracy. The answer is that under a strict application of *Shar`ia*, perhaps a democratic process and form of government may not be possible for there would be a hierarchical arrangement which would put Muslims at the top, with full legal rights and access to public office. Next would be the *ahl al-kitab*, those who believe in God according to revealed scripture or within "divinely revealed religions," that is, religions with revealed scripture with primary reference to Jews and Christians. Those would be given *dhimma*, a grantee of security of their person and property, freedom to practice their religion and law on personal matters. These freedoms would be given to the *dhimmi* in return for willingly submitting to Muslim sovereignty and as a token of their submission, they would agree to pay a poll tax or *jizya*. The *dhimmi* are not citizens but subjects, therefore they have no right to participate in government of the state. People whose religion is not considered revealed, indigenous religions, for example, would not enjoy the privileges given to the *dhimmi*, but they would be allowed to stay in an Islamic state on the basis of good conduct, *aman*, and after a year of residence with good conduct they would be treated as *dhimmi*.

Under *Shar`ia*, justice is divided in three divisions: offenses which demand strict punishments according to the stipulation of *Qur'an* or the *sunna* (the practices of the Prophet), the *hudud*. In such cases, neither the judge nor the victim is allowed to change the specified punishment in the *Qur'an* or the *sunna*. Included in this category are: theft, robbery, fornication, unproven accusation of fornication, and drinking (alcohol), but also apostasy and rebellion. The second category of cases covers inflicting bodily harm, whose judgment may be retaliation by the victim or monetary payment for restitution. These are known as *Qisas*. The last class of cases of offenses fall under *ta'zir*, cases whose punishment is not prescribed by either the *Qur'an* or the *sunna*, but is under the discretionary powers of the ruler or his representative.

CHRISTIANS AND MUSLIMS IN SUDAN

Religion has featured highly in the political crisis in Sudan, Africa's largest country. Unlike Nigeria, Christianity and Islam were in Sudan for centuries before colonization. When we discussed the Islamization of Africa it was mentioned that Nubians signed a treaty with Ibn Ali Sarh according to which the Nubians would give 300 slaves annually to the Arabs in exchange for grain. This treaty prevented Islam from moving further south of Sudan. Islam was not the first Semitic religion to penetrate Nubia, Christianity came first, in the sixth century. Concerning the presence of Christianity in Sudan, I have written in *Drums of Redemption* that Egyptian missionaries brought Christianity to Nobatia, Mukurra, and Aloa between the years 543–580. "The first missionary to go south from Alexandria was Julian. He was a presbyter (elder) of the Church who preached the Gospel to Nubians (Sudanese). In 543 Julian of Alexandria got permission from Empress Theodora of Constantinople to evangelize the Nubians. The Empress was happy with Julian's mission because it lessened border conflict and at the same time brought the Nubians into her empire. Julian was a missionary for two years."[18] Nubians built a strong Christian community which became monophysite following their Coptic neighbors to the north. When Egypt was overrun by the conquering Muslims, Nubia was cut off from the Christian world, and for six hundred years continued to survive on its own. "It was not until the thirteenth century that Saladin, an Egyptian Muslim ruler, conquered Nubia. . . . Although Nubia fell to Saladin in 1275, Christian influence continued for some time. For example, Soba did not become Muslim until 1504, and according to reports of Portuguese travelers in the sixteenth century, Christians in this region were seeking help from the king of Abyssinia."[19] The church used Nubian in its liturgy and literature and it also developed its own architecture and art suitable to the country. The influence of Nubian Christianity reached as far west as Lake Chad and Nubian pilgrims were recorded in Jerusalem.

The Christian kingdoms of Nubia maintained their independence for seven centuries before they lost to Islam, but even then both religions coexisted peacefully. Islam rose to dominance under the rule of Egypt Funj, the Sultanate of the Nile Valley (1517–1821) and the Dar Fur Sultanate (1650-1916). The rise of Islam to power is attributed to the Ottoman who were ruling Egypt and they extended their influence into the Nile Valley. It was during the rule of the Ottoman that the state began to reflect Islamic influences, and *Shar`ia* started to be practiced in private and personal law, although it was not applied universally. The Ottoman took the same approach to *Shar'ia* in Egypt throughout their rule there. The Turks continued to rule, except for a brief time at the end of the eighteenth century when British and French troops vied for power in the region. When the British left in 1802, Muhammad Ali Pash took control of the region and by 1805 he had established his authority. Neither Muhammad Ali Pash nor the Turco-Egyptian rulers introduced a universal and strict application of *Shar'ia*; that was done by Muhammad Ahmad ibn Abdullahi in his capacity as *Mahdi*, the chosen and guided one of Allah, ordained to purify Islam. The Mahdi set to purge Islam and rectify the believers through a religious and political revolution (1881-84) which ended with the capture of Khartoum and the establishment of an Islamic state in northern Sudan. In the middle of 1885, six months after the death of the *Mahdi*, Ta'ishi Abdullah ibn Muhammad, or Khalifa Abdullah, took office as the successor of the Madhi. He captured Khartoum and advanced Mahdist rule into the south. The rule was unpopular, and to keep themselves in power, the Mahdist rulers imprisoned or executed the native authorities. These abuses of power galvanized the people against the Mahdist rulers and made the north collaborate with Anglo-Egyptian effort to recapture Khartoum, which happened in 1898, thus establishing the Anglo-Egyptian Condominium in January 1899.

During the administration of the Condominium, Islam was excluded for fear that its influence in Sudanese politics might be negative. But the Anglo-Egyptian alliance did not hold because in the 1920s the British began to fear the growing influence of Egypt in Sudan. The British turned to Abd al-Rahman (and his Ansar Brotherhood), the son of the Mahdi, urging him to assume a political role in order to offset the growing Egyptian power. The Egyptians too, chose their own man for the politics of Sudan, al-Sayyid Ali al-Mirghani and his Khatmiya brotherhood. Through British-Egyptian political games, Islam was brought center stage although it had initially been excluded in Sudanese politics. The British and the Egyptians created the two political parties in northern Sudan: Umma Party (UP), of the followers of Abd al-Rahman, and the National Unionist Party (NUP) of the Khatmiya brotherhood. In various political configurations, these parties have ruled Sudan since the country's independence in 1956, and these parties have been the force behind the transitional constitutions of 1956, 1964, and 1985.

THE POLITICAL STRUGGLE

The Anglo-Egyptian control of Sudan ended on 1 January 1956, the date of the country's independence. By the time the country became independent, a civil war had already started in 1955 when the Equatorial Corps, the southern battalion, mutinied. The mutiny paved the way for the three non-

Islamic regions of the south, Upper Nile, Equatorial and Bahr el-Ghazal to fight to be on their own. The rebellion of the south, commonly called *Anya Nya* was to last seventeen years. The independence constitution did not help matters between the south and the north for the Constitution of 1956 declared that Islam would be the main source of legislation, although Christianity and Judaism were also cited as important sources. In the colonial era, the Christian south was protected, but this was no longer the case with the new constitution; actually, the constitution prepared a way for the government to set a policy that would make Islam and Arab culture dominant in the country. The first government was ousted by Abboud in 1958, and he ruled until 1964. He launched a vigorous plan to Islamize Sudan. Islamic schools were built in many places in the south; the rest day was changed from Sunday to Friday without any consultation with the south; and in 1962 the government introduced a new "Missionary Act" which was intended to check the spread of Christianity in the south. These activities were seen by the south as an attempt to Islamize and Arabize them, in spite of their insistence to keep their own culture and institutions. Besides these issues, the south saw the government of Abboud excluding them from the political process and power, but also not sharing equally the economic benefits of the country thus making the south underdeveloped.

There were no advances towards peace until March 1965, when for the first time since 1955, a roundtable conference was called in Khartoum to discuss the problems between the north and the south. The dialogue ended in a deadlock because the northern political parties were unwilling to grant the south autonomy within a Sudan federation. The discussions having fallen through, the northern political parties, UP and NUP, joined forces along with Islamic Charter, a fundamentalist group, to form a united front in a kind of *Jihad* against dissidents and communists in the north, and the secessionist south. As in 1958, the UP and NUP supported a 1968 draft constitution which sought to implement *Shar`ia*. This seemed possible in 1968 since the Constituent Assembly was dominated by the members of these two parties they managed to amend the constitution, ban communist activities, and communist Members of Parliament lost their seats to which they had been "democratically" elected. Having amended the constitution, leaders of the UP, NUP, the National Islamic Front, and the Muslim Brotherhood started advocating a move towards an Islamic constitution and Arab culture. Pushing this agenda, Hassan el-Turabi, leader of the Muslim Brotherhood argued that "The South has no culture; so this vacuum would necessarily be filled by an Arab culture under an Islamic revival."[20]

Both UP and NUP argued that *Shar`ia* applied in Sudan would fully recognize and safeguard the citizenship and rights of non-Muslims. This position seemed not to be supported by Articles 1 and 2 of the draft Islamic Constitution which stated that Sudan would be a "democratic, socialist republic based on the guidance of Islam" and that Islam would be the official religion. This position, was a move away from the 1956 Constitution which recognized other revealed religions. The southern members of the constitution committee objected to these constitutional changes which aimed at changing the running of the country but also changing southern culture. They finally walked out of the constitution drafting committee. The views of southern members of the committee were expressed by Abel Alier when he said that "We did not wish to be a party to a document that emphasized the Arab race, Islamic religion and Arab culture to the exclusion of other existing religions and cultures."[21]

The withdrawal of southern members from the drafting committee seemed to be heading the country into a constitutional crisis. Army officers took power in a *coup d'etat* staged on 25 May 1969. Colonel Jaffar Muhammed Nimeiri became the leader of the Revolutionary Council, thus the President of Sudan. Nimeiri got support from communists, and as one of his first steps as head of state he declared (on 9 June) that his government would promote diversity of cultures and beliefs. Following this ideology of diversity of beliefs, he attacked Aba Island, the stronghold of the Ansar sect, the fundamentalist element in UP. Imam el-Hadi al-Mahdi, the leader of the group, was killed in the assault upon the island. Nimeiri also declared the Muslim Brotherhood the enemy number one of the "May-Revolution." Concerning the civil war, Nimeiri sought a political settlement, but before a settlement was reached in the south his communist allies sought to oust him in a coup, which he narrowly escaped in 1971. Nimeiri had been an advocate of scientific socialism, but his communist supporters had seen him as putting the socialist agenda on the back burner and focusing on the political settlement of the civil war, which they considered as essentially an issue that could be solved by implementing socialist ideas. Once Nimeiri regained control, he killed many of the communists leaders, thereby ending his relationship with the communists.

Nimeiri then moved on with the political solution to the civil war. He allowed the World Council of Churches to mediate peace with the Sudan Liberation Movement. An agreement was reached on February 1972, and the Addis Ababa treaty was signed, giving the south regional autonomy. This autonomy included freedom from the enforcement of *Shar`ia*, having a regional president and a legislature, which required having a two-thirds majority before any changes to the agreement could be made. In addition, the agreement stipulated that the customs of the south would be respected. The only two areas in which the south would not be independent were foreign affairs and military installations. In March 1972, the agreement took effect and the civil war seemed to be over.

Having minted the Addis Ababa peace treaty, and with the war over, Nimeiri turned to constitutional matters and in 1973 the first Permanent

Constitution was enacted. On matters of religion, the new constitution declared that all heavenly religions, traditional beliefs and customs were crucial sources of legislation. The constitution also declared all people equal under the law, and it prohibited discrimination based on ethnic and cultural heritage. Even more important for the south, the Addis Ababa Agreement was incorporated into the Permanent Constitution.

Right from its early days, Nimeiri's regime did not get the support of the north. His anti-fundamentalist ideas, socialist sympathy, and his concessions to the south crowned in the Addis Ababa Agreement, worsened his position with traditional parties and the Muslim Brotherhood. In addition to having to deal with internal dissatisfaction, Nimeiri also had to deal with military and political opposition by Sudanese leaders outside the country. In 1977 Nimeiri decided to neutralize his opposition and consolidate his power; he signed an agreement of national reconciliation and he invited leaders of the Umma and Unionist parties as well as the Muslim Brotherhood to join the cabinet and the central committee of the ruling Socialist Union. Umma and the Muslim Brotherhood joined but the Unionists refused the offer. Within a few months, Umma left the government, but the Muslim Brotherhood went in with full force, entering the executive and legislative branches of government. Nimeiri appointed Turabi, leader of the Muslim Brotherhood to chair a committee charged with bringing the laws of Sudan in line with Islamic law. This move was aimed at pacifying Muslim Brothers who seemed to be gaining popularity with their push for Islamizing the country. In the meantime, however, Nimeiri developed his own plan for Islamizing Sudan. Nimeiri started embracing the idea of Islamizing Sudan because he needed the Muslim support since he had lost his strong support in the south. Problems had developed in the south as the result of his presidential decree to divide the region into three as a way of settling disagreements within the leadership there.[22] Nimeiri did not follow the stipulations of the Addis Ababa Agreement in passing his decree. The regional government had been dissolved in 1980 because of the disagreements among the southern leaders. A few months after his decree, Nimeiri used his presidential decree to establish *Shar'ia* as the law of the land in Sudan in September 1983.

The way *Shar'ia* was practiced as public law in Sudan under Nimeiri affirmed the worst fears of those against Islamic law, and even Muslims did not like Nimeiri's Islamic laws. After proclaiming *Shar'ia* as the law in Sudan, Nimeiri set a committee of lawyers to make changes in the legal system to match the stipulations of Islamic law. The areas which were affected by these changes included the Penal Code, the Code of Criminal Procedure, the Judiciary Acts, and Evidence Acts. In the Penal Code new penalties were added, among them were flogging, amputation of limbs, retribution, and crucifixion. These additional punishments were to be adhered to strictly, even crucifixion, the most well-known case of it being that of

Usatadh Mahmoud Mahammed Taha, the leader of the Republic Brotherhood and a scholar of Islamic law, who was executed on 18 January 1985, for advocating reform of *Shar`ia*. His argument was that there are two aspects of *Shar`ia*, one which speaks of eternal and universal justice and equality regardless of race, creed, and gender. The second aspect, and in which he interpreted the current practical implementation *Shar`ia*, teaches relative and transitional justice, that is, justice according to the quality of faith.[23] Mahmoud Taha maintained that the era for the second aspect of *Shar`ia* had passed, and that the time had come for implementing the universal dimension of *Shar`ia* where justice does not depend on the nature of faith. *Shar`ia* courts of Nimeiri interpreted this teaching as apostasy, whose punishment according to Islamic law is death by execution.[24]

Many people, Muslims included, felt that the courts under Nimeiri had been over zealous and harsh in their interpretation of *Shar`ia*, Islamic jurisprudence, and in administering penalties stipulated by *Shar`ia*—Mahmoud Taha's sentence was a case point. The Penal Code penalties introduced under *Shar`ia* prohibited execution of a pregnant woman, a breast-feeding mother, or persons over 70 years, yet the provision was not followed when Mahmoud Taha was convicted. Although the right of appeal was granted to individuals, the process was not very helpful because of the hasty manner in which the proceedings were done, beginning with the "Courts of Instant Justice" which Nimeiri Islamic laws had introduced.

To bring Sudan more in line with the principles of an Islamic state and jurisprudence, Nimeiri asked the National Assembly to carry out a range of constitutional amendments. Among the amendments were those that affected the south: the region lost its autonomy and it was no longer considered a single unit for it was divided into three regions. The division was supported by many Muslims because they always saw a united south as a barrier to an Islamic state. Nimeiri's constitutional changes also included replacing article 16 which stated that Sudan "shall endeavor to express the values of Islam and Christianity and show respect for the noble aspects of spiritual life."[25] The replacement for article 16 read "The Democratic Republic of Sudan is a unitary and sovereign Islamic republic."[26] In addition, the Islamic constitution would allow Nimeiri to be head of state by "divine right." Muslims saw Nimeiri's introduction of Islamic law as a political move to gain their support for Nimeiri to remain in power. Sadiq el-Madhi, leader of Ansar Brotherhood and grandson of the Madhi, denounced Nimeiri's introduction of Islamic law and administration of its punishments. His position was that the introduction of the law should have been preceded by Islamic education and that justice should prevail first. He further maintained that Nimeiri was not the person to have instituted Islamic laws in Sudan.[27] After a year of military rule, al-Madhi became Prime Minister in the first free election in 18 years, although voting was postponed in 37 constituencies in the south. Al-Madhi's government was ousted in June 1989 in a military coup led by Omar Hassan al-Bashir.

The Islamization of the constitution became a major concern for the non-Muslim south. Church leaders wrote a petition to Nimeiri expressing the threat that the south felt with the Islamization of the constitution. They said that an Islamic constitution "will be detrimental to the rights of individuals; detrimental to the equality before the law; detrimental to the administrative of justice in a society with a multiplicity of racial, ethnic and religious groupings."[28] The Christian south vigorously opposed the imposition of *Shar`ia* on the grounds that it abrogated their citizenry rights. Also strongly opposed to the Islamization of the law was the Sudan People's Liberation Movement (SPLM), an organization seeking national unity and a democratic secular state in Sudan. The SPLM maintains that the unity of Sudan can only come about by abolishing all forms of discrimination in the country and by liberating the south. Discontent from both Muslims and Christians with Nimeiri's Islamic laws, resulted in his overthrow on 5 April 1985, when he was on a state visit to the United States of America. Niemeiri's successor did not continue with the Islamization of the constitution.

CONCLUSION

It is virtually impossible to discuss in full the political problems that have emerged in Africa resulting from the encounter between these two Semitic religions. In this chapter we only looked at some of the major issues concerning the implementation of *Shar`ia* as public law, and the move towards Islamization of the state. It is true that for the most part, Muslims in non-Islamic states live under laws based on or heavily influenced by Christian ideals. Adherents of indigenous religions have to fight both Semitic religions for their survival and identity. A move to establish Islamic law raises the problem of democracy and citizenry rights as demonstrated in Nimeiri's Sudan. It is also questionable whether a real Islamic state, following strict application of *Shar`ia* is possible without the Islamization of the people, a problem made more complex by the multiplicity of cultures and faiths in modern Africa. On the other hand, is it possible for a Muslim to live his or her life according to the tenants of Islam as found in the Qur'an and the *Sunnah* in a "secular state" and particularly when the state is more inclined towards Christian values? Followers of Christianity and Islam must learn to live together, but will laws be able to reflect the values of these religions and indigenous religions as well? These are difficult issues and they will continue to impact politics in Africa for a long time to come.

NOTES

1. Quoted by Omari H. Kokole, "Religion in Afro-arab Relations: Islam and Cultural Changes in Modern Africa," in *Islam in Africa: Proceedings of the Islam in Africa Conference*, Nura Alkali, Awwal Yadudu, Rashi Motem, Haruna Sahili, eds. (Ibadan: Spectrum Books, 1993), 244.
2. See Harvey J. Sindima, *Drums of Redemption: An Introduction to African Christianity* (Westport, CT: Greenwood Press, 1994), chap. 1–5.
3. J. Spencer Trimingham, *A History of Islam in West Africa* (London: Oxford University Press, 1962), 29–30.
4. J. Spencer Trimingham, *Islam in Ethiopia* (New York, NY: Barnes and Noble, 1965), 58.
5. I. M. Lewis, ed. *Islam in Tropical Africa* (London: Oxford University Press, 1966), 38.
6. J. Spencer Trimingham, *Islam in the Sudan* (London: Oxford University Press, 1949), 61.
7. Peter B. Clark and Ian Linden, *Islam in Modern Nigeria* (Munchen: Grundwald Kaiser, 1984), 12.
8. R. A. Adeleye, *Power and Diplomacy in Northern Nigeria 1804–1966: The Sokoto Caliphate and its Enemies* (London: Longman, 1977), 38.
9. D. Cruise O'Brine, "Towards an Islamic Policy in French West Africa," *Journal of African History*, 8 (1967): 303.
10. Frederick D. Lugard, *The Dual Mandate in British Tropical Africa* (London: Oxford University Press, 1922), 223.
11. Ibid., 77.
12. Frederick D. Lugard, *Political Memoranda 1913–1918* (London: Oxford University Press, 1919), 124.
13. R. A. Adeleye, *Power and Diplomacy in Northern Nigeria 1804–1966: The Sokoto Caliphate and its Enemies* (London: Longman, 1977), 159.
14. John N. Paden, *Ahmadu Bello. Sardauma of Sokoto. Values and Leadership in Nigeria* (London: Hodder and Stroughton, 1986), 305.
15. For those reforms see J. N. Anderson, "Return Visit to Nigeria: Judicial and Legal Developments in the Northern Region," *International and Comparative Law Quarterly* 12 (1963): 282ff.
16. *Africa Confidential* 25, 9 (April 25, 1984):7.
17. "Nigeria: A National Council of Religious Affairs," *Impact International* (July 11–24, 1986): 3.
18. Sindima, *Drums of Redemption*, 5.
19. Ibid.
20. Abel Alier, "The Southern Sudan Question," in *Southern Sudan*, Dunstan Wai, ed. (London: Oxford University Press, 1972), 24.
21. Ibid., 25.
22. See Ann Mosely Lesch, "Rebellion in the Southern Sudan," *Universities Field Staff International Reports* 12, 8 (Africa, 1985).
23. Mahmoud Mohammed Taha, *The Second Message of Islam* (Syracuse, NY: Syracuse University Press, 1987).

24. Abdullahi A. An-Na'im, "The Islamic Law of Apostasy and Its Modern Applicability: A Case from the Sudan," *Religion* 16 (1986).

25. Abel Alier and Joseph Langu, "Letter to President Nimeiri," *The Horn of Africa* 25, n.d.

26. Ibid., 60.

27. Bona Malwal, *The Sudan: A Second Challenge to Statehood* (New York: Thornton Books, 1985), 15.

28. Petition to President Nimeiri on the Introduction of Shar`ia Law. Church Leaders, Khartoum, 21 September, 1983, 3.

8

Towards African Political Ethics

A growing number of African-centered scholars are troubled that Africans look elsewhere, rather than to their own context and tradition for solutions to their problems. We mentioned that Basil Davidson, among other Africanists, maintains that this is the direct result of colonialism. Ngugi wa Thiong'o, a Kenyan novelist and political activist, laments the effect of colonialism on African thought and language; he urges Africans to liberate themselves from this bondage.[1] It was mentioned in chapter two that modernists believe there is nothing in African culture that can deliver the people from the present crises. It appears Africans are the only people who do not draw from their own culture and heritage. Westerners do; Asians are very strict about cultural values and behavior. In Asia, social stratification, work ethic, and lifestyles are all based on culture. Some economic and political theorists and journalists believe that the success of Asia in spite of its ethnic, religious, and political problems, can partly be attributed to its adherence to cultural values.[2] Cultural values and practices are included in business ethics and courtesy, but in Africa, the educated despise their own traditional values, regarding them as a signs of backwardness.

In these days when the African church is challenged to develop political ethics it may be helpful to think of returning to the sources, and find therein appropriate cultural symbols to inform life together. These symbols may provide some insight into what it takes for a people to be constituted as a community and that knowledge may provide an understanding of the nature of politics, or what Africans politics should be about. Communities are created not given; it is therefore of utmost importance to know what goes into making them and to understand the dynamics needed to sustain them. African culture can provide all this knowledge via study of symbols. Having grounded the meaning of politics in traditional society, it is necessary to examine how traditional symbols can enhance or be enriched by what the various religious traditions say about life together. This is the method that will be followed in this chapter in an attempt to present a political ethics for the African church.

Ethics concern judgement of conduct or the nature of things. Ethics assesses whether they are right or wrong. In African thought, good is an attribute; things are not good in themselves. Good or goodness, concerns that which enhances human life or well-being. An act is good if it promotes life or human dwelling; conversely, that which destroys community, or reduces people to objects or the level of animals, is evil. Note here that evil and good are embodied in an act, a gesture, or a person. Rain is good when it comes at the right time and in the right amount for crops to do well, but rain is bad when it ruins crops and homes—the means of sustaining life. Similarly, one is said to be good if she or he encourages, helps, or leads others to experience dignity and fullness of life. A wicked person, whom Malawians call *mfiti* (witch), the highest embodiment of evil, is the person who harms others through deed, thought or speech; that person does not promote life and community. The bottom line is that good has to do with *life*, in particular human life because humans are the only meaning making creatures. As such, the human defines and determines whether a deed or thing is good or bad, thus ethics in African thought concerns a manner of living and conducting oneself to promote life and community. Since people are not only acted upon or towards, but are themselves (moral) agents, ethics also means responsibility and accountability of conduct. From this understanding, to speak of political ethics is to imply moral agency within human dwelling, that is, a manner of acting and living properly in society. We can say, then, that political ethics concerns organizing and controlling the distribution of goods in society, a stewardship of resources and regulation of social relations to produce peace, justice, and harmony among citizens of a given state. Good life of the state exists only in the life or well-being of its subjects. The subjects determine whether the action(s) of their leaders promote good life or destroy the community or the nation. It must be stressed, though, that political ethics does not focus on accountability of the leaders alone, but also of each member of society, since individually and collectively they are also moral agents. Moral responsibility extends to all institutions and organizations within society because these can be life enhancing or community destroying. This is where religion comes into the discussion on political ethics. As an institution, it can be an agent for enhancing the common good and increasing respect for life. Religion can do this by teaching adherents to uphold high moral standards and values that are informed by its sense of ultimate reality and meaning.

It cannot be overemphasized that for an ethic to be truly empowering it must draw or be based on what informs a people's way of life together. The African view of power or ethics must be informed by values resident in African culture, values which have sustained the people throughout the ages. Those are the values which form what I call spirituality,

> the organizing logic and principle of life . . . indigenous among people who share the same basic symbols and way of understanding the world. These symbols and their attendant manner of living become the common stock of the people and are passed on from generation to generation. New ideas may be introduced among these people, but their way of discerning ultimate reality and meaning still continues to be informed by their symbols which are rooted in their spirituality. . . . Resident spirituality runs deep in a people for it is this which distinguishes a people from any other. It forms their identity and collective consciousness. It is the power that make persons refuse to be broken or to be dehumanized, no matter the magnitude of their suffering, and it enables one to face death with dignity.[3]

True African political ethics, therefore, will have to be based on African concepts of the world and not on some borrowed concepts from outside Africa.

John Pobee has done exploratory work on African ethics; he has analyzed the concept of power in relation to the political structure of the Akan in Ghana. Pobee describes the Akan political structure as hierarchical, in which "the chief is the zenith of power." The chief rules with the help of councilors who are heads of families below him. The power which the chief has is not his own but of the people for "if they withhold their support, he cannot be chief."[4] Through the study of Akan wise sayings, Pobee shows the source and limit of the power of the chief. He says that the chief's power is under the ancestors and Deity. Power has a spiritual dimension, which implies that a chief is answerable not only to those who "instool" him (put him on the royal stool), the people, but to the ancestors and Divinity as well. This means "power is to be used for the benefit of society. With power goes responsibility to and for the people over whom it is exercised."[5]

What Pobee has said of Akan culture is true of most African cultures who have or had chiefs. Let us highlight some of the points from what he has given. Pobee has pointed out that power is of the people—a chief (or ruler) is not merely a person who can impose his or her will on others. Africans see a chief as the axis of their political relations, the symbol of their unity and an embodiment of their values. The chief is to ensure that moral values are upheld in society. We see here that political relations have a moral dimension, namely, regulating duties, obligations, and privileges. Pobee further states that this enormous responsibility on the shoulders of the chief is believed to have its origin in antiquity; it derives from the ancestors and is thus sanctioned by Divinity. The office entails duty and responsibility to Deity, ancestors, and the people.

Finally, Pobee has shown that there are always checks and balances within traditional African political systems; the power of the king though sacred has its limit. Traditional political systems insist that those in office must maintain the balance between power and authority, on one hand, and obligation and responsibility on the other. Anyone who holds office has responsibilities for the well-being and happiness of the people and these responsibilities correspond to the privileges of the office the person holds. For the privileges a king, queen or chief enjoys, there is the obligation to dispense justice to the people and ensure their well-being. Whenever a chief forsakes law and custom or puts personal interest before tradition and custom, the people are left with no alternative but to appeal to their elders or councilors (people through whom the chief exercises his authority) to remove the chief from office, for the chief no longer represents moral values, or a way of life together in their society. Even a mighty general like Chaka Zulu, who had a formidable army and had conquered many nations, had to submit to his own death when the people felt he no longer represented their values and interests. He had become ruthless, killing his own people. His own family felt a moral obligation to kill him.

In short, Pobee has shown that the concept of power in Akan society is closely connected with Akan understanding of community. This is to say that power in Akan thought is about regulating relations in life together; power is about life. Power is a creative way of life together; a way which seeks life and lets others be. If not used for enhancing life, power is force—it destroys life. Force is negative power for it diminishes life and destroys possibilities for full life.

In African thought power has nothing to do with *having* or *producing*. Dignity and respect are constituted in being human and, particularly in depicting fullness of human qualities. While wealth and glory, determine one's "value" and "worth" in Western society, in Africa it is moral conduct, integrity, compassion, and generosity that earn one respect and dignity in traditional society. Success or failure, does not add or take away from one's dignity and respect. A person at a low paying job in the city or a jobless person returns home to the village to be greeted with great honor and respect among her or his people. One who becomes incapacitated, and therefore cannot "produce," does not forfeit dignity and respect. On the other hand, a wealthy, successful person may not be respected at all if her/his way of life lacks good qualities of personhood or humanness. Anyone whose life does not befit human dwelling is *chinyama*, an animal, flesh and blood without human characteristics! One main characteristic of animal life is self-interest. In humans, this characteristic turns power into force because it is self-seeking. In humans, self-interest destroys self and others for it does not know integrity, compassion, generosity, caring, mutuality, harmony, respect, and justice.

Power as a creative way of life together is about right relations or justice. Injustice is a negative power, a force which in its self-seeking diminishes human life. What constitutes right relations or justice in African thought is anything that promotes life, anything that encourages care and mutuality, and controls acquisitiveness, self-seeking, and abuse of power. These are the conditions that constitute justice. By understanding justice as right relations or mutuality, power emerges as the common stock of the people in the service of human life; domination is expropriation of the common stock. Put differently, injustice is expropriation of the shared. The concept of justice as right relations deals with social structures not just persons. It is impossible for mutuality to exist in an elevated social structure or situation of dependence. The idea of right relations then is about ordering social structures in such a way that life will flow and people will be affirmed.

POLITICS AND AFRICAN SYMBOLS

Politics is an art of living together or a manner of relating. *Art*, is here not used in an aesthetic sense, as something appealing to the eye but as a manner or mode of creative activity. I do not define politics as governance as most theorists do, this is because I feel such a definition makes politics the business of the few, the elite. Indeed governance implies the means of creating and sustaining relations, but by its very nature governance becomes the concentration of power in the hands of the political elite. To interpret politics as a creative act is to presume certain basic ways, ideas, meanings, behavioral patterns, and a concept of the world which promotes living together—a spirituality. These basic ways, or ideals and goals which inform community living are known and shared by all and these are represented by symbols. This is to say, community implies a configuration of shared symbols and these constitute the people's spirituality—the organizing logic and principle of life, and that which gives people purpose, meaning, and direction. When these basic ways, acts, and symbols are distorted or corrupted, the people's manner of living also becomes corrupt too because symbols fail to give directionality to their vision since their actions have no logic to organize and hold people together. Life loses its value or meaning when symbols are corrupted.

There are many symbols in every society but only a few of those symbols are comprehensive enough to stand on their own or to lead people in the right direction. A symbol is something that mediates purpose, meaning and solidus or intention. This can be material, a thing, but it can also be nonmaterial such as a word or gesture. A symbol invokes sentiments as well as a vision; it mobilizes people. There are many non-material symbols just as there are many meanings. One of the most common political symbols is the national flag. The flag reminds people about their past as well as mobilize them into the future as they seek to actualize and perpetuate the values represented by their flag.

We have said that basic symbols are those symbols which constitute a totality or a comprehensive understanding in conceptualizing the world and life together. In Malawi, the totality of meaning in the world is symbolized by *moyo*, life. *Moyo* is the foundation of all that is; without it there is nothing. *Moyo* refers to cosmological order or the universe.[6] *Moyo* as the foundation of all that exists is material as well as spiritual, and it has no end. People participate in it at material and spiritual levels. At the material or biological level, *moyo* is symbolized by breath and blood. *Moyo* also refers to nonmaterial things such as right relations between people, sharing openness, and spiritual well-being, all nonmaterial things which nonetheless are necessary to support biological life. To exclude the social and religious dimensions of *moyo* would be to neglect the fact that *moyo* is constitutive in the meaning of persons. In sum, *moyo* is the purpose, meaning and intention of creation, therefore, the basic symbol for understanding both the world and living together. Accordingly, *moyo* is an art of learning to live together by accepting and affirming one another as persons and establishing genuine communication—a historization process, if you will.

Moyo originates in God, giver of all life, therefore the Divine mystery is Life itself. "This relation between human life and the Divine mystery, allows people to discern divine intention for human life and the cosmos. We can therefore say that in Malawian spirituality, *moyo* refers to that part of the human that has the capacity for self-transcendence and the ability to seek and respond to sacred things or communicate with Divinity. This is the part of human life that can respond to divine presence or to the source of life itself—Divinity."[7]

Moyo manifests itself in different forms in creation such as animal and vegetation life. However, there is one form which is a prototype, one which embodies the meaning and purpose of all creation, human life or person (*munthu*) as a member of humankind or a particular community or people (*anthu*). In Malawian thought, as it is in other African thought systems, *munthu* is a macrocosm of creation. In Malawian thought, therefore, meaning and purpose are symbolized by *moyo* and *munthu*. In other words, for Malawians, to understand *moyo* and *munthu* is to grasp the meaning and purpose of creation. These symbols seem to be universal in Africa; we find them with slight variations in spellings among the peoples of east and southern African countries. For example, in Swahili it is *moyo* and *muntu*; *muoyo* and *mundu* in Kikuyu; *moyo* and *ubuntu* in Zulu; in Sipedi it is *moya*, *mowa*, and *motho*; in Tsonga it is *moya* and *munhu*.

What relevance has the discussion of *moyo* and *munthu* to the development of political ethics? A great deal! We have asserted that politics is the art of living together, a manner of relating. It was further argued that this way of life is informed by basic symbols. Therefore, an interpretation of politics in Malawi, indeed in the whole of Africa, must be informed by the symbols of *moyo* and *munthu* for these are the overarching symbols of meaning and life together. When we speak of *moyo* in connection with *munthu*, we do not refer to the state of being alive or existence alone. These symbols have a much more broader and deeper meaning in Malawian thought. There are certain conditions that are below human life. There are also certain basics or necessities that befit human life: food, home, and clothing, but also emotional and spiritual needs. There is also a way of behaving and relating which reflects being human. In short, the concept of *munthu* includes a quality of life which enables one to realize full humanity, personhood (*umunthu*). *Umunthu* symbolizes all that is good and worthy in human life or a historization of *moyo*. In other words, *umunthu* stands for basic values of human life, or that which gives human life meaning. By articulating basic human values, the term distinguishes people from the cosmos or nature and other creatures with whom people share a common life. *Umunthu* is rooted in Malawian spirituality and it is about subjecthood of persons. As with *moyo*, *umunthu* is about the meaning of relations in a given community. Relations are determinative; this is to say that relations both provide or limit possibilities for self-discovery and actualization of *moyo*. In *umunthu*, then, we meet people as moral characters, and as such they can be agents of change when given a chance or when recognized as persons. To be recognized as a person is to have self-respect, or to realize self-determination. Here we see the need for character development or training in basic values and virtues of society, a practice which enables one to realize ones duties and responsibilities. Interpretation of politics in Malawi must focus on *umunthu* for this is the meaning of purposeful and responsible living. *Umunthu* is about character and moral agency.

From this discussion of basic symbols we observe that the primary aim of politics is to safeguard and promote *moyo*; to open or provide possibilities for the realization of fullness of personhood, *umunthu*. Politics can achieve this by creating opportunities for self-actualization. *Moyo* and *umunthu* would inform politics what to do or eliminate in society so as to enhance or create possibilities for *all* to lead a truly human life. In other words, *moyo* and *umunthu* reveal whether the aspirations of the people in the independence struggle, that is, freedom and dignity are being realized. Since these symbols are about the *what* and *what not* of life together, the task of decoding them, would also have to involve questions of power and justice as they affect fullness of life, *umunthu*.

AFRICAN SYMBOLS AND BIBLICAL INTERPRETATION: THE HERMENEUTICS OF POWER

We have said basic symbols mediate meaning and purpose in life. In Malawian thought everything in the cosmos is sacred. Accordingly, all meaning and purpose must be grounded in Divinity. The implication of this concept for any work of interpretation is that all symbols have to be ontologically grounded since they are about ultimate reality and meaning. To ground basic symbols in ultimate reality and meaning is, for Africans, to relate symbols to the sacred itself. It is to make the sacred the foundation of values the symbols represent. For the present project, this means examining and understanding the basic symbols informing community life, *moyo* and *umunthu,* from a biblical perspective since we are dealing with the relation between African values and Christianity. The aim of this exercise, is to see how these basic Malawian symbols interact with biblical teachings concerning life and being human. Biblical understanding of basic symbols will be edified and enhanced by traditional symbols. The exercise can enable people to develop a traditionally and biblically based interpretation of politics. Such an interpretation of politics would guide, but above all, enrich the Christian community in its attempt to live a responsible Christian life. Such a hermeneutic of power should also be engaged in Islam by examining the *Quranic* interpretation of African symbols. Unfortunately, I have no expertise to engage in such a task.

The term "politics" does not appear anywhere in the Bible. How then does one develop an interpretation of politics in line with the scriptures? The task involves two levels of interpretations: first, developing a clear understanding of what politics and the symbols informing it are and, secondly, subjecting those symbols to biblical examination. We have covered the first level of interpretation and we have defined politics as the art of living together that involves communicating and relating. The aim of this art is to preserve life and safeguard the dignity of persons. Drawing from traditional Malawian thought, we have said the task of safeguarding and preserving life and dignity of persons is informed by the overarching, all embracing symbols of living in the world, *moyo* and *umunthu.*

Having thus defined politics, now the task is to subject *moyo* and *umunthu* to biblical examination. The Bible opens and closes with the theme of life; it is its central theme. All people know God first as a creator and preserver of life. Creation is about bringing life into being. God creates *moyo* by divine command, says the writer of the first account of the creation story (Genesis 1:3-25). The second creation narrative says human life is special, for it came from the very breath of God (Genesis 2:7). To underscore how special human *moyo* is, divine authority is given to *munthu* to name and enjoy all things in creation. When *munthu*, through self-seeking, limits the potential for transcendence of life (the Fall is such limiting act), God provides the necessary means for *moyo* to continue. Here the Bible shows that creation involves preservation of *moyo*. In Genesis and the other four books of the Pentateuch, reference is made to the idea that human life ought to be preserved. People are asked to "choose life so that they may live" (Deuteronomy 30:15, 19). It is not just living, existing, that God is interested in, it is life befitting those who received divine breath. Laws are given to prevent human life being reduced to a nonhuman level.

Preservation of life, dignity, and respect of persons, *umunthu*, is the primary focus of the laws in Exodus, Deuteronomy, and Leviticus. The Deutronomic writer emphasizes that obedience to those laws leads to blessings (Deuteronomy 28:3–6). What does blessings mean in the Old Testament rather than happiness as the result of good health, material as well as spiritual well-being, that is, fullness and dignity of life, *umunthu*? The main thrust of Wisdom literature is living in the world as created by God and as a member of the human community. Wisdom literature is full of instructions on how to communicate and relate to others or let others be, which is another dimension of *umunthu*. This literature is against dehumanization; it hails respect and dignity of persons. In so many words, it encourages preservation of *moyo*. The prophetic writings repeat the words of the Deutronomic writer that obedience to divine laws earns one *moyo* and *umunthu*. Amos 5:14–16, for example, "Seek good and not evil; that you may live [that is, have *moyo*]; and so the Lord, God of Hosts, will be with you" [or you will experience fullness of life—*umunthu*]. The prophetic writings exhort and encourage the people to establish and execute justice (Amos 5:15; Jeremiah. 21:12; 22:3) or "to hold fast to love and justice" (Hosea. 12:6), or give the reminder to "let justice roll down like mighty waters" (Amos 5:24) and Micah adds, "the Lord requires you to do justice" (Micah 6:8). All these seek to ensure that *moyo* is preserved and all people offered equal possibilities to realize *umunthu*.

Moyo is the controlling symbol of New Testament narratives and *umunthu* is the bedrock of all New Testament ethical teachings. The message of Matthew is about finding (eternal) *moyo* (compare 6:25; 7:14; 10:39; 16:25–26; 19:16–17; 20:28; 25:46). We get the same concern in Mark and Luke. John says Jesus understood his mission as bringing *moyo* to people so that they may have it abundantly (John 10:10). Jesus himself is *moyo* who was at the beginning (John 1–18) and accordingly, he is the bread of *moyo* (John 6). Bread of life here refers to that which constitutes and maintains *moyo*. Other New Testament books also focus on *moyo* and *umunthu*.

The question of political power is indeed a very difficult one to deal with. Fortunately for Africans there are vast resources to draw from, including culture and the scriptures. The prophetic tradition provides plenty of examples concerning how people should be as a holy priesthood, God's own people. The symbols that have guided the way of life in traditional society can today also inform political conduct and behavior. *Moyo* and *umunthu*, for example, still remain central in Malawian daily experience. These symbols taken seriously could inform not only social policy but also political conduct and moral life and behavior. *Umunthu* informs people how to "let others be" by limiting personal power so as not to hurt others. *Umunthu* is about using power creatively, that is, promoting fullness of *moyo*. At the same time, *umunthu* rejects anything which is dehumanizing such as injustice, greed, or poverty due to unequal distribution of goods. How can *umunthu* be realized in a detention cell? No wonder traditional society did not have prisons—they dehumanize. Violation of human freedoms is an infringement of God's desire for humanity, which is *umunthu*, fullness of *moyo*. Human life is too sacred to be compromised and the scriptures agree with African tradition that *moyo* must be preserved at all cost.

Moyo is from God. God is *MOYO*. Therefore, we cannot give uncritical obedience to authorities when *moyo* is at stake. The church is a community called for the redemption and preservation of *moyo*. The task of the church is to empower people for fullness of *moyo* as its creator intended. Political religion is never interested in preserving *moyo*; neither is it ever interested in the creator of *moyo* itself. Political religion consumes people, filling their minds with false hopes and bad faith. People begin to believe it is the state, which they worship, that will redeem them from all perils of life. The state becomes a god; therefore people break the first commandment which prohibits the worship of anything or anyone other than the Creator.

The scriptures oblige Christians to announce divine discontent against human suffering. The word of God constrains the church to address questions of the moral responsibility of political leaders. The prophetic tradition gives examples of contributions by the ministry of the church to the sociopolitical order. It is a sin for the church not to tell political leaders to change their way of life when they are corrupt. It is a sin because in essence, the church says God is pleased with the life of corrupt rulers. If the church keeps silent, it will not be spared when God's wrath visits the political leaders, for the priesthood will have failed God, the people, and political authorities. How can the church in good conscience condone evil? The cost for condemning evil is no doubt high, but what other choice do the people of God have other than to obey God? In fulfilling their task as partners in creation and preservation of *moyo*, christians are compelled to announce divine discontent at human suffering and to seek ways of life together which will preserve *moyo* and promote *umunthu*.

NOTES

1. Ngugi wa Thiong'o, *Decolonising the Mind: The Politics of Language* (Nairobi: Heinemann, 1986).

2. Richburg, Keith B. "Why is Africa Eating Asia's Dust?" *The Washington Post National, Weekly Edition*, 20–22 July, 1992, 11–12.

3. Harvey J. Sindima, "Bondedness, *Moyo* and *Umunthu* as the Elements of Achewa Spirituality: Organizing Logic and Principle of Life," *Ultimate Reality and Meaning: Interdisciplinary Studies in the Philosophy of Understanding* 14, 1 (March 1991):6.

4. John Pobee, *Towards African Theology* (Nashville, TN: Abingdon, 1979), 144, 145.

5. Ibid., 146.

6. Harvey J. Sindima, "Community of Life" *The Ecumenical Review* 41, 4 (1989); Reprinted under different title in Charles Birch, William Eakin, and Jay MacDaniel, eds. *Liberating Life:Contemporary Approaches to Ecology Theology* (Maryknoll, New York: Orbis Books, 1990). Also see my book, *Africa's Agenda*, chap. 8.

7. Sindima, "Bondedness, *Moyo*, and *Umunthu*," *Ultimate Reality and Meaning*, 14.

9

The Kingdom of God

THE SILENT REVOLUTION

Jesus taught his disciples to pray: "Our Father . . . Your Kingdom come. . . . Give us today our daily bread . . . for yours is the kingdom, the power and the glory." Given the untold suffering of many Africans, unending political conflicts which bring misery and hunger, one wonders what it means to pray using these phrases which assert the power of God. Where is God's power when millions are condemned to die of war, starvation, and destitution? How long will people wait before God's kingdom finally arrives to set them free from poverty, illness, detention? The suffering of Africa presents serious questions of faith and theology. Put simply, what does it mean to be a person of faith amid the contradictions of life present in Africa today? In this section I want to make a theological reflection on the meaning of these phrases of the Lord's prayer.

The earliest manuscripts of the Lord's prayer do not contain the doxology, "yours is the kingdom, the power and the glory." The early church may have added these words to the original prayer to express and affirm the power of God as it ventured into a hostile world, where powers and principalities would challenge its mission and existence. The doxology is relevant to the African church, which as a pilgrim church faces challenges from powers and principalities of this world.

Some may perhaps wonder what relevance does prayer have to economic and political problems? In his late years, Karl Barth, a distinguished Swiss theologian, is said to have been heard many times saying, "to clasp the hands in prayer is the beginning of an uprising against the disorder of the world."[1] How so? I suppose Barth was not referring to prayer as faith statements or religious language alone, but as the first step in *doing* something about the disorder of the world, or better, being a partner in God's plan to end human suffering and destroy evil by bringing divine kingdom. A prayer that does not initiate one into some kind of action, a transformation, a conversion, is empty talk. At best such a prayer is therapy, an emotional catharsis that makes one feel good because deep inner feelings have been verbalized. That cannot be talking and listening to God, but a need to hear oneself. Prayer is a commitment to bring God's kingdom, to begin it with the one praying. Prayer is not a form of flight from the world, but getting involved in the world by being God's agent for change.

Prayer is a silent revolution against evil in all its manifestations, individual and structural. To pray is to say the world is not as God intended it to be; it is no longer as good as it was at creation. To pray is to acknowledge that people have corrupted the world, and that the whole creation groans as it awaits liberation. Prayer is ushering the rule of God into one's life and the world. What is prayer? A colleague and friend, Augustine Musopole, once told students that Christians pray because God has given prayer value. The words uttered do not give prayer value, God does. A secular parallel of this idea is that the value of a currency bill, say a dollar, pound, or kwacha, for example, is not in the quality of paper out which it is printed. The paper itself may not be expensive at all, but the currency itself has value because the government (U.S.A., Britain, Malawi) has given it value. It is the government, not the paper, that gives value to the currency. So too, human words do not give prayer its value, God does. It pleases God to give human words value. John Calvin, in his *Institutes*, expresses this idea concerning the value of prayer when he says, "For if our prayers were to be commended to God by our worth, who would dare even mutter in his presence?"[2] This value that God places on human words gives people hope. People pray because they have hope. It is indeed true that those who do not have hope do not pray, for prayer means nothing to them, it has no value. Hope comes from the understanding that God "hears" prayers, meaning God responds, indeed not always according to human will, but to divine wisdom and plan.

"YOUR KINGDOM COME"

The socioeconomic and political situation of Africa can lead to two opposite positions: emphasis on the here and now alone, or flight into otherworldliness, that is, existentialism or a pietistic faith, which is often a stale faith—mere religiosity. Many have this faith that produces a life of prayer that neither changes them nor transforms the world. Others have a faith that focuses here and now; that, too, is mere religiosity. None of these positions produce an authentic human, *munthu*, or Christian existence for they suggest a division between the external world and inner life—a very unbiblical view. People in the Bible, as in African culture, are of a piece, and are also social beings, "the souls of their bodies, and the fellows of their fellow creatures."[3] This is to assert that authentic human life, *umunthu*, in the Bible means taking seriously the material conditions of *moyo*, the concrete social, economic, and political realities. To retreat into piety or an inward form of life, is to announce a vote of no confidence towards the external world, which is also a vote of no confidence in God who is at the beginning and end of history. On the other hand, to throw oneself into the here and now alone, is to depend on personal ethics to transform the world, and thereby to exclude God, a humanistic kind of approach, which is antithetical to Christian life. In both cases the kingdom of God is prevented from coming.

To pray for God's kingdom to come is to ask God to intervene in human history and establish divine rule, that is, to liberate people bound by socio-economic and political powers—this advent of God into history is liberation. The Hebrew word for "to save," from which the idea of liberation develops, is "to create room." So to liberate or save is to create room for people to realize their *umunthu*, thereby their destiny. Thus to pray "Your kingdom come," is to imply a new beginning, when old powers and structures fall, and the captives are set free to realize their *umunthu*. The writer of Genesis makes a very interesting point that God does not restore the sinful world to a new order by giving it spiritual things alone, but by material means as well. When Adam and Eve broke their relationship with their maker, God's first move in restoring the relationship was to provide them with an apron of leaves to cover themselves. God gave them the material things they needed to exist in the world. God's liberation is always complete: freedom from both physical and spiritual bondage. This is what happens when God intervenes in human history. People cannot realize their *umunthu* without material things.

To pray for God's kingdom is to ask God to set in motion a resistance movement against the current social, political, and economic order, which by its very nature is oppressive because it is permeated with sin. Jan Lochman says to petition God for divine rule is to ask God to enter into confrontation with the powers that be, but also to initiate hope in those who have been made powerless, those who live in fear, feeling impotence and anger. When God's kingdom comes a new order is established: *the poor*, materially and spiritually, *are fulfilled* for they realize their true humanity (*umunthu*); *the captives*, those who have been robbed of their freedom and their dignity (*umunthu*) in the name of law and order, *are set free*; *the blind*, those hampered in body and spirit, the sick—those whose possibilities in life have been shortened—*see*, that is, experience a fullness of life (*moyo*). God is never neutral in the face of human suffering and oppression. On the contrary, God has a commitment to the helpless. "To oppress the poor is to insult their creator," says Proverbs 14:31. Exploitation and corruption demand that the people speak out (Amos 8:4–8). They cannot remain indifferent as the elite and the powerful rob and crush the poor (Psalms 10:8–10; Amos 5:11, 8:6, 2:6).

"Your kingdom come," encourages Christians not to surrender to the current powers or become immobilized by fear, but challenges them to set in motion a movement which resists ideas that dehumanize them. The phrase, "Your kingdom come," challenges Christians to become instruments of God in bringing a new order, which essentially is the rule of justice. Christians must not be afraid to seek justice for the Lord's prayer impels them to be involved in creating a new society; they must denounce corruption and all forms of injustice for God's reign to begin, but God's reign cannot be initiated by people who have not repented from inaction and fear. The church in Africa is called to this repentance. God's rule can only be established by people of faith, those who have repented of their inaction and fear; for faith casts away fear. The church is called to lead people to faith by providing hope and promise, and it fails in its task when it accedes to the powers of this world, an act which reduces Christianity to an ideology, a fetish of the powerful, useless to the oppressed, or at best, a drug that temporarily drowns their misery and suffering.

"GIVE US TODAY OUR DAILY BREAD"

Today Africa is in the grips of hunger; thousands have died as drought sweeps across the Sahel and the whole of southern Africa. Thousands more will die as development policies focus less on agriculture, creating malnutrition and high infant mortality rates. Yet in the homes of Christians, in prayer meetings and in Sunday worship the petition is said: "Give us today our daily bread," even as this sad situation continues. Some of those who recite this petition have nothing at all to eat, but perhaps in defiance to the conditions that bring about their indignity, they still pray: "Give us our daily bread." The question we must ask is: Why did Jesus teach his disciples to ask God for daily bread, when God gives it anyway, whether people pray for it or not? How many people ever went to bed hungry some night because they did not pray for their food that day? One third of the world, the West, has more food, so much so that weight is a problem for many, while people in the rest of the world are mere walking skeletons. Yet Christians throughout the whole world pray for daily bread even though only a third have too much to eat. What does it then mean to pray, "Give us today our daily bread?" What was the lesson Jesus wanted to teach his followers?

Food is one of the most important basic human needs, so essential that when Jesus taught his disciples to pray, he made it the first petition people could ask God. "*Give us today our daily bread,*" comes after honoring God's name, "*Hallowed be thy name,*" asking for the coming of God's rule, "*thy kingdom come*" and requesting God's complete control of the heaven and the earth, "*thy will be done in heaven and on earth.*" There are six petitions in the Lord's prayer. The first three are about God, and second set of three is about people. The first thing people can ask from God is for daily bread: "Give us today our daily bread."

"Give us *today* our *daily bread.*" There are two words which are very central in this petition: *today* and *daily*. Note that these two expressions put bread between them, and limit the question of bread even as they take it seriously, both in quality, *today*, and quantity, *daily*. The expressions put what is essential to life at the center: our *daily bread*. These expressions: *today* and *daily*, set priorities and limitations to what we should ask of God. We are not to ask God for everything in the world, but only those things which are essential for life or *daily living*. "Our daily bread" constrains us from seeking all our passions but focuses on *need*. Setting priorities is a very difficult thing in life and yet this is what Jesus teaches us to pray for and do every day. The term "bread" here could be understood as need, but above all I believe it means *moyo*. We must ask God for our daily need and not extras, but only those things which we need to sustain *moyo*. Why not extras? They can only lead to greed and the quest for power and more power to get extras. Jesus warns: "Watch out and guard yourselves from every kind of greed; because a person's true life (*moyo*) is not made up of the things he or she owns, no matter how rich the person may be" (Luke 12:15). "Give us our daily bread," teaches us to rethink our priorities in life. African leaders must guard against their own greed but they must also rethink the development process so that emphasis is placed on food production to stop importing food or to end the degrading situation of food handouts. It is God's will that people should be fed (Genesis 42:1–2, 43:1–2). The church must be involved in the ministry of food. This involvement does not mean being distribution agents for foreign aid grains, but teaching, encouraging, and engaging in farming itself. Development in Africa must focus on food production, poverty alleviation, health, and education. These are basic needs that leaders must strive to achieve and for which the faithful must pray and work.

"Give *us* . . . *our* daily bread." *Us* and *our* are two other words in the petition worth thinking about. In the fourth petition, Jesus teaches people to ask God for daily needs, not just theirs alone, but also those of all people. Indeed, the bread God will give will be theirs, but it is bread that must be shared. This goes against individual accumulation and the ethos that the poor suffer because they are lazy. Who misappropriates public funds? Certainly not the poor. The fact of the matter is that there are many who are poor despite their hard work. Individualism plays a great role in human suffering. When people believe that what they have is theirs and theirs alone, suffering begins to mount; the gap between the rich and the poor increases and all evils follow. This is what the Malawian bishops lamented in their pastoral letter and why they asked the authorities to curb and limit the greed of the rich and powerful so as to narrow the gap between them and the majority poor. The bishops wanted to let the authorities know that the widening gap was the direct result of a corrupt social system and not laziness or hard work. There must certainly be something wrong with a society when farmers are not compensated equally for the hard work they do. The fourth petition teaches everyone, the rich and powerful in particular, not just to be mindful of the lot of the poor, but to share in their suffering: to do something about it, beginning with controlling greed. So the fourth petition teaches us to ask God for our bread but also to give practical help, to share what we have with others. Even small steps count. To pray is to be converted, to become a partner with God in bringing divine kingdom.

"YOURS IS THE POWER"

The world is full of people seeking power, and they use power to establish fear and control. People believe that "might is right." In such a power-laden world, it can be confusing to Christians to say the doxology, "Yours is the power." How is divine power manifest in this power-laden world? Despite Christian confession of divine power, they and most of the people in the world live in fear; fear of losing one's livelihood; fear of poverty, sickness and death; fear of what might happen to them or their loved ones in times of economic and political uncertainty, as in Africa now.

Fear is the result of feeling or seeing no way out, no possibilities of overcoming the present circumstances to realize *umunthu*, thus the hopelessness that accompanies fear. Fear emerges from powerlessness. Hope comes by having a sense of power, a confidence in oneself or in those around. Religion is based on a deep sense of power that derives from "beyond," from God. For all religions, God is the power that transcends and exceeds all powers; people can tap into this power and transform their condition. Religion gives hope. For Christians to confess, "Yours is the power," is to declare faith in God; to believe in God's liberating power. God is the mobilizing energy, a power that provides alternatives to all earthly authorities, a liberating power. To ascribe power to God is to recognize that no matter how glorious earthly powers may be, they all perish and only God's power endures forever. This understanding of power does not deny earthly authorities their power, on the contrary, earthly power is taken seriously but denied the feeling of omnipotence. Power of earthly authorities is demystified and emptied by the power of God; this is the message of the cross of and Easter. Earthly powers thought they had destroyed the influence and power of Jesus by hanging him on the cross and burying him, but on the first Easter, God demystified the power of civil authorities by raising Jesus from the grave. Christianity must demystify the power of the state, and Christianity exceeds in this only when it analyses the religious situation of those who according to the present order of things have no status. Christianity was not founded as a national religion; God is a stateless God. Though a stateless God, Christianity did not begin as a private religion, and its God is not an apolitical God.

Christians must always remember that where the power of God is recalled, there it is known that what is real in our world is not merely existing power relations, but also the power that does not lie at human disposal, yet is accessible to them through faith in God. This power is not manifested in spiritual things alone; it takes seriously the present human condition, the suffering of the powerless. Thus Jesus heals the sick and multiplies bread to feed the hungry. For Africans to say the doxology, "Yours is the power," is to do something about the ills that do not seem to go away. Since the suffering is the result of injustice, Christians will have to engage in the work of creating justice relying on divine power. Christians must do this to rekindle hope among the powerless. The kingdom of God begins in this world; Jesus initiates the rule of God by coming into this world. God's reign does not wait for the poor in the hereafter but comes to them in the here and now. Christians are the instruments for bringing God's reign in the here and now.

NOTES

1. Jan Milic Lochman, "The Lord's Prayer in Our Time," *Princeton Seminary Bulletin*, Supplementary Issue 2 (1992), 19. The Lord's Prayer was the focus of the 1991 Frederick Neumann Symposium on the Theological Interpretation of Scripture at Princeton Theological Seminary. A few insights are drawn from the proceedings of the symposium.
2. Calvin, *Institutes*, III, 20, 47.
3. My reflections on the doxology are informed by Jan Milic Lochman's book, *The Theology of Praise* (Atlanta, GA: John Knox Press, 1982), 5.

Appendix A

The Confession of Alexandria

In February 1976, the General Committee of the All Africa Conference of Churches (AACC) met in Alexandria, Egypt, to reflect on Christian faith in Africa. Men and women from 114 member churches of the AACC representing 33 countries of the continent attended the meeting. After their reflection they drew up a document, a declaration of faith called the Alexandrian Confession. The Confession was read for the first time at St. Mark's Coptic church in Alexandria, Egypt, before an audience of more than two thousand. The following is the full text of the Confession.

> We African Christian gathered from all parts of the continent in the General Committee of the All African Conference of churches, praise God for having brought us together in Alexandria, the holy city in which tradition places the martyrdom of St. Mark, the Evangelist.
>
> Therefore God calls us to repentance,
> He grants us forgiveness,
> He leads us to confess our faith with joy,
> in the fellowship of the saints
> brought through the ages:
> The Christian community of Africa gives praise to God for His revelation through Jesus Christ, His Son and His constant presence among His people through the Holy Spirit.
>
> As members of Christ's church in Africa today, we have become conscious of the fact that we are inheritors of a rich tradition.
>
> Our current concern with issues related to: peace in Africa, as well as contemporary search for authentic responses to Christ as Lord over the whole

of our lives have led to a deeper understanding of the heritage delivered to us by the Fathers of the Early church in North Africa.

Our commitment to the struggle for human liberation is one of the ways we confess our faith in an Incarnate God, who loved us in our human form, suffered, was crucified for our redemption and was raised for our justification. Such undeserved grace evokes a response of love and joy that we are seeking to express and share in language, modes of spirituality, liturgical forms, patterns of missions and structures of organization that look beyond uniquely to our cultural context.

This is what the Fathers of the Early Church in North Africa did with the Gospel brought to them by St. Mark. As a result they were able to develop a Christianity that was orthodox and catholic both in its outreach and its cultural authenticity . . . and a church throughout the ages has endured persecution and martyrdom, and still survives with renewed strength, until our day.

It is this heritage which inspires us to confess that it is the same Incarnate Christ who is calling us to respond to Him in terms that are authentic, faithful and relevant to men and women in Africa today. His call is our present and our future.

As this future breaks into the present, Christians in Africa have every reason to be joyful. Through the continuing work of Christ, God is charting His highway of freedom (Isaiah 40: 3–5) from Alexandria to the Cape of Good Hope. By witnessing to the victorious power of Christ (Romans 8) we Christians in Africa are engaged to be co-workers with all those who are called by God to participate in His work.

The storms of history have sometimes led us astray. We have been too willing to rush off this way into dead-end paths. We have spoken against evil when it was convenient. We have often avoided suffering for the sake of others, thus refusing to follow His example (1 Peter 2: 21). We have preferred religiosity to listening to what the Holy Spirit might be whispering to us. We have struggled against colonialism and many other evils, and yet have built up again those things which we have torn down. We confess that we have been paternalistic towards others. We have often condemned these evils but we have condoned the same things by our people. We have turned a blind eye to the structures of injustice in churches and institutions. We have been a stumbling block for too many. For these and other sins, we are sorry and ask God to forgive us.

A full understanding of this forgiveness leaves us no choice but to continue the struggle for full liberation of all men and women, and the societies.[1]

NOTE

1. *A.A.C.C. Newsletter* 11, 3 (March 1976).

Appendix B

Country Profiles

Country	Date of Independence	From	Dominant Religion
Algeria	1962	France	Islam
Angola	1975	Portugal	Christianity
Benin	1960	France	Christianity
Botswana	1966	Britain	Christianity
Burkina Faso	1960	France	Christianity
Burundi	1962	Belgium	Christianity
Cameroon	1960	France	Christianity
Cape Verde	1975	Portugal	Christianity
Central African Republic	1960	France	Christianity
Chad	1960	France	Islam
Comoros	1975	France	Islam
Congo-Brazzaville	1960	France	Christianity
Congo, Demo. Republic	1960	Belgium	Christianity
Djibouti	1977	France	Christianity
Egypt	1952	Britain	Islam
Equatorial Guinea	1968	Spain	Islam
Eritrea	1991	Ethiopia	Christianity
Ethiopia	—	—	Christianity
Gabon	1960	France	Christianity
Gambia	1965	Britain	Islam
Ghana	1957	Britain	Christianity
Guinea Bissau	1974	Portugal	Islam
Ivory Coast	1960	France	Christianity
Kenya	1963	Britain	Christianity
Lesotho	1963	Britain	Christianity
Liberia	—	—	Christianity

Country	Date of Independence	From	Dominant Religion
Libya	1951	Italy	Islam
Madagascar	1960	France	Christianity
Malawi	1964	Britain	Christianity
Mali	1960	France	Islam
Mauritania	1960	France	Islam
Mauritius	1968	Britain	Christianity
Morocco	1956	France	Islam
Mozambique	1975	Portugal	Christianity
Namibia	1990	South Africa	Christianity
Niger	1960	France	Islam
Nigeria	1960	Britain	Christianity Islam
Rwanda	1962	Belgium	Christianity
Sao Tomé	1975	Portugal	Christianity
Senegal	1960	France	Islam
Seychelles	1976	Britain	Christianity
Sierra Leone	1961	Britain	Islam
Somalia	1960	Italy/Britain	Islam
South Africa	1994	White Rule	Christianity
Sudan	1956	Britain	Islam
Swaziland	1967	Britain	Christianity
Tanzania			
Tanganyika	1961	Britain	Christianity
Zanzibar	1963	Britain	Islam
Togo	1960	France	Christianity
Tunisia	1956	France	Islam
Western Sahara	1976	Spain	Christianity
Zambia	1964	Britain	Christianity
Zimbabwe	1980	Britain	Christianity

Works Cited

Acta Proconsularia Sancti Cypriani

Adeleye, R. A. *Power and Diplomacy in Northern Nigeria 1804–1966: The Sokoto Caliphate and its Enemies*. London: Longoman, 1977.

Africa Confidential 25, 9 (April 25, 1984).

Ajayi, J. F. A. "The Place of African History and Culture in the Process of Nation-Building in Africa South of the Sahara." *Journal of Negro Education* 30, 3 (1961).

Al-'Amal (Beirut), 8 September, 1981.

Alier, Abel. "The Southern Sudan Question." In *Southern Sudan*, edited by Dunstan Wai. London: Oxford University Press, 1972.

Alier, Abel and Joseph Langu, "Letter to President Nimeiri, *The Horn of Africa*: American Field Staff Report, 25. n.d.

All Africa Council of Churches Bulletin (1974).

All Africa Council of Churches Newsletter 11, 3 (March 1976).

Althaus, Paul. *The Ethics of Martin Luther*. Translated by Robert C. Schultz. Philadelphia, PA: Fortress Press, 1978.

Anderson, J. N. "Return Visit to Nigeria: Judicial and Legal Developments in the Northern Region." *International and Comparative Law Quarterly* 12 (1963).

An-Na'im, Abdullahi A. "The Islamic Law of Apostasy and Its Modern Applicability: A Case from the Sudan," *Religion* 16 (1986).

Aquinas, Thomas. *Summa Theologica*. Vol. I. Edited by Thomas Gilby. New York: Image Books, 1969.

_________. *De regimine principum*. Toronto: Pontifical Institute of Medieval Studies, 1949.

Aristotle, *Nicomachean Ethics*. Translated by and with introduction and notes by Martin Ostwald. Indianapolis, Indiana: Bobbs-Merrill Educational Publishing, 1962.

Augustine. *City of God* (Abridged). Introduction by Etienne Gilson; translated by

Gerald G. Walsh, Demetrius B. Zema, Grace Moahan and Daniel J. Hownan; forward by Vernon J. Bourke. New York: Image Books, 1958.

Bammel, E. and C. F. D. Moule, eds. *Jesus and the Politics of His Day*. London: Cambridge University Press, 1984.

Barker, Ernest. *The Political Thought of Plato and Aristotle*. London: Oxford University Press, 1906.

_________. *The Politics of Aristotle*. London: Oxford University Press, 1958.

_________. *Greek Political Theory: Plato and His Predecessors*, 4th. ed. London: Methuen, 1961.

Bates, Robert H. "Ethnic Competition and Modernization in Contemporary Africa." *Comparative Political Studies* 6 (January 1974).

Beti, Mongo. *The Poor Christ of Bomba*. London: Heinemann, 1971.

Bettenson, Henry, ed. *Documents of the Christian Church*, 2nd ed. London: Oxford University Press, 1963.

Bienen, Henry. *Armies and Parties in Africa*. New York: Africana Publishing Company, 1978.

Brown, R. E. and J. P. Meier. *Antioch and Rome*. London: Chapman, 1983.

Buchanan, Scott. ed. *The Portable Plato*. New York: Penguin Books, 1981.

Bujo, Bénézet. *African Theology in Its Social Context*. Translated by John O'Donohue. Maryknoll, NY: Orbis Books, 1992.

Calvin, John. *Commentaries on the Epistle of Paul, the Apostle to the Romans*. Grand Rapids, MI: Eerdmans, 1948.

_________. *Institutes of the Christian Religion*. Edited by John T. McNeill and translated by Ford Lewis Battles. Philadelphia, PA: Westminster, 1960.

Carlyle, R. W. and A. J. Carlyle. *A History of Medieval Political Theory in the West*. 6 vols. London: Blackwood, 1903–1906.

Childs, Brevard. *Old Testament Theology in Canonical Context*. Philadelphia, PA: Fortress Press, 1986.

Chipendo, José B. "Theological Options in Africa Today." In *African Theology en Route*, edited by Kofi Appiah-kubi and Sergio Torres. Maryknoll, NY: Orbis Books, 1979.

Church Leaders, Khartoum. Petition to President Nimeiri on the Introduction of *Shar'ia* Law. (21 September, 1983).

Church of Ethiopia: An Introduction to Contemporary Church of Ethiopia. Addis Ababa: Ethiopian Orthodox Church, May 1973.

Clark, Peter B. and Ian Linden. *Islam in Modern Nigeria*. Munchen: Grundwald Kaiser, 1984.

Coleman, James Smoot, ed. *Nationalism and Development in Africa: Selected Essays*. Berkeley, CA: University of California Press, 1994

Christian Messenger 4, 3 (March 1982).

Cumont, F. *Oriental Religions in Roman Paganism*. New York: Dover, 1956.

Davidson, Basil. *The Black Man's Burden: The Curse of the Nation State*. New York: Time Books, 1992.

_________. *The Search for Africa:History, Culture, Politics*. New York, NY: Times Books, 1994.

Dent, M. J. "Corrective Government: Military Rule in Perspective." In *Soldiers and*

Oil: The Political Transformation of Nigeria, edited by S. K. Panter-Brink. London: Frank Cass, 1978.

Donfried, K. P. ed. *The Romans Debate*. Minneapolis, MN: Augsburg, 1977.

Doro, Marion E. and Newell, Stultz M., eds. *Governing in Black Africa: Perspectives in New States*. Englewood Cliffs, NJ: Prentice Hall, 1970.

Duignan, Peter and Robert H. Jackson, eds. *Politics and Government in African States: 1960–1985*. London: Croom Helm, 1986.

Ejizu, Chris I. "Ethics of Politics in Nigeria." *Nigerian Journal of Theology* 1, 4 (1988).

Ela, Jean-Marc. *African Cry*. Translated by Robert Barr. Maryknoll, NY: Orbis Books, 1986.

Ethiopian Review (August 1992).

Eusebius, *Historia Ecclesiastica*. Lipsie, 1827

"Evangelical Witness in South Africa." *Transformation* (1987).

Fauré, Y. A. "Côte d'Ivoire: Analysing the Crisis," in *Contemporary West African States*. Edited by D. B. Cruise O'Brien, J. Dunn, and R. Rathbone. London: Cambridge University Press, 1989.

Ferguson, Everett. *Backgrounds of Early Christianity*. Grand Rapids, MI: William Eerdmans, 1987.

Fieldhouse, David. *Black Africa, 1945–1980: Economic Decolonisation and Arrested Development*. London: Allen and Unwin, 1986.

First, Ruth. *The Barrel of Gun: Political Power in Africa and the Coup d'Etat*. London: Allen Lane, Penguin Press, 1970.

Gelasius, *Tractatus*, IV, 11.

Gerth, H. H. and C. Wright Mills, trans. and ed. *From Max Weber: Essays in Sociology*. New York, NY: Oxford University Press, 1980.

Gill, Robin. *A Textbook of Christian Ethics*. Edinburgh: T. and T. Clark, 1985.

González, Justo L. *A History of Christian Thought*. 3 vols. *From Augustine to the Eve of the Reformation*, vol. 2. Nashville, TN: Abingdon, 1988.

Grindle, Merilee S. *Challenging the State: Crisis and Innovation in Latin America and Africa*. New York: Cambridge University Press, 1996.

Hadjor, Kofi Buenor. *On Transforming Africa: Discourse with Africa's Leaders*. Trenton, NJ: Africa World Press; London: Third World Communications, 1987.

Harbeson, John W., ed. *The Military in African Politics*. Westport, CT: Praeger, 1987.

Hetherwick, Alexander. *The Romance of Blantyre*. Dunfermline, Scotland: Lasodine Press, n.d.

Hobbes, Thomas. *Leviathan*. Edited by R. A. Waller. London: Cambridge University Press, 1904.

________. *De Civitate*. New York: Appleton-Century Crofts, 1949.

Hollenbach, David. *Claims in Conflict: Retrieving and Renewing the Catholic Human Rights Tradition*. New York: Paulist Press, 1979.

Hourtart, Francis and Andre Rousseau. *The Church and Revolution*. Maryknoll, NY: Orbis Books, 1971.

International Missionary Council of Nyasaland. Memorandum submitted to the Bledisloe Commission, April 1938.

Jackson, Robert H. and Carl G. Rosberg. *Personal Rule in Black Africa: Prince, Autocrat, Prophet, Tyrant*. Berkeley, CA: University of California Press, 1982.

Jaffé, P. *Bibliotheca rerum Germanicarum*. Vol. II, Monumenta Gregorian.

Josephus, *Ant* 14.

Kameeta, Zephania. *Why O Lord: Psalms and Sermons from Namibia*. Philadelphia, PA: Fortress Press, 1986.

Kelly, J. N. D. *Early Christian Doctrines*. New York: Harper and Row, 1978.

Knox, John. *Appellation: Works*, I. Edited by David Laing. Edinburgh: Bannatyne Society, 1846–64.

Kokole, Omari H. "Religion in Afro-arab Relations: Islam and Cultural Changes in Modern Africa." In *Islam in Africa: Proceedings of the Islam in Africa Conference*, edited by Nura Alkali, Awwal Yadudu, Rashi Motem, Haruna Sahili. Ibadan: Spectrum Books, 1993.

Lamb, Geoff. "The Military and Development in Eastern Africa." *Bulletin of the Institute of Development Studies* 4, 4 (September 1972).

Lemarchand, Rene. "The Basis of Nationalism among the Bakongo." *Africa* 31, 4 (October 1961).

Lesch, Ann Mosely. "Rebellion in the Southern Sudan." *Universities Field Staff International Reports* 12, 8 (Africa, 1985).

Lewis, I. M. ed. *Islam in Tropical Africa*. London: Oxford University Press, 1966.

Liebenow, J. Gus. *African Politics: Crises and Challenges*. Bloomington, IN: Indiana University Press, 1986.

Lochman, Jan Milic. "The Lord's Prayer in Our Time." *Princeton Seminary Bulletin* 2 (1992).

_________. *The Theology of Praise: The Kingdom, The Power, The Glory*. Atlanta, GA: John Knox Press, 1982.

Long, Edward LeRoy. *A Survey of Christian Ethics*. New York: Oxford University Press, 1982.

Lugard, Frederick D. *Political Memoranda 1913–1918*. London: Oxford University Press, 1919.

_________. *The Dual Mandate in British Tropical Africa*. London: Oxford University Press, 1922.

Luther, Martin. "Whether soldiers, too, can be saved." In *Works of Martin Luther*. Vol. 6. Philadelphia, PA: Fortress Press, 1931.

_________. "Lectures on Genesis, Chapters 15–20." *Luther's Works*. Vol. 3, edited by Jaraslov Pelican. St. Louis, MO: Concordia Publishing House, 1961.

_________. "On Good Works." In *Werke*. Vol. 6, translated by W.A. Lambert. In *A History of Political Thought*, George H. Sabina and Thomas L. Thorson. Hilsdale, IL: Dryden Press, 1973.

_________. "Temporal Authority: To what extent it should be obeyed." In *Luther: Selected Political Writings*. Edited by J. M. Porter. Philadelphia, PA: Fortress Press, 1974.

Machiavelli, Niccolò. *The Historical, Political and Diplomatic Writings of Niccolò Machiavelli*, 4 vols. Translated by C. E. Detmold. Vol I, *Discourses on the First Ten Books of Titus Livius*. Boston, MA: Osgood and Co. 1882.

Maimela, Saimon. "The Concept of Israel." *Africa Theological Journal* 15, 2 (1986).

Malwal, Bona. *The Sudan: A Second Challenge to Statehood.* New York: Thornton Books, 1985.
Maquet, Jacques. *Power and Society in Africa.* London: World University Library, 1971.
Maritan, Jacques. *Man and the state.* Chicago, IL: University of Chicago Press, 1951.
Marsilius of Padua, *Defensor Pacis.* Translated by Alan Gewirth. Toronto: University of Toronto Press, 1960 [1324].
_________. *Defensor Minor* and *De tranlatione* Imperii. Edited by Cary J. Nederman. London: Cambridge University Press, 1993 [1342].
Mazrui, Ali A. *The African Condition: A Political Diagnosis.* New York: Cambridge University Press, 1980.
McCracken, John. "The Nineteenth Century in Malawi." In *Aspects of Central African History,* edited by T. O. Ranger, Evanston, IL: Northwestern University Press, 1968.
_________. *Politics, and Christianity in Malawi 1875–1940: The Impact of the Livingstonia Mission in Northern Province.* London: Cambridge University Press, 1977.
McManners, John. ed. *The Oxford History of Christianity.* New York: Oxford University Presss, 1993.
McNeill, John T., ed. with introduction. *Calvin On God and Political Duty.* 2nd. ed. Indianapolis, IN: Bobbs-Merrill Educational Publishing, 1980.
Meyendorff, John. *The Orthodox Church.* Translated by John Chapin. Crestwood, NY: Vladimir's Seminary Press, 1981.
Meyer, P. M. ed. "Papyri Hamburg," *Abhandlungen,* Preussiche Akademie der Wissenschaften, Berlin, phil-hist. Klase, 1910, Anhang, Abhdlg. V.
Miller, Allen O. ed. *A Christian Declaration of Human Rights.* Grand Rapids, MI: Eerdmans, 1977.
Miller, Patrick D. "The Prophetic Critique of Kings." *Ex Auditu* 2 (1986).
Moltmann, Jürgen. *On Human Dignity: Political Theology and Ethics.* Philadephia, PA: Fortress Press, 1984.
Morgenthau, R. S. *Political Parties in French-Speaking West Africa.* London: Oxford University Press, 1964.
M'uyinga, Elenga. *Panafricanism or Neocolonialism.* London: Zed Press, 1982.
Nicene and Post-Nicene Fathers. First Series 2. New York: Scirberner's, 1903.
"Nigeria: A National Council of Religious Affairs." *Impact International* (11–24 July, 1986).
North, Douglas C. and R. Thomas, *Institutions, Institutional Change and Economic Performance.* Cambridge: Cambridge University Press, 1990.
O'Brine, D. Cruise. "Towards an Islamic Policy in French West Africa." *Journal of African History* 8 (1967).
Okullu, Bishop J. Henry. *Church and Politics in East Africa.* Nairobi: Uzima Press, 1982. Reprint.
Optatus. *De Schismate Donatistarum.* Appendix III, V-VII, IX, X.
Osoro, R. *The African Identity in Crisis.* Hudsonville, MI: Bayana Publishers, 1993.
Paden, John N. *Ahmadu Bello. Sardauma of Sokoto. Values and Leadership in Nigeria.* London: Hodder snd Stroughton, 1986.

Panter-Brink, S. K. ed. *Solidiers and Oil: The Political Transformation of Nigeria*. London: Frank Cass, 1978.

Papal Commission. *Justitia et Pax. The Church and Human Rights*. 1975.

Pastoral Constitution on the Church in the Modern World. Vatican, 1965.

Pennington, J. D. "The Copts in Modern Egypt." *Middle Eastern Studies* 18, 2 (April 1982).

Pobee, John. *Towards African Theology*. Nashville, TN: Abingdon, 1979.

Ramet, Pedro, ed. *Eastern Christianity and Politics in the Twentieth Century*. Durham, NC: Duke University Press, 1988.

Rawls, John. *A Theory of Justice*. Cambridge, MA: Harvard University Press, 1971.

Receuil à l'usage des fonctionaries et des agents du service territorial au Congo belge. Bruxells, 1930.

Richburg, Keith B. "Why is Africa Eating Asia's Dust?" *The Washington Post National, Weekly Edition*, July 20–22, 1992.

Roman Synod of Bishops. *Message Concerning Human Rights and Reconciliation*. Vatican, 1974.

Rotberg, Robert I. *The Rise of Nationalism in Central Africa: The Making of Malawi and Zambia 1873–1964*. Cambridge, MA: Harvard University Press, 1965.

Rousseau, Jean-Jacques. *The Social Contract*. Translated by Henry J. Tozer. London: Allen and Unwin, 1920.

Russell, Philip and Arthur Gosling, *Resolutions of the Lambeth Conference, 1867–1978*. Secretary General for the Lambeth Conference, 1988.

Sabine, George H. and Thorson Thomas L. *A History of Political Theory*. 4th. ed. Hinsdale, IL: Dryden Press, 1973.

Schlier, H. "Die Beurteilung des states in Neuen Testament." In *Die der Kirche*. Freiburg: Herder, 1956.

SECAM. "Seeking Gospel Justice in Africa." *Spearhead*, 69 (December 1981).

Sherperson, George and Tom Price. *Independent African: John Chilembwe and the Origins, Setting, and Significance of the Nyasaland Native Rising of 1915*. Edinburgh: Edinburgh University Press, 1958.

Sindima, Harvey J. *Africa's Agenda: The Legacy of Liberalism and Colonialism in the Crisis of African Values*. Westport, CT: Greenwood Press, 1995.

_________. *Drums of Redemption: An Introduction to African Christianity*. Westport, CT: Greenwood Press, 1994.

_________. *The Legacy of Scottish Missionaries in Malawi*. Lewiston, NY: Edwin Mellen Press, 1992.

_________. *Malawi's First Republic: A Political and Economic Analysis*. (Forthcoming).

_________. "Africa's Christian Heritage: Notes on Ethiopian Christianity." *Africa Theological Journal* 20, 2 (1991).

_________. "Bondedness, *Moyo* and *Umunthu* as the Elements of Achewa Spirituality: Organizing Logic and Principle of Life." *Ultimate Reality and Meaning: Interdisciplinary Studies in the Philosophy of Understanding* 14, 1 (March 1991).

_________. "Community of Life." *The Ecumenical Review* 41, 4 (1989); Reprinted under different title in Charles Birch, William Eakin, and Jay MacDaniel, eds.,

Liberating Life: Contemporary Approaches to Ecological Theology. Maryknoll, NY: Orbis Books, 1990.

_________. "Liberalism and African Culture." *Journal of Black Studies* 21, 2 (December, 1990).

Smallwood, E. M. *The Jews under Roman Rule*. Leiden: Brill, 1981.

Stevenson, James. ed. *Creeds, Councils and Controversies: Documents Illustrating the History of the Church AD 337–416*. Revised by W. H. C. Frend. London: SPCK, 1989.

_________. *A New Eusebius: Documents Illustrative of History of the Church to A. D. 337*. London: SPCK, 1957.

Tacitus, *Ann* 2. 85. 4.

Taha, Mahmoud Mohammed. *The Second Message of Islam*. Syracuse, NY: Syracuse University Press, 1987.

Temple, William. *Christianity and Social Order*. New York: The Seabury Press, 1977.

The Kairos Document. Challenge to the Church: A Theological Comment on the Political Crisis in South Africa. Braamfontein, South Africa: Kairos Theologians, 1985; Grand Rapids, MI: Eerdmans, 1986.

Theobald, R. "Nigeria." *The Annual Register* (1989).

Thomson, John A. F. *Popes and Princes, 1417–1517: Politics and Polity in the Late Medieval Church*. London: Allen and Unwin, 1980.

Tordoff, William. *Government and Politics in Africa*. Bloomington, IN: Indiana University Press, 1993.

Trimingham, J. Spencer. *A History of Islam in West Africa*. London: Oxford University Press, 1962.

_________. *Islam in Ethiopia*. New York: Barnes and Noble, 1965.

_________. *Islam in the Sudan*. London: Oxford University Press, 1949.

Unger, Roberto Mangabeira. *Knowledge and Politics*. New York: Free Press, 1975.

wa Thiong'o, Ngugi. *Decolonising the Mind: The Politics of Language*. Nairobi: Heinemann, 1986.

Why Not Be Fair? London: Federal High Commissioner, n.d.

Wilckens, U. *Romer*. EKK VI/3; Zürich: Benzier/Neukirche: Neukirchener, 1982.

Winter, Gibson. *Liberating Creation: Foundations of Social Religious Ethics*. New York: Crossroad, 1981.

Wright, G. E. "The Nations in Israel's Prophecy." *Encounter* 26 (1965).

Young, R. A. "States and Markets in Africa," in *The Market and the State. Studies in Interdependence*. Edited by M. Moran and M. Wright. London: Macmillan, 1991.

Index

About the Author

HARVEY J. SINDIMA is Associate Professor of Philosophy and Religion at Colgate University. He is the author of *The Legacy of Scottish Missionaries in Malawi* (1992), *Drums of Redemption: An Introduction to African Christianity* (Greenwood, 1994), *Africa's Agenda: The Legacy of Liberalism and Colonialism in the Crisis of African Values* (Greenwood, 1995), and *Beauty and Politics: A Commentary on Esther* (1997).

CPSIA information can be obtained
at www.ICGtesting.com
Printed in the USA
BVHW041941310721
613145BV00002B/7

9 780313 307034